THE
INVISIBLE
PLAYER

Consciousness as the

Soul of Economic, Social,

and Political Life

Mario Kamenetzky

Park Street
Press

PARK STREET PRESS
ROCHESTER, VERMONT

Park Street Press
One Park Street
Rochester, Vermont 05767
www.InnerTraditions.com

Park Street Press is a division of Inner Traditions
International

Library of Congress Cataloging-in-Publication Data

Kamenetzky, Mario.
  The invisible player: consciousness as the soul of economic,
social, and political life / Mario Kamenetzky.
    p.   cm.
  Includes bibliographical references and index.
  ISBN 0-89281-665-1 (alk. paper)
    1. Economics—Philosophy.   2. Economics—Sociological
aspects.   3. Economic man.   4. Households.   I. Title.
HB72.K355   1999
330'.01—dc21   98-48848
                                                          CIP

Printed and bound in Canada

10 9 8 7 6 5 4 3 2 1

Text design and layout by Kate Mueller, Electric Dragon
  Productions
This book was typeset in Veljovic

Grateful acknowledgment is made to the following for per-
mission to reprint these excerpts:
The World Bank's *World Development Report 1993: Investing
  in Health.* New York: Oxford University Press, 1993.
Carlos Rubio Torres, for his poem "Planeta."

This book is dedicated to my grandchildren, Elena, Julia, and Alejandro, and to all of their age, with my hopes that, as they mature, they will build harmonizing, integrative structures of consciousness by digging through their rational, mythical, and magical layers until reaching the natural, hence divine, foundations of their beings.

Its pages evoke memories of three regions of the world that I have trod:

Santiago del Estero, the hot land of Northern Argentina, where I still feel my ever-present origin anchored.

France, which offered me the first broadening mental and emotional experience.

The United States of America, where my rationality evolved to the point of glimpsing the new integrative, harmonizing consciousness.

Contents

Acknowledgments

I should like to express my heartfelt gratitude to the many friends who have contributed to the evolution of my ideas, from Carlos A. Mallmann, who inspired my work on needs and desires in the 1970s, to Frederick Franck, who, in the 1980s, acquainted me with Jean Gebser's research and writings on the evolution of consciousness. These were the initial and final markers in the evolutionary path that led to this book. Many others lighted the road with the flames of their own work and their warm support.

A. T. Ariyaratne, the founder and leader of the Sarvodaya Shramadana Movement of Sri Lanka, made clear for me, through words and deeds, that efforts to transform consciousness must complement any social and economic restructuring efforts.

Professor Henry Margenau contributed his books on the philosophical foundations of natural science, and a beautiful afternoon of discussions that his spouse arranged despite the bad health that was afflicting him.

Herman Daly taught me about steady-state economics through his books, and through conversations we held while we were both working for the World Bank.

The idea of studying new forms of technology transfer and social organization that were emerging at bottom levels of developing societies was supported within the Bank by Visvanathan Rajagopalan, then director of its Projects Policy Department and later Vice President of Sector Policy and Research, by Charles Weiss, Jr., then the Bank's Science and Technology Advisor, and later on by James E. Lee, director of the Office of Environmental and Scientific Affairs.

Robert Maybury encouraged me to bring my budding unorthodox

ideas to papers he edited for *Science and Public Policy*, the journal of the International Science Policy Foundation, and to his teachings at the Netherlands International Institute for Management.

Paula Underwood Spencer, an educator of Oneida lineage, educated me about the Iroquois tradition and its Great Law of Peace.

Alberto Araoz introduced me to the late Jorge Sábato, the distinguished Argentine scientist and technology policymaker, with whom Alberto and I had delightful conversations about technology and human values. Since our early work for the Fundacion Bariloche and the National Development Council of Argentina, I have found in Alberto an enlightened partner that helped me to bring both my engineering experience and my interest on human issues to policy-making.

Jim Turner brought to my attention Adam Smith's *Theory of Moral Sentiments*. Knowledge of Smith's cultural philosophy greatly illuminated my understanding of his political economy, as expressed in *The Wealth of Nations*.

I had support for my ideas that economics is more than just figures on the flow of money, resources, products, and services from my dear friend Hazel Henderson, who, in her thoughtful books, expresses clearly her belief that there is a life beyond economics and global economic warfare. Hazel shares with me the vice of dotting "serious" books with poems, and I am grateful for the opportunity of having her close by, in the little lovely town of St. Augustine, with its street cafes that invite conversation.

My sons, Ricardo and Eduardo, as young engineers and scientists, keep me in touch with the fast-moving world of modern science, technology, and entrepreneurial organization—a world from which I started diverging in the late 1960s. Through them, I also learn about the difficulties of organizing families and rearing children in our modern, conflicted society.

My little library of Palm Coast ably supplied me with some rare books, which I enjoyed consulting while developing my ideas. When I moved out of Washington, D.C., I could not imagine that, retired in this beautiful place of Northeast Florida, I would be able to read, for instance, a 1671 edition of *Erasmus' Colloquies* on microfilm, and print the desired pages for my records.

ACKNOWLEDGMENTS

After I completed my first manuscript, Jack Heidenry made valuable suggestions that promoted a change in the initial structure of the book. The next version was read by five distinguished scholars who provided detailed comments that helped enormously in shaping this final version. For having undertaken with love this onerous task, I express my gratitude to the late Willis Harman, and to Georg Feuerstein, Frederick Franck, James Liebig, and Joel Kurtzman. They all contributed to shape my thought forms.

Willis Harman did it through his books, conversations, and activities at the World Business Academy and the Institute of Noetic Sciences.

Georg Feuerstein provided the safe swimming pool where I could exercise my understanding of Gebser's work before daring to dive into the deep waters of the master's writings.

I have already mentioned Frederick Franck, but his contributions were not limited to reading my manuscript and acquainting me with Gebser's work; his own life, his Pacem in Terris project, and his writings and drawings were equally inspirational.

James Liebig shared with me the results of his interviews with ninety businesspeople in fourteen countries. In addition to long phone conversations, our encounters at Latin American events provided opportunities for long peripatetic exchanges of ideas and experiences.

Joel Kurtzman found time to discuss with me his ideas on economic flows, although he read the manuscript under the pressures of his job as editor of the *Harvard Business Review,* and later of *Strategy and Business.*

Ehud C. Sperling, president of Inner Traditions International, decided to publish this book after a stimulating exchange of ideas and perceptions about the subject. I express my gratitude to him and to those at Inner Traditions who, afterward, provided their enthusiastic support and advice, especially Jon Graham, acquisitions editor; Rowan Jacobsen, managing editor; Anna Chapman, copyeditor; Laura Schlivek, proofreader; Peri Champine, art director; and Kate Mueller, designer. Our interaction left me with the feeling that they are not doing simply a job, but an enterprise undertaken with love and understanding.

The initial intuition that launched me on this evolutionary path, and the ideas that developed while I was trudging along it, might have remained without external, organized expression if I had not had the invaluable help of Sofia, my closest companion for the last forty-five years. Often, my excitement with a subject would make my intellectual creativity overflow in too many directions. Sofia's advice would then help me to channel my energies in a positive, productive, and joyful way.

Despite Sofia's own activities in the marketplace as physician, teacher, and advisor on population issues, she managed to accompany me on many of my World Bank travelings, providing me with more sensitive eyes and ears to capture the often kaleidoscopic reality of the new places that I had to visit.

After I retired from the World Bank, Sofia suggested that I organize my thoughts on the role of consciousness in shaping societies and economies in book form, instead of conveying them through articles dispersed throughout different publications. I am thankful to her not only for reading different versions, providing comments and suggestions, and gathering the bibliography for my work, but, more so, for her partnership in developing new ways of thinking about our lives, our family, and the world. I should like to express this gratitude with one more loving hug and kiss—this time a book-mediated one.

INTRODUCTION

This is a book about the games we play in social forums and economic markets. It focuses on a key, and often invisible, player in all those games: our own consciousness. Consciousness is our ever-present, although often unacknowledged, companion. It fires our vision of human nature; reveals our feelings; burns with our loves; flashes intuitions; strives to keep simultaneously satisfied our instinctive drives and our social needs; transmits messages from and to the spiritual forces that animate the whole universe and helps us to translate them into our rational languages; listens to each cell of our bodies, caring for the integrity of their structures and functions; processes data from our perceptions; and with these data creates science, technology, art, literature, and social and economic organizations.

It was a rich experience lived some twenty-five years ago in Sri Lanka that sowed in my consciousness the first seeds of this book. Sri Lanka was then, and still is, torn by war between two ethnic groups: the Buddhist Sinhalese and the Hindu Tamils. As the Science and Technology Specialist of the World Bank I was exploring ways for increasing efficiency in the transfer of technical resources to the poorest sectors of a country's population. Previous bibliographic research had told me that the Sri Lankan Sarvodaya Movement had demonstrated high effectiveness in that task. My field work told me that this increased effectiveness was the result of intensifying and expanding the people's consciousness. The transferring of resources for development was accompanied by what the Sarvodaya leaders called an awakening of awareness, which essentially meant to help villagers overcome limitations from previous enculturation patterns.

Yet, the most impressive experience of that trip was not that. It was to see that within the Sarvodaya villages, Tamils and Sinhalese were working together, in peace and with joy, thanks to their evolved consciousness. A few miles outside these villages, Sinhalese and Tamils were at each others' throats. Within the Sarvodaya villages, Sinhalese and Tamils were ably perceiving the unity and common spiritual origin of the human race, seeking to make the most of the space they shared. Outside those villages, Sinhalese and Tamils were programmed into seeing one group in competition with the other—a competition that could end only by occupying separate spaces, or by one group dominating the other.

I then better understood Jean Jacques Rousseau: Human nature is not perverse, it is society that perverts it. I also better understood Albert Einstein: Problems cannot be solved by the same consciousness that created them. My reasoning went as follows: If people of two extremely different cultural backgrounds and religious beliefs could work harmoniously together in one place, while ten miles away they were killing each other, the multifarious problems of violence, poverty, hunger, pollution, and overpopulation that humankind faces might be products of deficient states of mind rather than scarcity of resources or perversity of nature.

Since then, I have tried to learn more about the structure of our consciousness, its evolution, and its role in shaping households, societies, economies, and international relations. However, mine is neither a work on economics, nor sociology, nor psychology. Its subject is consciousness. By laying out a better understanding of its structures, my book attempts to better interpret the economics, the sociology, and the psychology of the world as it is and as it may become.

For this book, I have developed metaphors and graphic representations that help us sense how different parts in the structures of our consciousness fulfill different functions, and how nature and society influence those structures. Metaphors and graphics are also used to describe the evolution of the structures since the emergence of the first hominids on Earth, some 1.5 million years ago. Jean Gebser's studies suggest that humankind advanced from the archaic con-

2

sciousness of the hominids to our present rationality through two intermediate steps: the magical and the mythical consciousness. He also found that humankind was moving beyond rationality to a more integrative consciousness. This new consciousness may help us to harmoniously integrate in our behavior the urges from our ever-present origin as creatures of nature with the demands from societies of our creation. It may also help us to blend concerns for humans and ecosystems—concerns that are necessary for our survival as a species and for our enjoyment of life as individuals—into the technical and financial rationality required to organize and manage successful businesses and economies.

New structures do not destroy the old ones. We all are born with the archaic consciousness of the hominids, and we all go through periods of magic and myths in our infancy, talking to our toys and believing that Santa Claus or Papa Noel comes down the chimneys to fill our stockings at Christmas. On these foundations—the archaic layers of the newborn and the magical and mythical layers of the child—the enculturation process builds the structures that prevail in the society where the child is born. In most present societies, this means that enculturation takes us to rationality in much less time than it took for humankind to advance to this stage. We do not yet see, anywhere, enculturation processes designed to move us equally fast beyond rationality to the new integrative harmonizing consciousness.

In chapters 1 through 3, I discuss these ideas about the evolution of consciousness and describe the main patterns of enculturation that societies follow in shaping its structures. In chapters 4 through 6, I focus on the state of households, societies, economies, and the international order as we see them, full of risks and shadows. They are products of a rationality that has exiled the spiritual forces from our beings. It is a rationality that believes that nature, in which we include our bodies, is a domain that we can control and exploit at will. It is a rationality that we have chosen to enculturate into competing for power and wealth.

However, it is not utopian to think that we can do differently and choose to move, individually and collectively, to the new integrative consciousness. We can do this by enculturating our rationality into mastering the forces of love, enjoying life, and relinking with the exiled spirit, the scorned body, and the neglected nature. New forms of households, societies, economies, and global relationships are already budding among us. They result when people decide individually to undertake the task of restructuring their minds.

Chapters 7 through 9 discuss the extent of the changes that are possible in the organization and management of households, economies, and international relations. Chapter 10 describes some ongoing experiments, and chapter 11 tells us the stories of two nations that, by reforming their educational systems, built a strong rationality among populations that were still imbued with magic and myth. Other stories tell us of cases in which nations attempted to introduce changes in their social and economic systems but failed because they neglected to simultaneously change the mind-set of their populations. Because education is the main tool in the enculturation process, hence the main agent of change, the last chapter is devoted to a critical analysis of the prevailing form and content of education. It is through a reform of their educational systems that nations can speed the way to a new consciousness. A new education may bring out from within ourselves a new vision of who we are. Instead of seeing ourselves as products of an original sin that condemned us to guilty suffering, we may start seeing ourselves as products of an original blessing that endowed us for playfulness and happiness. However, changes in education alone will not be sufficient to realize the new vision. To allow a new consciousness to bring conviviality, justice, and freedom to households, economies, and the global order of nations, we will also need to change social codes, norms, and regulations.

However, even if we take all these measures, we will not build a paradise on Earth. Gebser warned against creating this myth. He said:

> The world will never become a paradise. If it did, its existence would become illusory. Let us not deceive ourselves and succumb to false hopes. The world will not become much better, merely a little different,

4

and perhaps somewhat more appreciative of the things that really matter.[1]

I wrote this book wishing the generation of my grandchildren to mature in that "little different" world. I also hope that we all may even now become more appreciative of the things that really matter by cementing our partnership with our ever-present companion, whom this book tries to make more visible and graspable.

PART I

THE EVOLUTION
OF CONSCIOUSNESS

A description of consciousness,

the functions of its components,

its evolution, and the main patterns that

societies follow in building its structure.

1

TOWARD THE RATIONAL AND BEYOND

W e do not yet know what consciousness is. We do know that consciousness is one element of reality. Moreover, it is the element that allows us to relate to our inner reality, the world around us, and the cosmos. Different structures of consciousness will produce different perceptions of all these realities and different ways of acting on them, but we can never hope to know what these realities would be without our consciousness.

We often seek to define, and whenever possible quantify, the external, observable causes that we believe are producing certain effects on our personal lives, our societies, or our economies. We forget that many of these effects result from particular behaviors and world visions that respond to our particular structure of consciousness. There is no phenomenon in our complex reality in which this invisible participant does not play a crucial role. It is invisible because consciousness cannot be separated from the observer studying and acting on this reality.

Inspired by a materialistic, deterministic philosophy, some scientists are researching the material bases of consciousness. They ask, for instance, how electrochemical signals come together as mental events. They attempt to relate different structures in our brain with steps in our evolution as species. I prefer simply to see consciousness as an element of reality, trying to make it more comprehensible through pictorial representations and metaphors.

We all perceive that regulatory commands to our biological functions, certain behavioral impulses, and some knowledge about ourselves and our external reality come to us neither through our senses nor as a product of our will, but from a source that seems to permeate the totality of our body and spread beyond it. We call that source the unconscious of our consciousness.

It also is clear to us that knowledge, whether inferential or noninferential, whether personally acquired or received from others, is stored somewhere in our consciousness for future retrieval. We call that "somewhere" the subconscious of our consciousness.

Finally, it is universally accepted that another part of our consciousness retrieves, interprets, and uses knowledge; influences behavioral impulses; and can even modify the usually involuntary commands that control certain biological functions. We call this operational part of our consciousness the conscious of our consciousness.

THE COMPUTER AS A METAPHOR FOR CONSCIOUSNESS

The workings of a computer can be used as a metaphor for the roles that the three parts play in structuring our consciousness (see Figure 1).

The conscious, which is the logical processor of external data, internal feelings, socially programmed values and beliefs, and unconscious messages, can be compared to random access memory (RAM).

The subconscious is like a disk on which society loads programs of values, beliefs, and behavior and where self-acquired and transmitted knowledge is stored. All these bytes of information are recalled as needed by the individual operator when working with the RAM.

The unconscious can be compared to a read-only memory (ROM) in which operating procedures inherent to the condition of humans as creatures of nature are stored by the creator.

Figure 1. A PICTORIAL DESCRIPTION OF CONSCIOUSNESS

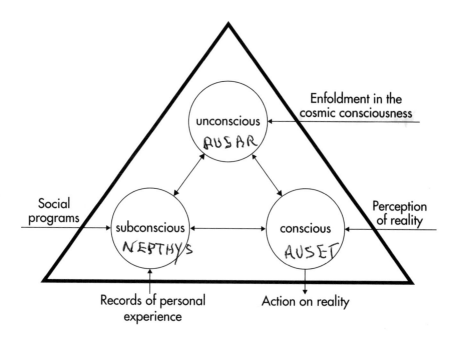

Depending on our particular system of beliefs, we name this creator God, nature, cosmic consciousness, or the universal spirit.

COSMIC CONSCIOUSNESS

I have no intention of convincing readers that there is a cosmic consciousness or universal spirit. I only propose to call cosmic consciousness the primary cause—whether an energy, a will, or a
mind—that set in motion the evolution of the universe, and at a certain point in the evolutionary process created the conditions for the
emergence of a human consciousness on planet Earth. Human consciousness is still evolving in partnership with its creator. This fact is
denied by many, especially by positivistic scientists, and is given
scant attention even by deeply religious people.

Experience from my seminars and lectures has taught me that the
metaphor of a cosmic consciousness interacting with our individual

consciousness is quickly grasped by people from different cultures. It is a metaphor that is easily translated into the metaphors of different religions, whether based on a unique anthropomorphic god, a divine trinity that embodies material and spiritual energies, or a full society of gods. In the same way that the luminiferous ether helped us understand light, the idea of a cosmic consciousness can help many people reconnect with what Gebser calls our ever-present origin, our origin as creatures of nature.

It would not be difficult to relate to this metaphor in the context of some African religious systems. Robin Poynor, an assistant professor of art history at the University of Florida, states:

Of utmost importance is the concept of vital force, an energy that emanates from the cosmos and is inherent in all beings and in all things. The Bamana people of Mali call this power nyama. Among the Yoruba of Nigeria it is ahse. All are essentially the same—an energy created by the High God, necessary for creative life, a dynamistic force which energizes all things. It is neither good nor bad in itself but is entirely neutral.[1]

Expanding on the latter concept, Poynor remarks:

A useful analogy for understanding this concept is electricity. Electrical energy is an impersonal force. It exists in the atmosphere, but it can be generated through a number of means. It can be harnessed and localized and made to flow from one object to another. It can be channeled in specific directions. As a force, it is neither positive or negative, but depending on the ways in which it is manipulated, it can be used effectively for good or bad. It can be stored for future use; it can be increased or decreased as needed; it can activate matter. Out of control, or in the hands of the untrained, it can maim or destroy. The vital energy of the universe is much the same. It can be channeled, directed, stored, increased, decreased, and used for good or bad.[2]

We cannot say whether or not cosmic consciousness is experimenting with the universe according to a preconceived plan. However, our present knowledge of the physical world leads me to believe that creation is not the work of an omnipotent and omniscient designer who has conclusively determined the nature of all things, including the evolutionary process to be followed by those things. Creation and its evolution seem instead to be the result of chaotic forces that are sometimes random, at other times probabilistic, and at still other times deterministic. These forces seem to be visible products in our earthly domain of a much larger energy field that we cannot yet fully comprehend. They seem to pop out from a sort of quantum field of infinite dimensions. We can look at these forces in a spiritual way akin to the intuitive concept of African religious systems. But we can also think of them, as materialist philosophers do, as products of matter that is evolving according to its own laws.

Even when we see these forces as products of a cosmic field, our rational consciousness still asks: Is this field in itself the cosmic consciousness, or is it manipulated by a supernatural conscious being? Will humans ever be able to find the answer? And does it really matter? I suggest that instead of worrying about finding an answer, we should concentrate on not blocking our consciousness from continually learning the ways by which, within the universal field of energy, chaos gives birth to form and form vanishes into chaos. Nor should we allow our consciousness to become deaf to the whispers through which this field of energy is continually trying to converse with us.

When we, as conscious operators, clear our random access memory from all the information momentarily stored, and put the hard disk of our subconscious to sleep, we can reach the depth of our unconscious. Once the regulatory commands and records of personal experiences have been deactivated, and the conscious mind emptied, we can receive intuitions and increase, at least temporarily, our links with the life forces at play in the cosmic field. Later on, by reactivating our hard disks and our random access memories, we can translate the noninferential knowledge that we have received into our particular languages, work to perfect it through inferential processes, and finally save it on the hard disk for future use.

The cosmic field seems to be learning, together with us, about the effects of technological progress on nature and humans, trying to

Figure 2. INNER LIFE, COSMIC CONSCIOUSNESS, PHYSICAL REALITY, AND THEIR ENFOLDMENT

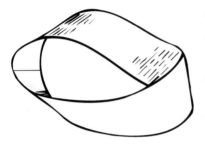

- The universal shaping the individual
- The inside matching and mating the outside
- The infinity of dreams limited by understanding
- Fantasy and reality mixing without boundaries

help us maintain our personal homeostasis and the homeostasis of our planet when our behavior threatens to disrupt them. At this point, my metaphor of a cosmic consciousness rejoins J. E. Lovelock's metaphor of Gaia, the mother Earth, which he sees as a complex living being of which all other living things are parts and partners. Gaia "has the power to maintain our planet as a fit and comfortable habitat for life."[3] To this end, Gaia may be desperately trying to move our consciousness to a higher structural level, as we shall see later.

For the moment, we can only speculate that if cosmic consciousness is embodied in a supernatural being, this being probably has a subconscious where plans and experiences are recorded, an unconscious that is tuned to the energy field of infinite dimensions, and a conscious operator through which the supernatural being creates and experiments within this field and even dialogues with its creatures. If cosmic consciousness is the energy field itself, creator and creatures, designer and design, experimenter and experiments, the cosmic operator and the earthly operators become the same. This last image of the cosmic consciousness can be described also in the beautiful words of a Christian priest, Jean Yves Leloup, who said: "God is not an object that we seek, it is a space that we share. The space is empty, but it contains everything."[4]

When we follow this last metaphor, the boundaries between humans and the cosmos, and between inner and outer reality, vanish, although for each there are limits. A Möbius strip[5] thus can also illustrate life (see Figure 2).

THE EVOLUTION OF CONSCIOUSNESS ACCORDING TO GEBSER

Our consciousness was not cast as described above from the beginning of evolution. The process of shaping a human consciousness started long after the Earth began transforming from a mass of rocks and molten minerals into a living planet. The first structures of human consciousness appeared millions of years ago, and their evolution accelerated during the last few thousand years, especially in the last few centuries.[6]

Jean Gebser has described this evolution through four main stages: the archaic, the magical, the mythical, and the mental/rational structures.[7] Gebser also saw a shift slowly taking place in contemporary society from the rational toward a new stage that he called arational, aperspectival, integral consciousness. In the evolutionary process, old structures never disappear; they remain as foundational layers for new structures, and they continue influencing our patterns of behavior and belief. The intensity and characteristics of these influences vary from one individual to another, responding to particular constitutional types and educational processes. Myths and magic still influence our rationality, while the archaic structure keeps reminding us of our ever-present origin as creatures of nature. Moreover, we will continue to feel the power of the archaic, magical, mythical, and rational structures as we move beyond rationality to integration.

The image in Figure 3 attempts to convey the ideas of permanence, interconnectedness, wholeness, and unity in diversity among the different evolutionary structural levels. In the next chapters, when discussing both the role of consciousness in socioeconomic life and the influence of society in shaping its structures, I will try to assign to each level its relative weight in the decision-making processes or activities under analysis. I hope to succeed, although it is not an easy task. It often happens that the levels are confused. It also

Figure 3. THE PERMANENCE AND
INTERCONNECTEDNESS OF THE
STRUCTURES OF CONSCIOUSNESS

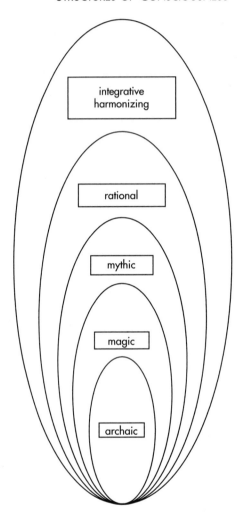

integrative
harmonizing

rational

mythic

magic

archaic

happens that the influences of one or more of them on a particular mind-set or thought form are neglected. We will see especially that rationality, which is the prevailing structure, is often assaulted and distorted by myths and magic visions that reason finds a way to rationalize and disguise.

Each evolutionary level supports the next and becomes enfolded in it. At present, rationality provides support to the building of the new integrative, harmonizing structures. Because I am neither a python nor an oracle, I do not know what will develop in turn from this new structural level. What I do dare to affirm is that evolution never stops, neither on this planet nor elsewhere in the universe. It would be deplorable if our repeated mistakes led to our final disappearance as a species, leaving the creative spirit without a mind on Earth that can reflect on its evolutionary task. But the spirit may already have other consciousness in other places on whom to reflect itself.

16

Rationality often poses little resistance to magical and mythical thoughts running into its structures. Yet it has stubbornly refused to integrate elements from the archaic consciousness into its thought forms. This stubborness has severely handicapped our perception of reality and our acting on it. The archaic level is the foundation stone on which the whole structure was able to develop. It is with this level that the creation of the human form and the human mind started, and it is through it that we are still in touch with the creative spirit. The structural layers that we have built and are still building over it should not hide our intrinsic spiritual origin. Without that foundation stone the whole consciousness collapses.

Evolution is a long learning process in which each stage responds to particular external physical and social environments and to internal biological conditions. Each stage produces positive as well as negative results for human beings and their environment. The positive results provide the tools, and the negative results supply the motivations for changes that lead to the next step.

The evolutionary process also is nonlinear. Although statistically we can describe societies as living predominantly under one or another of the prototypical structures, elements of more advanced structures may appear at earlier stages. Mythical Greece displays the rationality of its philosophers. Magic and myths keep encroaching in the Jewish rationality that Moses started organizing. The Iroquois society that the Pilgrims met was the product of strong mythical and magical structures, and an incipient rational structure of consciousness that had not yet blocked the channels through which the conscious mind communicates with the cosmic consciousness. Moreover, we can perceive among the Iroquois some elements of an integral consciousness that we have still to develop.

THE ARCHAIC STRUCTURE: HUMANS FEEL THEIR BODIES BUT DO NOT OWN THEM

When the first hominids emerged, their consciousness had not yet developed a conscious mind that could conceptualize reality and make decisions. They could freely express their emotions and feel

Figure 4.   THE NATURAL BEING:
             THE ARCHAIC STRUCTURE OF CONSCIOUSNESS

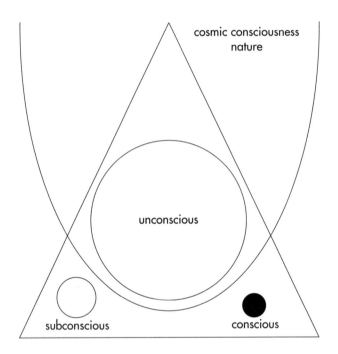

- Humans receive guidance from nature through the unconscious, the read-only memory of consciousness.

- Feelings are freely expressed but not conceptualized.

- An incipient subconscious records individual experience.

- There are neither enterprises nor households, and
  hence there are no markets. Nature is the only productive enterprise that supplies all the goods and services
  necessary for subsistence.

their bodies, but they did not own them. Under their archaic structure of consciousness, they could only follow the commands written by nature in the read-only memory of their unconscious. They could not design behavioral programs of their own, but they started saving memories of their experiences on the hard disk of their subconscious, which then had a very low storage capacity (see Figure 4).

At this stage, there was an undifferentiated union with the cosmic consciousness. There were no ideas of time and death. Life was a succession of "heres." Hominids did not entertain propositions of good and bad. There was perhaps a felt, though unexpressed, aesthetic, but there was no sense of ethics. Hominids could not decide how and when to follow their instinctive drives. They were guided by nature as trees are when shedding their leaves, or as birds are when undertaking their seasonal migration.

Ethologists are finding that animals do not just follow set routines. They seem to have "conscious experiences" and can solve unprecedented problems or design strategies for the satisfaction of their needs. An anthropocentric enculturation, and an unfamiliarity with the studies on the evolution of human consciousness, lead many scientists to reject those findings as irreproducible, anecdotal observations.

An analysis of the archaic consciousness helps in understanding the inner life of animals, because at that stage we were not very different from them. The fact that an archaic structure does have a rudimentary subconscious, an embryo of conscious mind, and a dominant unconscious explains that hominids could do some planning, develop deceiving tricks, solve unexpected problems, and express their feelings and emotions through sounds and gaze. Hominids then, like animals now, could receive information for all those activities through unconscious receptors well tuned to the cosmic consciousness.

It is no wonder that most of the cultures that emerged when humankind evolved to the next stages of consciousness developed stories of a lost paradise. It was a paradise because we could not do otherwise than just be, hence avoiding the discontent and pain but also the joys of becoming. We left paradise not because of being punished but rather because of being blessed. Humans had to develop

Figure 5. THE SORCERER'S APPRENTICE:
THE MAGICAL STRUCTURE OF CONSCIOUSNESS

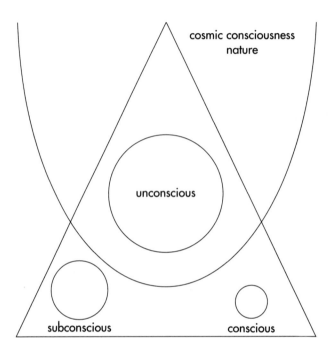

- The conscious operator slowly develops skills for using the random access memory of the mind.

- Nature, hence people as part of it, is seen as entrusted with magic powers.

- Intuitively and empirically gained knowledge and the first social rules are stored in the subconscious space, the hard disk of the mind.

- Feelings begin to be conceptualized.

- Relationships between events, internal forces, and forces in the external physical and social environment are thought of.

- People start manufacturing things, which are bartered among households and tribes in incipient markets.

knowledge about the world and themselves, shaping themselves into conscious partners of the cosmic consciousness for the task of guiding the evolution of planet Earth, a tiny part of the awesome cosmic creation. Moreover, they had to become independent partners, acquiring the capacity to make decisions about their own lives.

THE MAGICAL STRUCTURE: HUMANS BEGIN TO OWN THEIR BODIES AND MINDS

The hominids who began to analyze inner and outer life and its interrelations shaped the first paradigmatic shift. With them the first elite was born. They were the magi and wise persons who thought that mental projections could influence physical reality. They emerged from the hordes, organized the first communities, and led the change from archaic to magic (see Figure 5).

Living under new behavioral and perception-processing programs, people of magic painted figures of animals on cave walls to help them catch desired prey and to ward off dangerous species. Intuitively, these more evolved beings discovered how to heal with plants and make fire with wood. They began to conceptualize their feelings, especially those related to death and risk, creating sometimes complicated rituals to deal with these situations. They began to make connections between events, internal forces, and forces in the external environment.

The magi and wise persons became the keepers and transmitters of the knowledge that they were intuitively developing, and of the magic principles of their conscious creation. Magi and wise men designed behavioral programs and systems of values and beliefs that they read into the hard disk of the subconscious mind of new generations. These programs created the first conflictive tensions between social requirements and natural needs.

Paradise was lost. New creatures emerged from the womb of nature to feel the pain and the joy of human life. These human creatures began to own their bodies and minds, but society increasingly tended to control and standardize the bodily and mental functions of its members.

Figure 6. THE CREATION OF THE GODS:
THE MYTHICAL STRUCTURE

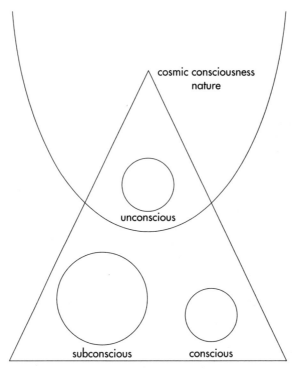

cosmic consciousness
nature

unconscious

subconscious   conscious

- Instead of nature perceived as empowered with magic, it is seen as animated by extraordinary beings.

- Behavior in society and nature is consciously explored.

- The relations between love, sex, and reproduction are better understood.

- Feelings are increasingly conceptualized, and their expression is strongly codified.

- The read-only memory still provides unconscious guidance from inside each being, but tensions between the internal voice and social commands increase.

- The capacities of the hard disk (the subconscious) and the random access memory (the conscious) are increased.

- The economic flows become more sophisticated with the creation of money; products and services are still bartered, but they are also traded.

We have already seen how magical structures led African people to think that the vital energy of the universe could be channeled, directed, stored, increased, decreased, and used for good or bad. Ritual was created for this purpose.

> Ritual may include the use of words, music, dance, objects, magical substances, special arts and actions which have been prescribed by someone with special knowledge and training. Sculpture often assumes a role of importance in such ritual acts. It may serve to store great amounts of energy, a sort of battery which might be used and then recharged as necessary. . . . Those trained in ritual have the power to unleash potent supernatural forces that radically affect the agricultural, animal, and human environments. These forces may be used to prevent misfortune and to bring about well-being and good for the entire community, or they may be directed against persons or communities, causing destruction and sickness and ill fortune.[8]

This period of weaning from nature's nurturing and guidance was very long. It lasted hundreds of thousands of years. Slowly, magi and wise persons began to wonder whether the visible world was shaped and reshaped by the direct activity of supernatural invisible beings rather than by mental projections. From thinking that it is possible to control the forces of nature through incantations, conjurations, and the like, humans shifted toward the belief that those forces were manifestations of mythical heroes, gods, and goddesses, and that control could be exercised only by an alliance with them.

THE MYTHICAL STRUCTURE: AN INCREASE OF SOCIAL CONTROL OVER BODIES AND MINDS

The magi and wise persons slowly changed into priests and priestesses whose task was to turn the deeds of the mythical heroes in favor of their own group by making sacrificial offerings. The behavioral and perception-processing programs that they designed increased the tension between social and natural commands, the first often trying to override the latter (see Figure 6).

During the transition from magic to myth, humans learned to cultivate the soil and to domesticate animals. Markets were organized, and money was created. Until that moment, households had gathered and hunted the produce of nature, which was a cosmically managed, productive enterprise. Nature did not request payment for its outputs and provided all the inputs. From the mythical stage on, human enterprises began to produce the necessities of life with the support of nature, which still provided the land and raw materials, and still cleaned the waste from biological activities by humans, animals, and plants. Now, in addition, nature started cleaning the waste of the primitive production processes that humans were inventing.

Slowly more and more functions, including sex,[9] were commercialized. The creation of money originated a new concept: wealth. A few people began to possess, accumulate, and parade riches. Fellow beings were exploited and enslaved to produce this wealth and the services required by the few for the enjoyment of their leisure and intellectual pursuits.

As I said before, evolution never follows a linear path. Some tribes that used magic also had slaves, and also paraded riches in the form of body ornaments. There were, among the people of magic, fewer possibilities for accumulating wealth, but certainly the wielding of social power had already awakened ambition.

An alliance of religious and money elites convinced their mythical communities that the social rules imposed upon them were necessary to gain the favors of the supernatural heroes, the giants, and the gods and goddesses who otherwise might send down all sorts of plagues. Humans felt powerless facing the overwhelmingly strong, and often awesomely violent, forces of nature. They knew so little about themselves, and about the workings of their bodies and minds, that they believed everything was the result of supernatural activity. For instance, they were led to believe that fire had been stolen by Prometheus from the gods, rather than seeing it as a discovery by a human who, by following a deep intuition, linked several observations: first, that when lightning strikes wood, it generates fire; second, that there is no fire without heat; and third, that rubbing one's cold skin causes it to become warm.

In the mythic structure, the role of the unconscious as the

24

communication channel with the cosmic consciousness was further reduced, but the subconscious memory and the skills of the conscious operator grew, especially among the powerful elite who seized control over nature and other humans. This control was increased and perfected during the next stage.

THE RATIONAL STRUCTURE: THE SPLIT BETWEEN THE MATERIAL AND THE SPIRITUAL WORLD

This stage began with the replacement of mythological heroes, who embodied the spiritual forces that animate nature, with single powerful male deities. These, unlike mythological heroes, would not consort with humans and nature. Single male gods were exiled to a custom-made realm, whence they would judge the activities of nature and humans. However, from their exile they could offer humans a second chance: an afterlife that would not be subject to the complexity of life on earth—a kind of return to the lost paradise of the archaic consciousness.

The exile and masculinization of the gods meant a separation of humans from nature. Because most of the bodily functions are apparently not controlled by the mind, the body was considered part of nature. Hence, the human body and mind were also divided (see Figure 7). The earlier, often creative inner tensions between social demands and natural requirements were symbolically transferred to an external conflict between God's influence over his terrestrial subjects and the Devil's manipulations. The heavens became the abode of God, while earthly and human nature were seen as the seat of the Devil.

Dogmas, ideologies, and creeds replaced myths in the subconscious records. The behavioral programs that were read into the hard disk of the mind became increasingly oppressive, and ended up suffocating communications between the conscious mind and the unconscious, through which the cosmic consciousness was still trying to send intuitions for the advancement of this planet and its creatures.

Gebser calls this step in the evolution of human consciousness the

Figure 7. THE EXILE OF THE GODS AND NATURE:
          THE RATIONAL STRUCTURE

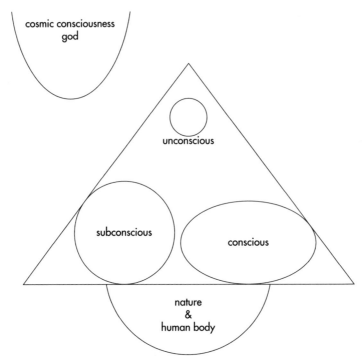

- The cosmic consciousness, nature, and the human body are all separated from the mind.

- Spiritual messages are now seen as issuing from an external domain, where magical and mythical events may still happen.

- Instinctive messages are seen as relayed by the body from the larger domain of nature and are often considered as products of an antispiritual force, the Devil.

- Nature is the realm of causality, where forces can be controlled by discovering the mathematical relationship that holds among them.

- The capacities of the hard disk (the subconscious) and the random access memory (the conscious) are considerably expanded, but the operating capacities are biased toward thinking and acting rather than feeling and intuiting.

- Populations and economic flows grow without concern for the limited capacity of nature to provide resources and to clean waste.

mental structure of consciousness, reserving the term *rational* for its recent manifestations, which are taking place in our present societies. The rational is seen by Gebser as a deficient mode of the mental structures. I prefer to simplify the wording and include, under the name *rational,* all the structural developments that took place after the mythical stage.

Mental usually pertains to the mind, implying the idea of being performed by or existing in the mind. The word *mental* also connotes intellectuals or intellectual activities. Magic and mythical structures also pertain to the mind, while the enculturation programs that built these structures were designed by intellectuals of those respective ages. *Rational* denotes, instead, the reasoning power and its proceedings. What really happened in the evolution from myths to our present rationality is that reason overpowered intuition and spiritual guidance. At the start, during the period that Gebser calls mental consciousness, this process was slow. Later on, the process sped up and led to the distortions and existential pains that will be analyzed in more detail in Part II of this book.

In the last few centuries, a new elite, the scientific aristocracy, has helped to consolidate the changes that leaders of monotheist religions initiated some five thousand years ago. Scientists share with theocrats the belief that there are three separate fields of human perception and action: the spiritual field, where the battle between God and the Devil takes place, the mental field of human consciousness, from which religions, science, and technology emerge, and the material field of nature, which includes the human body with its instinctive urges.

After a period of bitter struggle, scientists and the priesthood of the new religions reached an understanding: the priests would preside over the spiritual domain; the scientists would look after the material world. While the role of theocracies was to rationalize myths and devise means of controlling instinctive drives, the role of scientific aristocracies was to control nature and the body, and use them, through powerful technologies, for the constant growth of the economy. The control of instinctive drives would contribute to this growth by channeling most human energy toward the production and consumption of wealth. When theocracies remain antagonistic

Figure 8. HUMANS BECOME HUMANE:
THE INTEGRATIVE HARMONIZING CONSCIOUSNESS

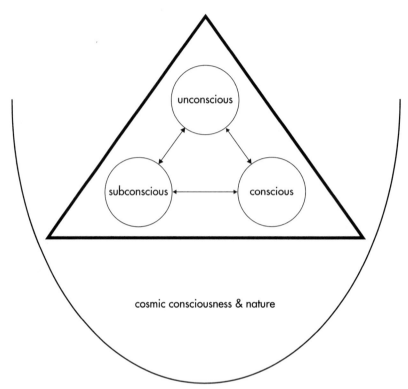

cosmic consciousness & nature

- Humans take individual control of their minds and bodies, which are reunited with the spirit and nature at a more evolved level than under the archaic structure.
- Nature's scripts of the read-only memory are consciously recognized as an integral part of the mind.
- Attuned to spiritual messages from the cosmic conscousness, the conscious operator strives to balance social and instinctive needs.
- The knowledge-storing capacity of the subconscious (the hard disk) keeps expanding, but the capacity of the conscious operator to apply knowledge wisely also increases.
- Life-enhancing programs replace behavioral programs that restrict physical, emotional, and intellectual communication.
- Societies organize their economies within the limits set by their environments and with the aim of satisfying needs rather than creating desires.

to scientific aristocracies, economic and social progress is arrested.

The Next Step: The Harmonizing Structure

Gebser suggests that we are now evolving toward an integral, aperspectival, arational consciousness. It is aperspectival because the world is conceptualized by humans from within the complexity of the world itself, not from the outside reductionist perspective of the human mind as master of the Earth. It is arational because it lets feelings, intuitions, and instinct mix with logical thinking in the conceptualization process. Perspective was a great achievement of reason. By separating the observer from the observed reality, perspective could draw on a two-dimensional plane the image of a three-dimensional world. To move to an aperspectival world does not mean to go back to the pre-Renaissance age, when people and nature were represented together in a painting that had no volume. The art of the aperspectival world will instead attempt to represent as closely as possible the spiritual and mental multidimensionality of beings inhabiting a multidimensional space.

Although Gebser's terminology is intellectually appealing, I prefer to define the new stage as the stage of a harmonizing, integrative consciousness. The word *integral* as used by Gebser denotes belonging as a part of the whole, and certainly the new consciousness should make us feel and think as part of the whole. However, I favor the word *integrative* because it brings the idea of an effort to reunite what rationality has separated. I add the adjective harmonizing because the task of the new consciousness also is to create trade-offs and to build compromises among opposites, converting them into polarities that when linked yield useful energy. One of the main tasks of the new consciousness is to work out a more user-friendly balance between the social requirements that we impose on ourselves and our natural needs.

We then consciously recognize nature's scripting in the read-only memory of our unconscious as an integral part of the mind, and we perceive nature's intuitive, instinctive, and spiritual messages as emerging from the field of infinite dimensions of the cosmic consciousness that envelops every individual consciousness. This is pictured in Figure 8, where I again make use of the equilateral triangle and the links among the three parts of consciousness depicted in Figure 1. But now the restricted triangle that represents human consciousness is fully enveloped by the larger field of the cosmic consciousness and nature. Consequently, the closed lines that limited the triangle in Figure 1 have been replaced by open lines.

When we are spiritually attuned, we can better harmonize our social and instinctive needs, transforming our present arrogant and abusive control over body and nature into cooperation with both. The old subconscious programs which support the oppressive control of both human nature and nature at large, interfere in communication with the spirit and restrict physical, emotional, and intellectual communication among humans. By eliminating them, we simultaneously increase our access to information and our creativity to transform information into knowledge and wisdom. This happens because we start feeling more free to tune into and act on our intuitions, letting all our senses become involved in the process.

Humans become more humane when an integrative, harmonizing human consciousness meets the cosmic consciousness in a unified field of consciousness where body, mind, and spirit are reunited, and separateness among humans and between humans and nature vanishes. The integrative, harmonizing structure reminds us that it is suicidal to ignore our cosmic partner when we either act on our external reality—the reality of nature and society—or delve into the inner reality of our individual lives.

We shorten our lives by ignoring cosmic advice when molding our internal reality. If we neglect such advice when dealing with our external reality, our disappearance as a species may be at stake. A harmonizing structure humbles us enough to enable us to understand that the cosmic consciousness can leave us out of the cosmic experiment. We can neither enjoy our individual experiments nor achieve the experiment of building a human community on Earth without keeping a close dialogue with our cosmic partner, however we choose to visualize this partner.

By transcending the incantations and conjurations of the magical rituals, the mythical dalliances with the gods, and the rational toying with matter and thoughts, the harmonizing structure can lead us to

30

realize Pierre Teilhard de Chardin's dream of mastering the forces of love that arise from the depths of our spiritually linked unconscious.

THE MAKING OF OUR INDIVIDUAL STRUCTURE OF CONSCIOUSNESS

To the making of each individual consciousness, nature contributes two structural foundations. One is the individual biological terrain—that is, the particular genetic, metabolic, constitutional type that will condition to a large extent the life of the person. The other structural foundation is the read-only memory with its records of our natural needs and its communication channels with the cosmic consciousness. It is on these foundations that society will build the structure of consciousness it has decided to adopt. Once a child emerges from the paradise of the womb,[10] society ushers his or her passage from the archaic structure to the prevailing structure through the enculturation process.

In most societies today, this enculturation process develops a rational structure, with magical and mythical components whose structural weights vary from one society to another. Also different from one society to another is the degree of repression of the instinctive drives that emerge from the archaic structure of our ever-present origin. Present societies design their enculturation patterns on the basis of a preanalytic vision of human nature that considers us as products of original sin. Hence, we believe ourselves to be intrinsically perverse, and in this life we cannot but suffer and feel guilty for that original sin. All the instinctive drives that are related to that original sin, especially those connected with sex and sensuality, are seen as dirty manipulations of the Devil to make us sin again and again. Those societies then try to discipline the instincts and allow them to be sometimes never satisfied, sometimes only partially satisfied.

I have yet to find a society whose enculturation patterns are based on a preanalytic vision of human nature that sees it as a product of an original blessing whose spiritual purpose is to create on Earth a partner of the cosmic consciousness. In such a society, the drives emerging from our ever-present origin as creatures of nature would never be considered devilishly dirty. Indeed, those drives may at times bring too much chaos to society, but this does not justify repression, especially not total repression and denial. The enculturation may instead lead to the mastery desired by Teilhard de Chardin and other theologians and philosophers whose proposals I will discuss in later chapters. If we manage to advance globally to the new integrative harmonizing consciousness, we may see more and more societies adjusting their enculturation patterns to the new vision of human nature. In my short visits to The Netherlands, Sweden, Finland, and Denmark, I saw efforts to move toward the new consciousness. These countries have started modifying their legal systems and public morality codes so as to weave a more healthy social tissue with less repression.

However, the enculturation process can do more than just build structures with different mixes of magic, myths, and rationality, and different degrees of support from the archaic foundations. Enculturation can also favor either a power-controlling, wealth-accumulating behavior based on an egotistic self-love *(amour propre)* or a love-mastering, life-enjoying behavior supported by a healthy self-esteem *(amour de soi)*.

2

Amour de Soi and *Amour Propre*

*A*mour de soi and *amour propre* are two distinct psychological attitudes. Each promotes a different pattern of behavior. *Amour de soi* encourages enjoyment of life and assists in mastering the forces of love that are strongly anchored in our archaic consciousness. *Amour propre* strives to control power and promotes the accumulation of wealth. It considers that this is rational behavior and tries to stop the archaic forces from interfering with its objective.

Despite the tremendous importance of these concepts in understanding economic theories and analyzing economic practice, psychologists and sociologists do not place great stress on clearly describing their denotations and connotations. Jean Jacques Rousseau made a clear distinction between the two concepts:

> Love of oneself is a natural sentiment which inclines every animal to watch over its own preservation, and which directed in man by reason and modified by pity, produces humanity and virtue. *Amour propre* is only a relative sentiment, artificial and born in society, which inclines each individual to have a greater esteem for himself than for anyone else, inspires in all the harm they do to one another, and is the true source of honor.[1]

Discussing this statement, Allan Bloom, translator of Rousseau's *Emile* and commentator on it, notes that

Rousseau, instead of opposing love of self to love of others, opposes two kinds of self love, a good and bad form. Thus without abandoning the view of modern political philosophy that man is primarily concerned with himself—particularly his own preservation—he is enabled to avoid Hobbes' conclusion that men, as a result of their selfishness, are necessarily in competition with one another.[2]

A healthful love of oneself is not opposed to love of others. On the contrary, it is supported by the love of others toward oneself and supports in return the expressions of love toward the others. *Amour de soi* reminds us of the biblical injunctions "You must love your neighbor as yourself"[3] and "treat others as you would like them to treat you."[4] We will see later, when discussing the role of consciousness in the organization of our economies, that Adam Smith, the father of the the free-market theory, rejoins Rousseau and makes of *amour de soi* the basis of healthy market behavior.

Since we emerged from our archaic origin, some individuals have been intent on developing the capabilities of the human body and the human mind. They have tried to understand human feelings and to discover how nature works and how it can help humans to increase their enjoyment of life. These individuals have usually approached the objects of their work with love and have developed the concepts of physical, mental, emotional, and spiritual health.

Yet, other individuals have been intent on controlling the social organizations they were designing. They soon discovered the concept of wealth and found that by controlling power they could simultaneously create and accumulate wealth.

Are both psychological attitudes and their corresponding behaviors intrinsic to human nature or products of the enculturation process? Or is *amour de soi* natural while *amour propre* is culturally acquired? My answer is that both attitudes and behaviors seem to be present in human beings, their enculturation reinforcing one or the other. However, *amour de soi* appears to be strongly anchored in the archaic levels of our consciousness, while little of *amour propre*—if any—seems to issue from our origin as creatures of nature. We often say that our conscience reproaches us for unjust or unloving acts inspired by *amour propre*. Does the conscious mind find those acts reproachable after comparing its behavior with enculturation codes recorded in the subconscious? Or is the cosmic consciousness reminding us, through the unconscious, that nothing in our read-only memory tells us to behave in that unjust and unloving way?

Rousseau answers the second question with a resounding yes! "Let us set down as an incontestable maxim that the first movements of nature are always right. There is no original perversity in the human heart."[5] And he finds it "quite strange that since people first became involved with raising children, no instrument for guiding them has been imagined other than emulation, jealousy, envy, vanity, avidity, and vile fear—all the most dangerous passions, the quickest to ferment and the most appropriate to corrupt the soul, even before the body has been formed."[6]

Instinctively—meaning cosmically—our tendency is to love and protect ourselves, and to enjoy loving others and being loved by them. This latent trend can be either developed or distorted by the enculturation process. However, as the cosmic field is essentially probabilistic, atypical manifestations occur, and some human beings develop *amour propre* even if we attempt to enculture them into *amour de soi*, mastery of love, and enjoyment of life. Conversely, other beings will remain faithful to the messages of *amour de soi* that they receive from their unconscious despite all the enculturation efforts that aim to strengthen their *amour propre*. In these beings, the enculturation is unable to block or jam the communication between the conscious mind and the cosmic field of consciousness from which, errors apart, more impulses toward *amour de soi* than toward *amour propre* are sent to our individual consciousness.

Amour propre, power control, and wealth accumulation were already powerful elements of social reality during the magical and mythical stages of humankind's development, and they have strongly influenced the building of our present rational structure of consciousness.

Love and Power in the Development of Rationality

During the mythical period of humankind's development, people encultured into *amour propre* and power control thought that their gods and goddesses were also fighting among themselves to acquire more power and enjoy more pleasure. Sometimes gods and goddesses would involve humans in their rivalries, jealousies, and passions. As rational structures began to program the Western mind with the notion of a unique anthropomorphic male god, and as these structures further separated humans from nature, humans began to fight for their specific god, who would promise them a particular piece of land.

Since then, as we have frequently seen, armies of men have fought armies of other men who have a different image and idea of a god. These warriors think that they are fulfilling commands of their god. They seek through acts of heroism—which do not exclude such barbaric acts as mass murder, rape, and torture—to win the favors of the god who, if they are killed, will take them back into the lost paradise of the archaic consciousness. Equally tragic and barbaric are the conflicts among people who follow the same god but whose leaders have different rational interpretations of their god's commands and various earthly interests.

In the East, the building of rational structures had a different start. In China, about the sixth century B.C.E., Confucius started building the rational structure by using legal and organizational rather than religious blocks. Meanwhile, Lao-tsu, with his metaphor of the Tao, was trying to include large windows open to cosmic universal energies among those stifling rational blocks. The Tao is a concept and a feeling that rejoins the description of the cosmic consciousness described in the previous chapter. It is a creating principle and an invisible, formless guide of the evolutionary process. It speaks to those who can tune into it by emptying their minds of thought but also by making conscious efforts to perceive the whole of reality. It speaks to people who can look not only at the measurable causes and effects of a particular event but also at the perennial energies at play, which in the next moment, or in another space, can assume a different configuration and produce a different event.

Rationality often denies the rich multifariousness of cosmic forces, attempting to jail them in underground dungeons built within the structures of consciousness. Lao-tsu tried to prevent this from

Accumulated knowledge and wisdom from the magical and mythical development of humankind feed

Love-mastering traditions
- try to remove the violent from the erotic and the beautiful
- perceive love as the main force between and within human beings
- have an androgynous vision of human nature: the feminine and the masculine working harmoniously together

Power-controlling organizations
- develop male-dominated cultures
- consider the erotic, and even the beautiful, as devilish and associated with the feminine
- condone violence on nature and in society

Art and science emerge from the love-harnessing traditions and generate

Secular humanism
- quickly increases knowledge of nature
- originates powerful technologies for the exploitation of natural resources
- attempts to include large masses in the appreciation and practice of beauty
- creates the notion of self-regulating markets

Power-controlling organizations accumulate power and generate

Institutionalized theism and the nation-state
- organize households into nation-states and religious congregations around mythic symbols
- cement the division between nature and society
- institutionalize violent competition

When secular humanism dogmatically adheres to the idea that matter evolves by itself, following its own laws, it becomes

Scientific fundamentalism
- sustains the dominance of humans over nature
- considers only what can be measured as part of reality
- believes that the observer is independent of the observed
- exiles the erotic and the beautiful from the domain of science
- accepts the use of violence to silence iconoclastic scientific work that may disturb the ossified mind-set of the scientific hierarchy, threatening its privileges

When institutionalized theism dogmatically adheres to the idea of an external supernatural being as the creator and master of an unchangeable universe, it becomes

Religious fundamentalism
- sustains dominance of humans over nature
- represses the erotic and sees the beautiful as threatening society because it evokes the erotic
- accepts the freedom of science to develop all kind of technologies for the marketplace, but doesn't allow science to discuss religious beliefs
- sees violence as an intrinsic part of human nature and accepts its use for preventing heterodox behavior and repressing the erotic and the beautiful

When the nation-state dogmatically adheres to the idea of being different and superior to the others, it generates

Nationalism
- considers people from other nation-states as potential subjects of slavery and serfdom
- sees violence as an intrinsic part of human nature and uses it to prevent political opposition, market practices that threaten prevailing privileges and interests, and social behavior that is not accepted by either its religious fundamentalist allies or its own ideological dogmas

When harmonizing structures of consciousness lead secular humanism, institutionalized theism, and the nation-state to accept the notion of oneness of humans with nature and unity among human beings, humankind evolves toward

Integration
- respects the limits set by nature to economic growth
- continues increasing the pool of knowledge through observation, experimentation, and intuition
- seeks to cancel violence by liberating the erotic and the beautiful from social constraints
- promotes cooperation rather than competiton, whether in the local marketplace or in the international arena
- uses advances in science and technology to establish a balance between the Earth's carrying capacity and the number of people

happening in the East. He was echoed in the West by some Greek thinkers like Heraclitus, who clambered over the rational walls that were beginning to surround Greek society, and looked at nature with fresh eyes. For Heraclitus, everything was in constant change, new totalities were constantly emerging from opposites, and everything was part of God, the indestructible energy of the world. Harmony, for Heraclitus, was a healthy tension between different elements in which no single element wins but all function together inescapably. However, two centuries later,[7] other Greek thinkers closed Western minds back within the dry walls of rational, hierarchical categories. Among these thinkers were Aristotle, whose abstract logic influenced Western thinking for millenia, and Democritus, who, preannouncing our deterministic science, claimed that "nothing is produced by chance; everything starts with a reason, and obeys to a necessity."[8]

Since these early beginnings, rational thought has progressed along two main paths: the cultivation of love-mastering traditions,[9] and the building of power-controlling social organizations. This development is summarized in the flow chart on page 37, which is a simplified view of the complex evolution followed by humankind under the rational structure of consciousness. In the multifarious reality of our world, systems of values, beliefs, and behaviors never evolve along simple, singular, linear patterns, like those depicted in the chart. They often intertwine, converging at some points and diverging at others. Progress seems to follow a sort of sinuous path. At some points it advances quickly, then stops, and even regresses, only to accelerate again and reach even further.

Ideas and practices that one society adopts under early rational structures of consciousness could be revived much later by another more sophisticated society. In the process, those early ideas and practices can be either improved or distorted. For example, laissez-faire policies entertained by the Taoist love-mastering tradition were reintroduced in the eighteenth century by Western secular humanists and were misinterpreted and misused by the power-controlling organizations that emerged after the Industrial Revolution.

In other cases, primitive rational practices inspired by power control were subsequently modified when a change in the modes of production allowed for the release of repressed love energies. For instance, slavery was first openly practiced by rationally organized societies and later guiltily disguised as serfdom. But over time, technological progress made it possible for most power-controlling organizations to exclude both slavery and serfdom from their social codes.

There are always strong interactions between both lines of thought and behavior. For instance, science and technology inform the ideology and praxis of nation-states, and these ideologies and praxis in turn affect scientific and technological development.

SCIENCE: A PRODUCT OF LOVE THAT PROVIDES SUPPORT TO POWER

Many scientists have explicitly acknowledged that their discoveries were guided by an intimate and often unconscious liaison with nature. Love of nature and love of knowledge about her gave birth to science. As a footnote in the Jerusalem Bible says, "in biblical language 'knowledge' is not merely the conclusion of an intellectual process, but the fruit of an experience, a personal contact; when it matures, it is love."[10]

Science usually clothes the deterministic and probabilistic mathematical relations it discovers in nature with sometimes beautiful, and other times obscure, metaphors and parables.[11] These metaphors and parables are closer to the poetic language of love than to the dry language of the laws, regulations, and codes of power-controlling organizations. For these latter, matter is as solid as rock, or as light as air. For them, the scientific discovery that a hard and beautiful diamond is mainly made of empty space sounds like a puzzling paradox and an unproductive statement. Power-controlling organizations are structured around the notion that time always follows a linear evolution from a past, which made it possible for these organizations to emerge, to a future that if properly planned will ensure further control. For science, there may be a time arrow coming from the future to our present.[12]

The erotic[13] vibrations of the universe were not alien to many scientists. Despite Isaac Newton's undeniable influence on the development of our prevailing materialistic, positivistic scientific paradigm, John Maynard Keynes sees him not as "the first of the age of reason," but as "the last of the magicians, the last of the Babylonians and Sumerians, the last great mind which looked out on the visible and intellectual world with the same eyes as those who began to build our intellectual inheritance rather less than 10,000 years ago."[14]

To Newton, "the universe and all that is in it" was "a riddle, a secret which could be read by applying pure thought to certain evidence, certain mystic clues which God had laid about the world to allow a sort of philosopher's treasure hunt to the esoteric brotherhood."[15]

More recently, Albert Einstein provides another good example of a loving attitude toward nature. He says: "The most beautiful experience we can have is the mysterious. It is the fundamental emotion which stands at the cradle of true art and true science. Whoever does not know it and can no longer wonder, no longer marvel, is as good as dead, and his eyes are dimmed."[16]

G. J. Whitrow summarized Einstein's philosophical position well when he wrote that "although Einstein rejected the churches, he had a Spinoza-like belief in a cosmic religious force. He regarded this as an eternal spiritual being that communicates small details of itself to our weak and inadequate minds." Whitrow concluded that Einstein "had no more use for the shallow materialism that is the most widely accepted philosophy of scientists and others today than for the authoritarian views of the churches that once were so powerful."[17]

Yet, Einstein is also a good example of the crisscrossing cultural influences between the two lines of thought and action along which our rational structures of consciousness evolved. Einstein's theories overcame the weaknesses of old explanations, but they shared with the latter the underlying deterministic rationale on which, on one hand, secular humanism was building modern science, and on the other hand, power-controlling organizations were conceiving modern religions and societies. Einstein was in love with nature, but his relations with her were under the influence of the programs he had received in his formative years. Hence, when quantum physics challenged the notion that everything in nature was determined by a cause-and-effect relationship, he bitterly argued with Niels Bohr and Max Born, saying in a letter to the latter: "You believe in the God who plays dice, and I in complete law and order in a world which objectively exists, and which I, in a wildly speculative way, am trying to capture."[18]

Mystics Try to Reunite What Rationality Separates

In another entwining of the two main rational evolutionary currents, mystics have often tried to introduce the notion of oneness between humans and nature in organized religion.

Angelus Silesius, a seventeenth-century European mystic, who experimented with Lutheranism and Catholicism, said that "In God all things are one. He does not separate; with me as with a gnat does He communicate."[19]

Kabir, a fifteenth-century Indian mystic, who bridged Hindu and Moslem traditions, wrote: "O friend, Kabir has looked for him [the divine] everywhere, but to no avail. For Kabir and he are one, not two. When a drop is submerged into the ocean how is it to be seen as distinct? When the ocean is submerged in the drop, who can say what is what?"[20]

Arthur I. Waskow, a modern Jewish mystic, writes:

As the kabbalists say, the Tree of Life and the Tree of Knowing Good and Evil were one tree; but Eve and Adam could not experience them as one tree. If they had been able to eat knowing that the trees were one, history would at the beginning have achieved its goal. But how could they experience flow and separation as one whole? It was not until childlike human beings had grown up enough to experience separation, alienation, that they could desire to flowing wholeness and search toward it. And that is still our task. For the history we live in is the history of alienation. God sends us out; the Garden disappears, and we begin the history in which human beings do battle with nature; in which human beings sweat to win a living from the earth; in which men rule over women and give them their names; in which we are exiled from our land; in which we kill each other. It is not that these are the commandments for our walking on the path of life; they are descriptions of the path. Only institutions seeking to defend and entrench the rule of men over women would have taken "and your husband should rule over you" to be a positive command. Only institutions seeking to justify and prolong the toil of some people in the service of others would have taken "and you shall eat bread in the sweat of your brow" to be a positive command. Like the other conditions of life outside Eden, these were sad facts, described in sadness. They are meant to be overcome, not celebrated.[21]

PROSPECT OF A CONVERGENCE

For the moment, we see a sad exacerbation of fundamentalist, nationalistic currents, rather than an effort to master love and achieve integration. If those narrow-minded patterns of thought and behavior in science, religion, and politics—which foolishly attempt to fight nature within and outside us—prevail, I see two scenarios for the future of our evolution. In the most optimistic, we enter a prolonged dark age from which we painfully emerge, full of bruises and sorrows, into a new renaissance. In the most pessimistic, we end by destroying ourselves. Instead, if our efforts to evolve toward new harmonizing integrative structures of consciousness grow and coalesce, we may see a convergence of love-mastering traditions and power-controlling organizations into new forms of social and economic organization.

There is a fascination with efficient procedures among power-controlling organizations. The focus of love-mastering traditions, instead, is on seeking knowledge; developing wisdom; becoming masters of our physical, mental, emotional, and spiritual life; and peacefully enjoying the erotic powers of nature. The convergence of the two trends would blend the human and ecological concerns of the love-mastering traditions with the legitimate interests for technical and financial efficiency of the power-controlling organizations. It would also harmonize the satisfaction of needs, which is of main concern to followers of the love-mastering/life-enjoyment paradigm, and the creation of desires, which is an instrument used by those who control power to increase their wealth.

3

NEEDS AND DESIRES

C arlos A. Mallmann defines needs as those requirements that we always find when we analyze human behavior, irrespective of culture, race, language, creed, color, sex, or age.[1] Needs do not depend on the value system of specific social structures, nor are they conditioned by the natural environment in which a community evolves or by its degree of technical and social development. Needs cannot be programmed by society or modified by the will of the conscious mind. Needs, which are part of our read-only memories, have been recorded by nature in the unconscious since our archaic origin.

Desires can instead be modified—even suppressed—by acts of will because they are products of the interaction of the conscious mind with subconscious behavioral programs and existential records. Not only do desires differ from one society to another and among individuals in the same community, they change within a given society as the technologies and the cultural patterns of that particular society change. Moreover, desires are different for each individual at different stages of life.

Needs are like the base material of a photographic film, which produces different pictures depending on the nature and intensity of the light to which it is exposed. Acting as beams of light that influence photosensitive material, values and beliefs modify the simple and replicative configuration of human needs to produce complicated sets of desires. Human beings always need shelter and food, but some may prefer to save on good food to buy luxurious homes, whereas others may feel comfortable in modest homes and splurge on sophisticated meals. The need for a dialogue with the spirit may, according to the early programming of the mind, awaken desires for meditating, contemplating nature, or praying according to one rite or another. The need for clothes to protect ourselves from cold weather should not be confused with the compulsion to cover the body, even when soaking in the warm waters of tropical beaches, to avoid chastisement for breaking the taboo of nudity. Nor should this need be confused with the desire to dress in attire that denotes a certain social status or identifies us as belonging to certain groups.

An Integral View of Human Needs

In Figure 9 I draw a set of independent needs derived from my original proposal published in 1976 and reproduced later in other articles and books.[2]

Specific satisfiers of psychological and sociocultural needs work efficiently only when biological and biopsychological needs have also been satisfied. At the same time, satisfaction of the psychological and sociocultural needs enhances the satisfaction of biological and biopsychological needs. When discussing the degree of satisfaction of needs within a society, economic analysis should neither forget to prioritize the biological level nor neglect any of the levels above it.

Biological Needs

Biological needs are those which, if not satisfied, lead either to the physical disappearance of the individual (energy-renewing requirements) or to an imbalance in the individual's life-supporting systems (energy-balancing requirements). Among this group of needs, sexual activity is unique because it is linked with the satisfaction of more than one need. It is always deeply rooted in the biology of individuals, and while assuring the perpetuation of the species it also contributes to maintaining the energetic equilibrium of the individuals, and it satisfies both the psychological need for recreation and the so-

Figure 9. SET OF NEEDS

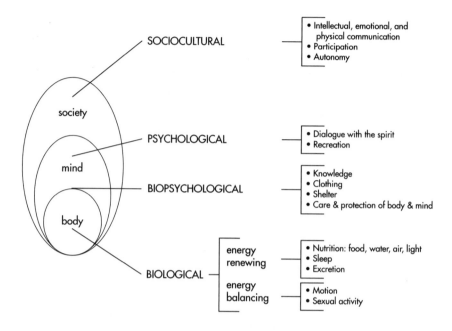

ciocultural need for communication. However, institutions inspired by the power-control/wealth-accumulation paradigm still attempt to limit this rich activity to its contributions to the reproduction of the species.

BIOPSYCHOLOGICAL NEEDS
Biopsychological needs seem to have been written by nature in our read-only memories to compel us to emerge from the archaic structure of consciousness and start processing natural elements for the increased protection of our existence. To accomplish this purpose, we had to interrogate nature and develop knowledge about her.

PSYCHOLOGICAL NEEDS
The needs for recreation and a dialogue with the spirit aim at increasing life enjoyment and reducing the stress produced by the efforts that our survival and development entail. Exhaustion from

using up all the energy in the task of survival may lead us to temporarily repress recreation and spirituality. These needs can be postponed, but never suppressed, and even their temporary repression may cause disease. Whether enculturated to believe in generative powerful spiritual forces, or in the evolution of matter following its own laws, we all feel the smallness of the planet in the vastness of the creation, and the even smaller size and power of our beings in the often awesomely powerful natural world. These feelings lead us to interrogate ourselves about our origin, the aim of our existence, and the meaning of life and death. Responses to these questions are found by dialoguing with the creative spirit through external social rituals and internal personal practices. Re-creation of the life pleasures bestowed by the creative spirit upon its creatures also helps us find answers.

The recent revival of spiritual expressions in formerly Marxist countries, where organized rituals were previously banished, further corroborates this truth: that the spiritual dialogue is a universal and invariant need, not a programmed desire. Marxist leaders identified the spiritual dialogue with the oppressive practices of some religious groups that supported particular interests. Following their own scientific dogmas, those leaders banished the expression of all systems of belief instead of empowering the people to decide by themselves which elements of the old systems hindered their personal and socioeconomic development and which satisfied their spiritual needs. Marxist leaders did not expand and intensify people's consciousness. They just changed the nature of the fences within which consciousness was corralled. In chapter 12, I discuss the consequences of this action on the Russian experiment.

SOCIOCULTURAL NEEDS
These needs, although still anchored in each individual's unconscious, require humans to build societies as another step in their emergence from the archaic structures of consciousness. The search for satisfiers for all other needs can be the task of a single person. Communication, participation, and autonomy speak instead of activities that involve at least two persons.

In a captivating re-creation of Robinson Crusoe's adventure, the French novelist Michel Tournier describes the whole process by which a person left alone on an isolated island first survives by discovering natural elements with which to satisfy his biological needs, and then slowly perfects his life by learning to satisfy biopsychological and psychological needs. But only when Friday joins him does he again become a complete human being.[3] At this point, Crusoe can establish physical, emotional, and intellectual communications with another human. Crusoe and Friday can then feel that they both should participate in further developing what has become a community while still remaining independent from each other to satisfy the need for autonomy.

Submission of one person to another, and dependence of one person on another, are not the result of satisfying natural needs. Submission and dependence are created by desires programmed into the hard disk of our subconscious during our enculturation. The desire to have power over others and to use others to increase one's own wealth promotes dominance. The desire to be protected from threats that we have learned to fear promotes submission.

The needs of communication, participation, and autonomy can be summed up in one concept: the need of love, of loving, and of being loved. The closer we are to our ever-present origin, the more intense is this need. Babies may have had all their biological and psychological needs satisfied, but if they lack love from others, the chances are that they will develop diseases and may even die. Without another person, it is still possible to love oneself, but it is with others and through others that love is displayed in all its liberating and nurturing dimensions. Although all other needs, as we have already said, can be satisfied by oneself, love from others makes their satisfaction more pleasurable and intense. For instance, knowledge delivered without love is difficult to acquire and unlikely to promote wisdom. The satisfaction of biological needs—the care of body and mind—without love are less than machine-shop work, because happy engineers and mechanics bring love and laughter to their work.

The conscious introduction of love into all our activities, but especially in the satisfaction of our permanent and invariable needs, is one of the axiomatic properties of the integrative, harmonizing consciousness. As Teilhard de Chardin says: "In spite of all the apparent improbabilities, we are inevitably approaching a new age in which the world will cast off its chains, to give itself up at last to the power of its internal affinities. We must believe without reservation in the possibility and the necessary consequences of universal love."[4]

THE REPRESSION OF NEEDS

When a need goes unsatisfied, human beings frequently express the pain associated with the deprivation of the corresponding satisfiers through oneiric symbols and distorted behavior. It has been shown that under conditions of sexual freedom and scarcity of food, images of food appear in people's dreams and in the arts as frequently as erotic arts and dreams are found in sexually repressed societies.[5] It has also been shown that the lack of satisfaction of the need for emotional and physical communication brings about violent behavior and strong drives for power, domination, and the accumulation and parade of wealth.

This may explain the explosion of consumption among rich but emotionally starved people. It may also be the root cause of the blind violence that threatens developed and developing societies alike. It is a violence that erupts day after day through diverse individual and governmental forms of terrorism, drug pushing, Mafia control of businesses, shootings, kidnappings, rapes, guerrilla activities, harassment of minorities, and sabotage.

This kind of violent behavior is exacted by a faulty programming of the minds. It is quite different from either a natural violent response to a life-threatening situation or the violent behavior that results from nutritional deficiencies and metabolic illnesses. At least three kinds of enculturation programs induce violent behavior. One such program handicaps the development of affectionate bonds of trust in parent-child relationships, and in the intimacy of relationships between teenagers. The resulting emotional deprivation is recorded in the subconscious, generating vicious, enraged responses.[6] Another family of programs promotes aggressive competition and makes each competitor—whether at home, school, church, playground, or marketplace—neglect the subjectivity of others.[7] The third group of programs is generated by political and religious groups that teach people to hate those who do not share the same ideology or faith. These lead the followers of one political party or one religion to believe that their socioeconomic well-being or their spiritual salvation is linked to the conversion or destruction of the others.

A heavy programming of minds against the satisfaction of needs transforms human beings into automatons by suppressing their instinctive needs for intellectual, emotional, and physical communication; participation; autonomy; knowledge; and a free, unhindered dialogue with the spirit. When these needs are not satisfied, humans cannot unfold their humanness. Humans cannot be fully human and feel fully alive when only their biological needs are appeased. This is precisely what has been happening during most of human history. Since the magi and sages transformed hordes into tribes, we have developed socioeconomic institutions of various kinds. These were aimed at reducing the risks and increasing our efficiency and effectiveness in obtaining satisfiers of our needs. The management of these institutions was soon appropriated by elite groups whose power was further reinforced by their appropriation of the means invented by humans for the production of satisfiers. The rules that these elites imposed upon society allowed them to acquire more satisfiers than those allowed the majority under their authority. They especially repressed the satisfaction by the latter of their needs for communication, participation, autonomy, and knowledge.

When technologies for the production of satisfiers and for warfare were based almost exclusively on human energy, the elites thought that any diversion of this energy from productive and reproductive uses toward "unfruitful," "sterile" recreational and relational activities had to be avoided. It was feared that an expenditure of energy for these purposes would adversely affect production by simultaneously decreasing the productivity of laborers and their cheap availability. It was also feared that a permissive attitude toward emotional and physical communication would adversely affect the waging of war by decreasing the number of available people and their aggressiveness.[8] At the same time, wanting to have clear and secure channels through which to transfer their accumulated wealth and acquired power to their own descendants, and unable or unwilling to repress their own sexual drives, the elites programmed patrilineal cultures in which women were divided into three groups: the privileged but dependent family-guardians of the upper classes, the reproductive machines and economy-keepers of the lower classes, and pleasure-giving courtesans and prostitutes.

The elites knew that despite repression, an analysis by the masses of the programs that were guiding their behavior would lead to revolt. Hence, they controlled the sources of knowledge that could empower people for this self-analysis of the interactions between their development and their surrounding environment. One of the controlled sources, often plainly barred to the masses, was education, because it facilitated people's access to knowledge by helping them acquire logical thought processes and skills for organizing sensory experiences. The other controlling source was religion: Elites transformed churches from institutions that could help people to establish a fruitful inner dialogue with the spirit, thus helping them gain intuitive knowledge, into competitive communities of formal, narrow-minded believers. Even war, the ultimate wastrel of satisfiers, was rationalized as being a God-sent command. When Napoleon started his Great Army, "in nearly every church the clergy called upon the youth of the nation to obey the call to the colors; they proved from Scripture that Napoleon was now under the direct guidance and protection of God."[9]

The English philosopher William Godwin (1756–1836), a lucid cultural critic of his time, said that English elites opposed the communication of knowledge to the people because "a servant who has been taught to write and read ceases to be any longer the passive machine they [the elites] require."[10] Godwin "repudiated the conservative contention [so often repeated even in our time] that the masses were congenitally inferior and always potentially murderous, and therefore had to be ruled by fable, terror, or force. He thought that most inferiorities were due to inadequate education, narrow opportunities, or environmental blight."[11] The problems with the masses have never been in their nature, but instead with the mind of the elites who separated themselves from their fellow beings, hindering—when not prohibiting—their pursuit of satisfaction for the full set of needs.

By the end of the eighteenth century, intellectuals and artists were trying to peel off absurdities from beliefs anchored in our magical and mythical structures. The Spanish painter Goya ridiculed superstitions in a series of small paintings, dated from 1797 to 1798, which he called witchcraft scenes. Goya was part of the enlightenment that viewed reason as the supreme guide of human society. Under its guidance, all people would find opportunities to satisfy all needs. Soon Goya would realize that with fables and fears, and by hiding knowledge, reason can easily be put to sleep. In its dreams, reason can rationalize monstrous atrocities and justify duplicitous actions. Goya then painted "El Sueño de la Razón Produce Monstruos" (The Dreams of Reason Engender Monsters).

When reason is guided by love and integrated with imagination and intuition, it perfects life and increases its enjoyment. When reason is constrained to serve the interests of power and wealth, it develops capabilities to rationalize even the irrational. Unfortunately, it is this last behavioral paradigm that has dominated the evolution of rationality and produced the pain that we now suffer.

PART II

OUR DIVISIVE, SLEEPY RATIONALITY

The effects of rational structures of consciousness patterned into *amour propre*, power control, and wealth accumulation on our societies and economies.

4

SAD HOMES AND UNSAFE STREETS

For centuries now, all societies have followed enculturation patterns that develop *amour propre* while structuring our rationality. The belief and behavioral programs written into the hard disks of our minds include many commands that repress the satisfaction of needs, working against the intuitions and instinctive drives that emerge from the archaic layers of our consciousness. It becomes easier to recognize the irrationality of those commands when we relate them to the particular needs whose satisfaction, or repression, they try to socially organize (see Table 1). The list of commands in the table is by no means exhaustive, but it contains enough examples to show how difficult it is for people to develop as fully human and fully alive beings after undergoing enculturation processes that instill those values and beliefs.[1]

FAMILY VALUES

Nowadays, everybody talks about family values. It has become a political issue. However, family values are about commitment and care, and those are products of love, not law. Unjust laws and inhuman economies are hindering the unfolding of love through commitment and care. They make commitment and care scarce commodities, even within families who, for the outside world, appear to be happy groups that get along quite well.

Table 1. ARMING RATIONALITY WITH AMOUR PROPRE

Needs	Frequently Used Commands in Our Enculturation Programs
Biological	• The body is seat of the devil and prone to be manipulated by it. Nudity favors the devil's work and excites low passions; hence it is a criminal act to let others see your body naked. Even when feeding their babies, mothers should not expose their breasts to the view of others. • Although excretory functions are inescapable elements of the living process, they are shameful. • Sexuality has no other purpose than to perpetuate the species, and even then it is another shameful chore of human life. Sensuality, and all sexual activities that bypass reproduction in favor of recreation and relationship, are criminal.
Biopsychological	• To have access to knowledge, good clothes and shelter, and premium care and protection for the body, we must have as much money as possible. • We should not attempt to solve problems in the functioning of our bodies and our minds by ourselves. Specialists licensed by society should be in charge of them. • With gentleness we can neither tame the wild instincts of the body nor develop its strength. No pain, no gain.
Psychological	• God is the only being more powerful than ourselves, but he is our ally and will lead us in the attempt to get power and wealth. If we become rich and powerful, it means that God loves us; if not, we have fallen from grace. • Recreation should avoid physical communication with other beings. A clear distinction should be made between chaste merriment and erotic delights. Society should punish the latter.
Sociocultural	• Our race, our religion, our culture are superior to all others. If the others do not accept a subordinate position in our society, they should be excluded, even by exercising violence on them. • All who do not share our perception of the world; our way of thinking, feeling, behaving; and organizing household, societies, and economies are against us. • Women are inferior to men and should submit to their authority. • Humans are here to put nature to service. • Our cars, our homes, our kids' achievements, our wives' beauty, all our possessions are part of ourselves and define our position in the world. • We should care for our own life and that of our immediate descendants without concern for the long-term future. If the flood comes after us, let us make sure that our names survive by inscribing them in as many statues, memorials, and stones as we possibly can. • It is immodest to openly express emotions. Men, especially, should never cry. • The more power and wealth we have, the more we can participate in social and political life, and the more autonomous our lives will be. • Physical, emotional, and intellectual communication, even among consenting adults, should be carefully controlled by society through government.

How can there be commitment and care when every touch among family members is suspect of perversion; when every sensual, tender moment between parents, kids, and relatives is lust; when the discovery of the body by toddlers and infants through ancestral games provokes anxious, intolerant, prejudiced reactions from parents and educators; when politicians, parents, educators, and priests ask teenagers to abstain from sexual relations at their peak of hormone production; when even masturbation is charged with guilt and fears; when courtship has lost romance and playfulness?

Children observe their parents, whether divorced or still living together, lose their lives in their attempt to earn an income. When one of the spouses decides to stay home and raise the children, the other has to multiply his or her activities in the marketplace to maintain a decent standard of living. This reduces their opportunities to exercise motherhood or fatherhood when children need both a male and a female model for their balanced development.

Any time someone is seriously injured or ill, families have to worry about bankruptcy. Then, the sick member of the family does not receive the tender physical and emotional support required for his or her recovery because the other members are rushing to find the extra money to pay the health care bills. Physicians cannot replace them in the task. They are too busy and feel too awkward to spend time just sitting beside the bed, talking and holding hands with the sick person.

Monogamic families and youth are the two social groups that suffer the most from the combined stress of highly competitive economies and laws that repress healthy instinctive drives emerging from our ever-present origin.

The monogamic family represents the most elaborate and sophisticated compromise between our archaic natural instincts and our social desire to have a solid base for the development of both partners and their offspring. To keep this delicate balance for the couple's lifetime requires a continuous renovation of the partners's erotic personalities. Integration and harmonization of the particular interests and potentials of the two members also require a just share of daily household chores and pleasures, and of market and social opportunities and responsibilities. The chances of reaching this balance increase when the household is formed after each member gets to know the other well at all levels: physical, emotional, intellectual, and spiritual.

None of these requisites can be easily fulfilled under repressive laws, feelings of guilt and shame instilled by the enculturation process, harsh economic struggles, social shortsightedness, and cultural ignorance. No wonder, then, that we keep only the appearance of a monogamic society through a succession of divorces and remarriages. More recently, the high financial costs, economic losses, and emotional pain associated with each divorce are leading to dating rather than remarriage after the first divorce.

Often, youth who have suffered the painful experience of their parents' divorce in their childhood are later assailed with troubles of their own. Quite often, we hear grim stories of teenagers' irresponsible behavior, which strains household budgets and social welfare systems. For instance, we hear of a twenty-year-old woman who already has five children and is living on welfare. Or we may hear of a twenty-year-old man who has fathered six children with different teenage girls and shows neither support nor affection for his previous partners or his offspring.

Mature people who complain about this situation can be heard saying, "We are fed up with having to support the irresponsibility of youth with our taxes." The first reflection that comes to mind when these complaints are heard is the amazing fact that few people refrain from paying taxes to sustain military adventures that kill blossoming youth. The second reflection is that most people seem to blame those problems on the perversity of human nature and the perversity of social welfare systems. Few voices are heard about the perversity of societies and educational systems that throw youngsters into the jungle of our harsh competitive economic systems and our disintegrating societies with neither knowledge nor wisdom about their chaotic instinctive impulses whose strong somatic persistence confuses them.

The youth of our hominid ancestors were in much better shape. Their archaic consciousness could receive, through widely open channels, the wisdom of the cosmic consciousness. Youth in our rational societies have been cut off from this source by the same education that also denies them scientific information on the most insistent and urgent aspects of their lives.

With neither knowledge nor wisdom, youth submit blind and deaf to the instinct, and refuse to become responsible participants in irresponsible social organizations. Taxpayers are as confused as youth are, and as a result they act as irresponsibly as youth do. Taxpayers pay happily for the wrong causes and are stingy when governments invest in the only instruments that could help youth channel their instinctive drives toward a healthy rationality—mainly art, culture, education, and recreation.

Even in 1776, Adam Smith thought that the best antidotes against superstition and enthusiasm were the study of science and philosophy and the gaiety of public diversions. He said:

> The state, by encouraging, that is by giving entire liberty to all those who for their own interest would attempt, without scandal or indecency, to amuse and divert the people by painting, poetry, music, dancing; by all sorts of dramatic representations and exhibitions, would easily dissipate, in the greater part of them, that melancholy and gloomy humor which is almost always the nurse of popular superstition and enthusiasm.[2]

The problem is with the different interpretations that followers of Adam Smith's economic and political ideas have given to the words *scandal* and *indecency*. After all, scandal and indecency are in the eyes of the beholder, and what for some is a scandalous and indecent representation or exhibition, to others is just a display or illustration of uninhibited, playful behavior, which is free of social conventions. I suggest that only representations and exhibitions of violent attitudes should be considered scandalous or indecent, because in present societies violence is another product of melancholy and gloomy humor. Violence in our societies is more toxic than superstition and enthusiasm. Moreover, technological advances in communications can now spread the three toxins—superstition, enthusiasm, and violence—with a power unknown in Smith's time, and advances in the technology of weaponry are making killing and maiming easier every day.

MELANCHOLY AND GLOOMINESS

Social regulation of private behavior has transformed our households into places of sad solitude. Rousseau perceived this in the eighteenth century and commented, "When home is only a sad solitude, one must go elsewhere for gaiety."[3] But where is that elsewhere in our times? Streets have become unsafe; markets and workplaces have turned dull and impersonal; the joy of meditative or recreational reading is being dampened by excessive divergent pressures on our limited leisure time; agape, the loving communion with the universal spirit, is hard to find in passive, listless, sanitized religious services; and Eros, the spirit of physical and emotional exchanges between humans, is discovered through and practiced in ways that kill its playful character because they involve mechanical initiations, culturally induced scorn of romantic tenderness and warmth, and socially created feelings of guilt and shame.

What, then, are the alternatives that may offer relief to our thirst for gaiety? Television and movies with their parade of violence? The deafening and somber discos? The stadiums where for each over-stressed player in the competitive game there are thousands of passive beer-gulpers? A pornography full of violence and repetitive sexual mechanics that hides from the young the tenderness, imagination, and playfulness of the erotic artistry that museums and art books display—an artistry practiced by ancient as well as modern cultures? It is no wonder that there is so much anger and frustration among the youth of our time and that so many youngsters are either being lured into becoming drug pushers or enlisted as warriors for deceitful dictatorships and religious fanaticisms.

Since the time of Adam Smith and Jean Jacques Rousseau, the divergence between what nature tells humans they need and what humans receive from society has grown (see Table 2). Thanks to Smith, Rousseau, and other philosophers of their time, we began to dream of a better future. Liberté, Egalité, Fraternité proclaimed the French Revolution. The rights to life, liberty, and the pursuit of happiness were written into the constitution of the United States. If we have only partially accomplished these dreams, it is because their fulfillment would have required the enculturation of people into *amour de*

Table 2. What We Need and What We Receive

Nature tells children to ask for	Children instead receive
Nourishment	Underfeeding among the poor Overfeeding with undernourishment among the rich
Close physical and emotional contact with their parents	Almost nothing; parents are too busy either trying to survive or accumulating and maintaining wealth; moreover, parents are programmed against close physical and emotional contacts
Information on how the spirit evolved into the wonders of the universe and how humankind is becoming human	Information on the mechanics of nature and history
Guidance, support, and help to explore the world and their bodies	Fears

Then children grow into teenagers

And when the teenagers ask for	They instead get
Opening up physical and emotional contacts with other bodies and other minds	Codes, norms, and regulations that block communication with others and introduce more fears
Romance	Incitements to practice mechanical sex and to think that relationship-building is a game in which there is always a loser and a winner
A joyful inner dialogue with the spirit	Devotional forms that are empty and boring

In turn, the teenagers become grown persons

And when the grown persons ask for	They instead get
Time to be	Time to work and use possessions and services
Time to share with those they love	Time to compete
Time to dialogue with the spirit	Time to get bored at churches
Food that will renew cells and energies	Junk food, empty of calories in the developed world Not enough food in the developing world

Finally the grown persons become elders

And when they call for	They instead get
The gentle and loving touch, the intimate caress that will keep the energy balanced and flowing	Cold family and institutional spaces where touching and caressing are taboo Scorn from society if they satisfy these needs by themselves
Nurturing food prepared and served with love and joy by themselves and others	Fast food and TV dinners at homes and restaurants of the developed world Scarcity of food resources and harsh conditions to transform them into meals in the developing world
Participation in society, opportunities to deliver their accumulated experience and to receive new information on changes in science, technology, and society, both the delivery and the reception taking place at a pace adjusted to their condition of reduced energy	Loneliness Learning opportunities submitted to rigid schedules and formalities in the developed world Lack of possibilities for adult education in the developing world

soi, empowering them to master the forces of love and life. Instead, the societies that emerged from those two great transformational processes in the Western world went in the opposite direction. They indoctrinated people into *amour propre,* power control, and wealth accumulation. "A higher value was attached to whatever could be shown in public according to the rules," while "any sign of inner life had become suspect."[4]

Indeed, we live longer in the industrialized countries, and those who have means live better than when Rousseau and Smith were alive, but we are increasingly discontented. Societies that see themselves as inheritors of the French and the American revolutions have still to understand that we need freedom, knowledge, and wisdom to master our physical, mental, emotional, and spiritual health through individual, diversified pathways. It is this mastery that may bring gaiety and loving care to our households, promote equity in the operation of the markets, and free streets from violence.

THE USE OF VIOLENCE UNDER THE POWER-CONTROLLING BEHAVIORAL PARADIGM

Governing elites needed large populations to provide docile warriors for external wars and internal struggles, cheap labor for the production of goods and services, and domestic servants for supporting the elite's leisure. Barring common people, men and women, from knowledge was not enough to keep them submissive within societies organized by and for the elites. It was also necessary to exercise violence, crush dissent, and impose blind obedience. To exercise violence it was necessary to have violent people, and to make people violent, it was necessary to do violence to their human nature by depriving them, from an early age, of external love and by making them fearful of the love impulses that spontaneously spring from within each being.

Table 3 gathers words on violence spoken by some outstanding programmers of the power-controlling paradigm.[5] For these programmers, the ideal society is a society of people who can live with only subconscious hard disks and no contacts with their cosmically enfolded unconscious. Thus, the conscious operators act only on the

Table 3.   PROGRAMMING PEOPLE FOR VIOLENT BEHAVIOR

Samuel (11th century B.C.E.)	• Now, go and strike down Amalek; put him under the ban with all that he possesses. Do not spare him, but kill man and woman, babe and suckling, ox and sheep, camel and donkey. (1, 15:3)
Ecclesiasticus (2nd century B.C.E.)	• A man who loves his son will beat him frequently so that in after years the son may be his comfort. (30:1) • Pamper your child, and he will give you a fright, play with him, and he will bring you sorrow. (30:9) • Bend his neck in youth, bruise his ribs while he is a child, or else he will grow stubborn and disobedient, and hurt you very deeply. (30:12)
The Koran (7th century C.E.)	• Garments of fire have been prepared for the unbelievers. Scalding water shall be poured upon their heads, melting their skins and that which is in their bellies. They shall be lashed with rods of iron.
Martin Luther (16th century C.E.)	• Heretics are not to be disputed with, but to be condemned unheard, and whilst they perish by fire, the faithful ought to pursue the evil to its source, and bathe their hands in the blood of the Catholic bishops, and of the Pope, who is the devil in disguise.
Adolph Hitler (20th century C.E.)	• The very first essential for success is a perpetually constant and regular employment of violence. • A violently active, dominating, intrepid, brutal youth—that is what I am after. I want to see in its eyes the gleam of pride and independence, of prey. I will have no intellectual training. Knowledge is ruin to my young men.
Leon Trotsky (20th century C.E.)	• Not believing in force is the same as not believing in gravitation.

basis of the strong commands in the software generated by the programmers. They become deaf to the whispers of the creative cosmic consciousness that question the sanity and rationality of those violent commands.

It is not that there was no violence during the long period when we lived purely as creatures of nature. Humans of the archaic consciousness responded to personal threats by either fighting or fleeing, but there was no programmed, organized violence. This started during the next evolutionary step, when the first magic-based societies were organized. Since then, violent behavior has become the rule among those who want to maintain power and possessions. This has engendered equally violent responses from the dispossessed and the repressed.

Scientific and religious fundamentalism and nationalism all indulge in violence. It is their means of curbing dissent and subduing other groups or nations. In more democratic and participatory forms of organization, violence is still a component of the social tissue but not its main thread. If violence occurs even within societies of this last type, it is because the enculturation of their members continues to instill power-controlling programs in citizens' minds, making them perceive love mastering and life enjoyment as threatening activities.

This obnoxious programming generates within our consciousness a struggle between our longing for the beautiful and erotic and our socially acquired fears of beauty and eroticism. The struggle is clear in the many who, on one hand, promoted the mastering of the forces of love and, on the other, supported the repression of the erotic. Take, for instance, St. John. In the first of three letters that are included in the New Testament, John preaches against the sensuality of the world. He says: "You must not love this passing world or anything that is in the world. The love of the Father cannot be in any man who loves the world, because nothing the world has to offer—the sensual body, the lustful eye, pride in possessions—could ever come from the Father but only from the world."[6]

John's words speak out clearly the division between the creator and its creation, between body and mind that is depicted in chapter 1. For John, the body is one more vile and vain material possession, and the lustful eye betrays one more competitive game to increase our possessions. However, John also speaks of a Father full of love for his creatures, a Father who tells them to love one another and never to kill one another: "My dear people, let us love one another, since love comes from God and everyone who loves is begotten by God and knows God. Anyone who fails to love can never have known God because God is love."[7]

The inner struggle and the resultant contradictions clearly appear. It is as if humans and the world have been created differently; while a human is the I who can communicate with God, the world, including our bodies, is the It that is the domain of the devil.

The struggle is visible also in St. Francis. He sensed within his own family that the wealthy and powerful had to use violence to retain their privileges. As a young man he told his bishop, "If we have properties we will need arms to defend them."[8] He also believed that humans and nature are both equally magnificent exponents of God's works. St. Francis thanked God for the creation of nature. He saw the latter as being made active by the same spirit that animates humans.[9]

Yet, St. Francis feared the erotic to the point of thinking that the mortification of the flesh was a way to happiness. It is said that he "never allowed his appetite to be completely satisfied; and once he commanded a fellow brother to drag him naked through the streets of Assisi to mortify his body."[10]

John and Francis did not realize that loving others and God feeds on a healthy love of ourselves as full persons. If we do not accept, understand, and care for our own bodies and minds, we will not care for the mind and bodies of others, and we will exercise violence even on those closest to us.

THE SITUATION OF WOMEN

Memories of free frolicking paradises buried in the archaic structure, and of the polyandric customs of early magic-based societies, were felt as threatening by the men who built the mythic structure and, later on, the rational structure of today's human consciousness. These men rationalized that women had to be made submissive through economic dependence, psychological terror, and even sheer physical force to avoid a return of society to the practices that prevailed under the archaic and magical structures. Table 4 collects samples of the "rational" arguments that conspicuous programmers used in the design of women-controlling programs.[11] For a long time, these programs have been read into the subconscious mind of males and females of each new generation.

Violence against women destroys many individual lives, dissolve households, breaks down social tissues, and increasingly affects our economies because it is becoming a health issue, as is stated in a World Bank report. It is worth quoting this report at length:

Table 4.   HOW MEN PERCEIVE WOMEN UNDER THE POWER-CONTROLLING PARADIGM

Confucius (ca. 500 B.C.E.)	Such is the stupidity of woman's character that it is incumbent upon her, in every particular, to distrust herself and to obey her husband.
Aristotle (4th century B.C.E.)	The male is more fitted to rule than the female [and] as long as one is ruling and the other is being ruled, the ruler seeks to mark distinctions in outward dignity, in style of address, and in honors paid.
Ecclesiasticus (2nd century B.C.E.)	Sin began with a woman and thanks to her we all must die. (25:24)
Tertullian (2nd century C.E.)	Do you know that each of you women is an Eve? The sentence of God on this sex of yours lives in this age; the guilt must necessarily live too. You are the gate of Hell, you are the temptress of the forbidden tree, you are the first deserter of the divine law.
The Koran (7th century C.E.)	Women are your fields: go, then, into your fields whence you please.
Martin Luther (16th century C.E.)	Men have broad shoulders and large chests, and small narrow hips, and are more understanding than women, who have but small and narrow chests, and broad hips, to the end they should remain at home, sit still, keep house and bear and bring up children.
Macchiavelli (16th century C.E.)	Fortune is a woman, and if she is to be submissive it is necessary to beat and coerce her.
William Blackstone (18th century C.E.)	Husband and wife are one person in the law; that is, the very being or legal existence of the woman is suspended during the marriage.
Joseph Goebbels (20th century C.E.)	The National Socialist movement is in its nature a masculine movement. . . . The outstanding and highest calling of women is always that of wife and mother.

Data from many industrial and developing countries reveal that anywhere between one-fifth and more than half of women surveyed say they have been beaten by their partners. Often, this abuse is systematic and devastating. In Papua New Guinea, for example, 18 percent of all urban wives surveyed had sought hospital treatment for injuries inflicted by their husbands. In the United States domestic violence is the leading cause of injury among women of reproductive age; between 22 and 35 percent of women who visit emergency rooms are there for that reason.

Research has shown that battered women run twice the risk of miscarriage and four times the risk of having a baby that is below average weight. In some places violence also accounts for a sizable portion of maternal deaths. In Matlab Thana, Bangladesh, for example, intentional injury during pregnancy—motivated by dowry disputes or shame over a rape or a pregnancy outside wedlock—caused 6 percent of all maternal deaths between 1976 and 1986. Research from the United States indicates that battered women are four to five times as likely to require psychiatric treatment as nonbattered women and are five times as likely to attempt suicide. They are also more prone to alcohol abuse, drug dependence, chronic pain, and depression.

Rape and sexual abuse also damage women's health and are widespread in all regions, classes, and cultures. In Seoul 17 percent of women report being victims of attempted or actual rape. In one study of U. S. women a history of rape or assault was a stronger predictor of how many times women sought medical help and of the severity of their health problems than was a woman's age or unhealthy habits (such as smoking). In addition to physical injury and emotional trauma, rape victims run the risk of becoming pregnant or contracting sexually transmitted diseases, including AIDS. A rape crisis center in Bangkok reports that 10 percent of its clients contract STDs as a result of rape and 15 to 18 percent become pregnant, a figure consistent with data from Korea and Mexico. In countries where abortion is restricted or illegal, rape victims often resort to unsafe abortion, greatly increasing the danger of infertility or even death.

Another form of violence against women and girls is female genital mutilation, popularly known as female circumcision. An estimated 85 million to 114 million women in the world today have experienced genital mutilation. The practice is reported in twenty-six African countries, among minorities in India, Malaysia, and Yemen, and among some immigrant populations in western countries. If current trends continue, more than 2 million girls will be at risk of genital mutilation each year.

Clitoridectomies account for 80 to 85 percent of cases worldwide. Infibulation, which involves removal of more tissue, is more common in eastern Africa. These initiation rituals pose a health risk to girls and women and are a threat to their psychological, sexual, and reproductive well-being. The consequences of both procedures can include hemorrhage, tetanus, infection, urine retention, and shock. Infibulation

carries the added risk of long-term complications because of the repeated cutting and stitching at marriage and with each childbirth, and
it can limit a woman's choice of contraceptive method.[12]

WOMEN ASSERTING THEIR RIGHTS

Not too long ago, women started reacting against the situation described above. Their movements often adopted patterns of thought
and behavior inspired by the same *amour propre*, power ambition,
and greed that inspire most of male behavior. Women challenged societies to give them opportunities and responsibilities equal to those
given to men in the market place and social fora. They became CEOs
of big corporations, supreme court justices, legislators, and elected
officials. However, their fundamental contributions to the organization and management of households remain unrecorded in the national accounts. When a mother heals a baby, are not her services
worth those of a well-paid nurse? Why would not cookies baked with
love at home command a plus over the market price of similar mass-
produced cookies? When a psychologist takes us out of a depression,
we gladly pay the corresponding fees. How much more should that
person deserve than a companion who does the same at home with
understanding, love, and tenderness?

Indeed, men can also perform all these tasks, and they are increasingly doing so. However, women have carried them out almost
exclusively for millenia, while men only recently started sharing
these responsibilities. Men's participation in household chores is
more the result of painful economic pressures and an increased rate
of divorce than a product of a conscious movement toward integrating and harmonizing the needs and potentials of both genders.

Women and men seldom join in asserting the right, which both
have, to freely use their bodies and minds as the wonderful instruments of life, love, deep spiritual contact with nature, and happiness
that the creator intended them to be. Women, like men, confuse the
ownership of bodies and minds with the ownership of two more
pieces of productive machinery. Even when they use their bodies
and minds for pleasure, women and men do so under subconscious
commands of competition and performance.

Gallantry, flirtatious remarks, and flattering compliments are still normal patterns in the relations between men and women in cultures where power-control and wealth-accumulation motivations have not completely obliterated the instinctive commands.[13] Games of love and sexual attraction have been played since time immemorial. Our long march through magic, myths, and rationality has slowly transformed them from the coarse manifestations of a compelling instinct to refined romantic games sung by poets, painted by artists, translated into music, and described by writers. Of course, many women—and certainly more women than men—have been and still are the object not of these refined games but of sometimes brutal, sometimes subtle pressures to submit to sexual advances and participate in unwanted sexual practices, both at home and in the workplace.

Intuitively, men and women sense the difference between fine expressions of gaiety and affection, which lead to further intimacy only if both parties consent to it, and coarse physical approaches by bosses and companions who do not distinguish friendship from courtship, and persuasion from brutality. However, the enculturation process does not give people, especially women, the capacity to heed those intuitive messages and hold the coarse suitors back. Our enculturation transforms gender relations into a bloody sport with winners and losers. Given women's submission to men since the time of mythic societies, women still constitute the majority among the losers.

Buying into the same repressive codes designed by men for women's submission, women attempt to correct the situation not through changing the enculturation rules but through punishment. As in many other domains, a male-developed rationality tells women that the law should protect them. Instead of becoming masters of their emotions, their bodies, and their minds by changing internally and promoting similar changes in their offspring, husbands, lovers, and associates at school and work, women shifted responsibilities to external sources. Just as doctors fix problems affecting the body and the mind, so the reasoning goes, lawyers should fix problems in relationships. For the rational consciousness, there is always an external fixer of problems: another person or persons, or an external

69

divinity. There is a neglect of the inside, whence the creative spirit still speaks through our ever-present origin.

If women would defend their rights by promoting deep changes in the structure of male and female consciousness, they would bedeck households, marketplaces, and workplaces with new colors. Instead, their insistence on sexual harassment and sexual abuse laws has driven both genders further apart and made marketplaces and workplaces duller than they already were. The fear of mischievous law suits for sexual harassment have added one more threat to the already long list that budding creative entrepreneurs, male and female alike, fear to face when thinking about entering business.

We have reached a situation in which physicians hesitate to let their fingers explore the naked bodies of their patients. They bring nurses to witness examinations, and we may soon see them asking their patients to point on a human-size doll—a Rambo boy or a Barbie girl—to where it is aching. Similarly, educators who hug their students are suspected of being perverts.

THE SEXUAL REVOLUTION

The sexual revolution was mainly a revolution in the mechanics of sex. It allowed more sexual contacts but did little to improve the relations between partners, whether of the opposite or the same sex. As with most sociopolitical rationally inspired revolutions, the sexual revolution was incapable of leading people to integration and harmony. It made people jump from the old, damaging repression to the chaos of a newly discovered freedom without enough knowledge and with even less wisdom to exercise this freedom in a responsible and joyful way. As happened with those other sociopolitical revolutions, this one, too, risks ending with a counterrevolution that may inflict on people an even harsher repression than that against which they initially rebelled.

At earlier stages of the development of the rational structures, there was a shameless approach to the body and its functions. Children grew up within an adult world that did not hide these facts of life from them. There was no adolescence at those historical times. In transiting from a tough childhood to a tough and short adulthood,

70

children would learn about sex not from reading academic treatises but from observing their environment and experimenting with their bodies. As soon as they were ready for reproduction they were declared adults, sometimes after complicated initiation rituals, of which the Christian confirmation and the Jewish bar mitzvah and bat mitzvah are watered-down mementos. "Most ancient Middle European tribes declared their children adults at the age of 12, the Angles and Saxons even at the age of 11. A 13th-century German legal code (Schwabenspiegel) still allowed males of 14 and females of 12 to marry without their father's consent."[14]

From the seventeenth century on, the situation began to change, especially within the moneyed class. Children began to be protected from sexual knowledge and programmed to consider the body as a shameful part of nature that had to be controlled by the mind and always kept covered from the view of others. The age of consent was increased, and the requirement for long studies created a new social group, adolescents, who were economically dependent on their families. They were supposed, and for some governments in today's world they are still supposed, to go through the height of their sexual responsiveness and well into their twenties without any sensual or sexual experience.[15] Even Rousseau, who suggested that the main objective of education should be to help children develop a healthy love of themselves, thought that children should be maintained in a happy ignorance of sexual matters to prolong their innocence.[16] How could he expect households to be joyful, spirited places when the main forces of life, the forces of Eros, were silenced? How could he hope that an enlightened, compassionate self-esteem would develop if the beauty of the body and its functions were veiled and considered to be debasing factors that interfere with the higher objectives of the mind?

The introduction of the "pill" and a somewhat more open, post-Freudian attitude toward sex and sensuality prepared the rational mind for a positive change toward accepting a more free and open exercise of activities that aim at satisfying needs of energy balance, relation, and recreation. However, guided by *amour propre* rather than *amour de soi*, the sexual revolution became a pursuit of conflicting love games rather than harmony, of quick, uncommitted,

71

mechanical pleasure rather than romance and mutual trust. For couples, whether heterosexual or homosexual, it became a search for a variety of sexual objects outside the household rather than a revitalization of life within the household through fantasy and playfulness.

On the other hand, the prevailing powers maintained, and even reinforced, a moral code, norms, and regulations that deny the diversity of sexual orientations and behaviors, even trying to intrude upon the intimacy of the households to enforce a uniform comportment. Because the polymorphic, instinctual drives of the archaic structure cannot be ignored, adjustment to the inflexible rules set up by society is often bypassed. When the bypass takes a consensual path, it creates the consensual crimes on whose persecution society needlessly invests huge amounts of money.[17] When the bypass takes a brutal path, it creates violent crimes, which society must fight and punish. A healthier, *amour-de-soi*-inspired rationality would easily realize that consensual crimes are not really crimes and that violent crimes do not disappear just by jailing or killing the criminals. Criminals are the product of either educational and social mistakes or errors of nature. We should prevent the first and learn about the latter by studying the violent criminal while seeking his or her rehabilitation under controlled conditions that protect society.

Masses because of ignorance, and political leaders out of prejudice and self-interest, neither see the evidence contributed by specialists in these matters of violence and its punishment, nor learn from the negative results of past experiments with harsh judicial systems. Masses and politicians do not see what is out there, in our surrounding reality; they see instead what is not there. Shortsightedness and delusions are wrecking our lives. We will see next that shortsightedness and delusions also are wrecking our economies.

5

UNSTABLE, UNFAIR ECONOMIES

Since 1917, and until very recently, the struggle between capitalism and Marxism has dominated economic and political life in most countries. However, the fight between the two theories is much older, predating Karl Marx's publication of his *Communist Manifesto* in 1848. These old geopolitical and ideological confrontations obscured the fact that the two economic systems are based on the same economic model, namely, a circular flow of money in one direction and of resources, products, and services in the opposite direction (see Figure 10). These flows take place between households and enterprises: household expenditures become business receipts, and business costs make up household income. Governments participate in the flow, buying resources from the households, and products and services from the enterprises. Governments also collect taxes and in exchange provide services to both households and enterprises. Finally, savings by the households sustain business investments.

Marx did not propose to change this simple model. He suggested that what should be changed is the locus of ownership of the means of production from private hands to the hands of the governments. In 1918, the Russian revolutionaries implemented his suggestion, so that in Figure 10, the rectangle labeled "enterprises" could read "state enterprises" in the Soviet Union. If this is the only prominent change

Figure 10.   THE CIRCULAR FLOW MODEL

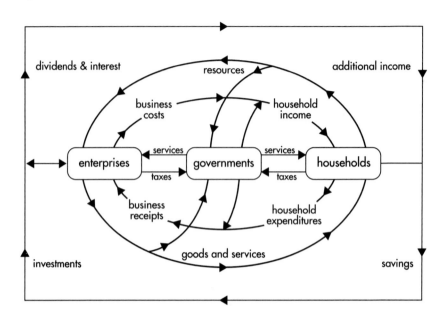

in the economic structure, why then all this long and costly confrontation? The answer is to be found in the links between the structures of our consciousness and market behavior. For Adam Smith those links were clear. As we will see, he suggested government interventions and reforms in education to promote behavior that would lead to the satisfaction of individual needs without affecting the common good. Marx thought, instead, that changing the structures of the markets would change the behavior of the people. History proved he was wrong. Marxist leaders had to use repression to keep the system functioning according to their model, and even with repression they could not satisfy all the needs of their populations. Moreover, they did not care to conserve the beauty and productivity of their natural environment. Instead, in democratic societies, free markets became increasingly efficient, and the consciousness of the population is slowly evolving toward a behavior that could increase freedom while reducing inequalities and respecting the regenerative and cleansing powers of nature.

THE IDEOLOGICAL DIFFERENCES

Adam Smith and Karl Marx clothed the simple, reproducible, mathematical model of the circular flow in two different ideologies. By the second half of the eighteenth century, when physics was still supporting the idea of a luminiferous ether, Smith believed that businesspeople, guided by an "invisible hand," would "make nearly the same distribution of the necessaries of life, which would have been made, had the earth been divided into equal portions among all its inhabitants, and thus without intending it, without knowing it, advance the interest of the society, and afford means to the multiplication of the species."[1] This statement reflects typical traits of the rational structures of consciousness at Smith's time. It misses the fact that a continuous multiplication of the species would end up reducing the piece of land available to each inhabitant to a miserable plot incapable of supporting anyone. It also fails to see that large portions of the planet can sustain no people, but are essential to the beauty and homeostasis of the whole Earth.

Marx became interested in political economy some fifty years after the publication of Smith's *The Wealth of Nations* (1776), which is considered the bible of capitalism. By then, scientific belief in such magical elements of reality as the luminiferous ether was slowly fading; science was becoming increasingly positivistic and materialistic. Seeing that markets were not operating in the equitable way that Smith had thought, Marx rejected the idea of an invisible hand as the organizing element of the circular flow. He proposed thrusting the full responsibility for the organization and guidance of the flow into the hand of governments. Knowing that entrepreneurs would not respond to state guidance on how to manage their enterprises, Marx proposed to transfer the ownership and operation of all businesses to the state.

Suggestions from the old magical and mythical layers in Marx's rational mind led him to adorn the simple frock he threw over the mathematics of the circular flow with appealing dentelles. Appropriation of the means of production by the state was presented as eliminating the old distinction between labor and capital, between workers and managers. Workers would participate in all the decisions required to produce and distribute goods and services effectively and equitably. Transformation of the state into the service-oriented representative of a classless society would assure equity and freedom in a measure never before known to the working class. Hence, the global appeal to this class to unite around Marxist ideology and to fight for the implementation of these new ideas.

Business owners felt extremely threatened in their interests and lifestyles when this appeal found a fertile ground for experimentation in the old Russian empire after the drain of financial resources and human bloodletting of World War I. Since then, economic and political leaders have engaged in world-wide hand wrestling that led first to the catastrophe of World War II and later to the economically destructive and socially annoying Cold War.

One side swore for the right hand, the invisible hand of the markets, which was efficient in increasing the circular flow but careless in assuring all participants a fair share of the flow's growth. The other side trusted the left hand, the heavy hand of the state, convinced that this hand would "provide to each according to his needs and demand from each according to his capacity."[2]

While the leaders were wrestling, the hands exchanged messages through signals subject to the codes of their respective systems. Some messages were pure propaganda; others had profound humane implications. Sometimes, messages of this last type were able to induce positive changes after being recoded along the patterns of the opposite system. At one point in the evolution of the Soviet Union, Lenin, inspired by capitalist signals, accepted the idea that cooperative forms of production might perform more efficiently than state-owned enterprises. Meanwhile, Marxist signals inspired labor unions in capitalist countries in their often painful task of obtaining humanization of the workplace.

Unluckily, the confrontation did not remain at that level for long. Soon the twin systems began to load their hands with deadly artifacts, testing them in other territories by hiring the unscrupulous hands of third parties as doubles in their fight. The whole of humankind then became involved in an ominous struggle, whose costs we will be paying for generations to come.

It has now become obvious that neither the invisible hand of the markets, nor the heavy hand of the state, or any combination of the two can efficiently deal with the economies of our time unless they are guided by an integrative, harmonizing structure of consciousness. The real invisible player in the marketplace is our consciousness. Its deficient structure created the problems that led one of the systems to destruction while the other, although the winner, is facing several options, some of which are threatening. Capitalist societies may fall into the abyss of an environmental catastrophe; may be swept by the winds created by the turbulence of a new world disorder; may retrograde to obscure, oppressive stages in the evolution of civilization where both reason and creativity were put to sleep by powerful interests and blinding dogmas; or may evolve to new, more humane ways of thinking and doing business and of creating, sharing, and enjoying wealth.

Capitalism won because its theory is based on a better interpretation of human nature, and the influence that society exerts on this nature, than the corresponding concepts that informed Marxism. However, for capitalism to survive and progress, it will need to bring its practice closer to its theory. Otherwise, it may achieve a Pyrrhic victory: a victory won at the cost of devaluing life and love.

ADAM SMITH'S THEORY WAS INSPIRED BY AMOUR DE SOI, BUT CAPITALIST PRACTICE WAS GUIDED BY AMOUR PROPRE

Adam Smith's rational mind was largely guided by ideas of a healthy self-esteem that motivates people, both consumers and producers, to harness the forces of love and enjoy life. The following quotes from Smith's *Theory of Moral Sentiments* clearly show this approach:

> Man, according to the stoics, ought to regard himself, not as something separated and detached, but as a citizen of the world, a member of the vast commonwealth of nature. To the interest of this great community, he ought at all times to be willing that his own little interest should be sacrificed.[3]
>
> The happiness of mankind, as well as of all other rational creatures, seems to have been the original purpose intended by the Author of nature, when he brought them into existence.[4]

77

It is not in being rich that truth and justice would rejoice, but in being trusted and believed, recompenses that those virtues must almost always acquire.[5]

Among those primary objects which nature had recommended to us as eligible, was the prosperity of our family, of our relations, of our friends, of our country, of mankind, and of the universe in general. Nature, too, had taught us, that as the prosperity of two was preferable to that of one, that of many, or of all, must be infinitely more so. That we ourselves were but one, and that consequently wherever our prosperity was inconsistent with that, either of the whole, or of any considerable part of the whole, it ought, even in our own choice, to yield to what was so vastly preferable.[6]

As we see, Smith does not separate the creative spirit from its creatures.[7] To him, the spirit talks to humans from inside their minds. If left free to follow this inner voice, consumers and producers would satisfy their individual needs without entering into conflict with the common good. Smith's idea of an invisible hand rejoins the concept of a consciousness whose structure neither blocks nor distorts the open flow of messages between the conscious and the unconscious. Hence, an unhindered *amour de soi* makes us feel, appreciate, and enjoy our unity with all the others. Smith thought that an invisible hand (which to me is consciousness) can bring order, freedom, enjoyment, and equity out of the apparent chaos of the marketplace.

In practice, capitalist leaders used their power to motivate their peers toward increasing their *amour propre*, seeking power control and wealth accumulation. Simultaneously, they indoctrinated the masses into submission and acceptance of the inequalities created by greediness and ambition. When indoctrination was not enough to assure submission, capitalist leaders would resort to brute force. Albeit for different reasons, the haves and the have-nots were to abstain from developing a healthy love for themselves.

Households that provided only labor were not given their fair share of the economic flow. The poorer they were, the less their share would grow with the growth in total flow. Some households were left totally outside the economic flow. Members of the latter made up the body of starving unemployed who would work for a pittance just to survive. Thus, the cost of labor was kept low, allowing the households that owned the means of production to appropriate most of the income originated by the flow.

Moreover, when the use of land by households interfered with the cheap production of material inputs, enterprises dispossessed their owners. John Kenneth Galbraith, in *The Age of Uncertainty*, describes the case of Scottish highlanders chased off by big landowners to make room for sheep.[8]

Smith was not blind to this divergence between capitalist theory and practice. In *The Wealth of Nations*, he denounced the oppressive behavior of business people and the fact that public education was facilitating neither the development of a healthy *amour de soi* nor the pursuit of happiness among the masses, promoting instead submission. I will analyze here only the first criticism, leaving the second for a later chapter on the role of education in the evolution of the structures of our consciousness.

SMITH'S PLEA FOR THE POOR

Despite his trust in the guidance of the invisible hand, Smith had to recognize the existence of injustice and exploitation. For thousands of years, societies have been programming minds toward a behavior quite contrary to that suggested by Smith. This programming replaced the self-preserving but compassionate attitude toward life with a possessive acquisitive disposition that led human behavior toward a destructive exploitation of other human beings and nature.

Smith speaks movingly of the miserable situation of the working class. He says that

> the man whose whole life is spent in performing a few simple operations, of which the effects too are, perhaps, always the same, or very nearly the same, has no occasion to exert his understanding, or to exercise his invention in finding out expedients for removing difficulties which never occur. He naturally loses, therefore, the habit of such exertion, and generally becomes as stupid and ignorant as it is possible for a human creature to become. The torpor of his mind renders him, not only incapable of relishing or bearing a part in any rational

conversation, but of conceiving any generous, noble, or tender senti-
ment, and consequently of forming any just judgment concerning
many even of the ordinary duties of private life. . . .[9] In every improved and civilized society this is the state into which the labouring
poor, that is, the great body of the people, must necessarily fall, unless
government takes some pains to prevent it.[10]

He perceived that this situation was a result of the gap in power
and wealth between the ruler and the ruled:

The masters, being fewer in number, can combine much more easily;
and the law, besides, authorizes, or at least does not prohibit their
combinations, while it prohibits those of the workmen. We have no
acts of parliament against combining to lower the price of work; but
many against combining to raise it. In all such disputes the masters
can hold out much longer. A landlord, a farmer, a master manufac-
turer, or merchant, though they did not employ a single workman,
could generally live a year or two upon the stocks which they have already acquired. Many workmen could not subsist a week, few could
subsist a month, and scarce any a year without employment. In the
long-run the workman may be as necessary to his master as his master is to him, but the necessity is not so immediate.[11]

I have said already that some seventy years after these writings,
Marx, building on Smith's and his own criticisms, started developing
a new economic theory on the basis of a different preanalytical view
of human nature and market mechanisms, but without changing the
basic mathematical model of the economy.

MARX'S VIEW OF HUMAN NATURE

Marx thought that Smith's call for government interventions that
would rescue the poor from despondency and alienation was of no
avail. To Marx, it was naive to call for justice from governments
whose interests colluded with those of greedy, narrow-minded business people.

Instead of appealing for justice to the private interests that created
the injustice, Marx recommended thorough planning and control of

all economic activities that produce the circular flow. Without this control, Marx maintained, the greed of owners of enterprises fouls the market's games, halting the achievement of the common good. Marx's recommendation was to transfer the property of enterprises to a state organized and administered by households, thus assuring that economic activities would serve all households, not just those of the entrepreneurs. We would then reach the type of society dreamed of by some prophets and mystics, partially achieved by some indigenous people before the European colonization, and romantically envisioned by some modern, pre-Marxist utopians.

Giving free rein to their imaginations, Marx and Engels describe their utopia as

> a communist society, where nobody has one exclusive sphere of activity but each can become accomplished in any branch he wishes, society regulates the general production and thus makes it possible for me to do one thing today and another tomorrow, to hunt in the morning, fish in the afternoon, rear cattle in the evening, criticize after dinner, just as I have a mind, without ever becoming hunter, fisherman, shepherd, or critic.[12]

As with capitalism, Marxist practice diverged considerably from its theory. Workers in Marxist societies did not exercise any of the options dreamed of by Marx and Engels, especially not the one that opened the possibility of becoming critics after dinner. As writers and filmmakers of the former Soviet Union have documented in harrowing books and movies, Marxist states augmented alienation with oppression, and workers could only aspire to become unidimensional Stakhanovite target-hunters.[13] Survival was assured, but a full human life became unachievable.

When Marx suggested that the rejection of the capitalist forms of production was a precondition for advancing individual freedom and economic equity, many thinkers in capitalist societies succumbed to the idea. These intellectuals were sickened by the overt reality of ignorance and subhuman conditions among large masses of the population, and alarmed by the discrimination against sexual, age, religious, and racial minorities. They soon realized, to their dismay, that in Marxist states fears went well beyond the fears of facing legal responsibility and social pressure for offbeat behaviors or beliefs. In Marxist states, with their secret police, ideological dissent and behavioral variation often meant arbitrary imprisonment, torture, and death.

An Interlude on Consciousness and Revolution

As I come from a scientific and engineering background, the word *revolution* always had for me the connotation of a geometric figure that starts from a point, then goes first upward, then downward, and finally backward before rejoining the starting point. Later on, my studies on consciousness and its evolution made clear to me that revolutions that spring from a rational structure of consciousness, especially from a structure that is enculturated into power control, can closely reproduce the geometric image. They usually do not end exactly where society was before the revolution; some evolution does take place through revolution. However, equally often, they end by worsening some social problems they were intended to correct.

Every attempt to violently and abruptly redistribute wealth has added rather than erased pain and oppression. As William Godwin said, "A revolution of opinion is the only means of attaining a better distribution of wealth."[14] But then it is not any more a revolution; it is an evolution to a more advanced structure of consciousness; it is one step further in the process of building on Earth a partnership with the cosmic consciousness. With these semantic distinctions, we should not say that the events that led to the formation of the United States of America constituted a revolution. Rather they were an evolutionary response of the white, propertied, American households to a distant king, who was exacting arbitrary taxes and denying his American subjects participation in policy-making. Thanks to this evolutionary response, those Americans became masters of their social, political, and economic life. It was a change from foreign tutorship to mastery by a local group. For the latter, the change meant taking important steps toward perfecting the rational structure of their consciousness. The first step was signalized by a declaration that all men are created equal, and that they are endowed by their creator with certain unalienable rights, among them being life, liberty, and the pursuit of happiness. Was this an attempt by Thomas Jefferson to bring the rational mind back in touch with the creative unconscious cosmic partner? Was the inclusion of the pursuit of happiness among the rights a recognition of our needs as natural beings? The other two steps in perfecting the rational structures of consciusness were also taken initially by Jefferson in his native Virginia. They were the separation of church and state and the promotion of public education. Later they became part of the Constitution and the political heritage of the whole country.

It was different with the two great European movements: the French and the Russian Revolutions. In the same way that "Rousseau's sovereignty of the people became, in the [French] revolution, the sovereignty of the state, then of the Committee of Public Safety, then of one man,"[15] Marx's dictatorship of the proletariat became the dictatorship of one party, and then of one man. It ended being a dictatorship *on* the proletariat and everybody else. Both revolutions started as love songs for liberty and compassion. In both cases, philosophers and educators recommended that leaders go slowly in the redistribution of wealth and power while making every possible effort to advance people's consciousness. In both cases, the revolutionary leaders—themselves with an unchanged consciousness, and too busy with consolidating power and responding to internal and external threats—neglected the advice. In both cases, because people did not know what to do with their newly acquired freedom, they generated chaos; and chaos called for repression. In both cases, a divisive rationality mutually fueled fears in both camps: the old and the new. In both cases, the revolutionary leaders attempted to further cut off the conscious mind of the people from the inner dialogue with the spirit. They lumped together this invariant and universal human need with previous exploitative excesses of organized religions that misappropriated their role of mediators in the dialogue.

In both cases, the world was ready for a change from old repression and exploitation. Many joined in the chorus to sing for liberty and compassion. Love of liberty and compassion led people like the historian Thomas Carlyle, the rich entrepreneur Baron John-

Baptiste du Val-de-Grâce, the essayist Mary Wollstonecraft, the writer Thomas Paine, and the poet William Wordsworth, among many others, to sing praises to the French Revolution in its initial stages. Later they became disappointed. Many entered into despair, caught between three equally discouraging options: the horrors of a popular movement co-opted by bloody leaders; the dictatorship of a former son of the Revolution, Napoleon; or the restoration of the old oppressive, insensitive Bourbon regime.

Love of liberty and compassion moved modern intellectuals— such as the British Bertrand Russell, the French Romain Rolland, the Chilean Pablo Neruda, the Argentines Aníbal Ponce and Lisandro de la Torre—to cheer the Russian Revolution.[16] None of them were seeking personal gains of power or wealth. After October 1918, they and thousands more felt as if a wind of fresh ideas were blowing in the world—a wind that would dispel the darkness of exploitation and bring new hope to humankind. The wind was used by skillful propagandists to create heavy clouds around "the workers' paradise." Reality had to be hidden from the rationality of the chorus members; otherwise they might get disappointed and change scores. Most of those intellectuals died before the clouds were pierced and the truth was known. Those who survived had to put up with the fact that the appropriation of the means of production by the state did not improve the human condition but rather allowed it to deteriorate. Some realized this very early. The German socialist Rosa Luxemburg (1870–1919) complained, "freedom for supporters of the government only, for the members of one party only—no matter how big its membership may be—is no freedom at all. Freedom is always freedom for the man who thinks differently."[17] And Harold Laski (1893–1950), a leader of the British Labour Party, warned, "the only permanent safeguard of democratic government is that the unchanging and ultimate sanction of intellectual decision should be the conscience. We have here a realm within which the state can have no rights and where it is well that it should have none."[18]

Love of liberty and compassion come from the depth of our spiritual ever-present origin. These sentiments are sometimes so strong that they lead certain individuals, usually those less encultured into competing for power control and wealth accumulation, to surround certain political events with a magic aura, blinding the rational consciousness to the fact that without a change in consciousness among the masses, a change of tutorship can only mean more of the old under a different banner. It happens especially with brilliant minds who, by personal decision or because of their enculturation, have blurred the cosmic vibrations that persist in bringing wisdom to our decisions. The more we deny our ever-present origin as spiritual creatures of nature, the easier it becomes for magic and myths to confuse our rationality.

Marx's proletarian paradise was a myth produced by rational analysis based on a faulty preanalytical vision of human nature. As we saw, the myth was later clouded in magic. Marx thought that a change in the external material environment was a necessary and sufficient condition to make individuals change the patterns of organization and management of households and enterprises. Marx failed to perceive that to reduce greed and promote compassion, it is necessary to teach *amour de soi*, love harnessing, and life enjoyment from a very early age, in an attempt to flexibly integrate and harmonize people's natural and social beings. Marxist education continued to develop *amour propre*, which was necessary to support the Stakhanovite competition with which Marxist leaders replaced capitalist competition. *Amour de soi*, love harnessing, life enjoyment, and the acceptance of our divinely created natural beings were perceived as threats to the building of communism. This approach ignored the truth that only a deeply felt and openly acknowledged self-love can lead to service to others. Then, the service is intentional, not compulsory.

Notwithstanding this negativism about revolutions, I should not allow my engineering mind to play tricks on my reflections and take the geometric analogy too far. Neither the countries where the first notes of the new liberty and compassion songs were heard, nor the world, went back exactly to the point from where it all started. In France, the Bourbons, the Napoleons, and the Republics that succeeded the first Napoleon were not the same as the old Bourbons. Most peasants kept the piece of land they got during the Revolution. Serfdom and compulsory church tithes could not be restored. In Russia, incipient democracy, with all its flaws, is light-years away from the obscurantism of the Czars. The world also gained from both experiments. The declaration of people's rights to liberty, property, security, and resistance to oppression is slowly penetrating even the most stout bastilles, those constructed by rationality with heavy mythical blocks and weighty bricks of greed. Most countries rid themselves of absolutist monarchs, and in only a few countries the link between churches and secular powers are still as strong as those kept by the Catholic church in prerevolutionary France. The idea that society should create opportunities for all to satisfy all their needs is also slowly permeating those blocks and bricks. We now find fewer business people displaying the cruelty recorded in the works of writers such as Dickens, Zola, Steinbeck, and Dostoyevsky than we could find in the period between the French and the Russian Revolutions.

RESULTS OF THE PROLONGED HAND-WRESTLING

During the forty years of hand-wrestling that followed World War II, the right hand, the victorious capitalist superpower and its allies, decided to fight "the evil of communism" everywhere in the world—never mind if, to achieve this purpose, they had to make alliances with spurious tyrannical systems. The left hand, the Marxist superpower, that also emerged victorious from the war aimed at "cleaning the world from the depravity of capitalism"—never mind if, to attain this aim it had to forge alliances with thieves and compromise with religious fundamentalisms. We have seen already that a sleepy and frightened reason can rationalize even the irrational and present to the unawakened mind the monsters of her dreams as angels of progress.

To achieve their respective geopolitical goals, both superpowers engaged in huge military expenditures and pressured smaller economies, which were within the orbit of one or the other, to do the same. Each superpower rationalized these expenditures as required to respond to the other's threat. The dependent economies rationalized them as necessary to respond to internal threats, any opponents to the government in place being labeled as communists, on one side, and as capitalist agents, on the other side.

Huge military expenditures produce strange effects on the simple mathematics of a regular circular flow (see Figure 11). The enterprises that produce the heavy equipment and sophisticated technologies of modern wars continue to buy resources from households, but their receipts are not made up of purchases by the households; their products are bought by the governments or paramilitary forces (guerilla groups).[19] This originates a sort of separate economic loop outside the normal flow of money, resources, goods, and services between enterprises and households. It is this loop that was denounced as the military-industrial complex by none other than the military man who led the Allied forces to victory in World War II. President, Eisenhower said in 1961:

> [The American people must be on] guard against the acquisition of unwarranted influence, whether sought or unsought, by the military-industrial complex. The potential for the disastrous rise of misplaced power exists and will persist. . . . We should take nothing for granted.[20]

More than ten years later, in 1974, a high official of the Department of State told Galbraith, "To understand this world you must know that the military establishments of the United States and the Soviet Union have united against the civilians of both countries."[21]

It was a conspiracy against the people because, as can be seen in Figure 11, the part of taxes that is invested in military expenditures does not have a counterpart of services provided by the government to the households. But the bad effects on households do not stop there. As the influence of the military-industrial complex increases and exploits the magical and mythical layers of people's consciousness, making them see threats everywhere, the military expenditures increase, soon exhausting governments' budgets. Governments then increase taxes, but when even this is not enough to cover expenses, they start borrowing, both internally and externally.

THE BURDEN OF DEBT

World War I was costly for the United States. The public debt jumped from $5.7 billion in 1917 to $14.5 billion in 1918 and $27.3 billion in 1919.[22] In World War II, indebtness was compounded by the start of

Figure 11. WAR EXPENDITURES AND THE CIRCULAR FLOW

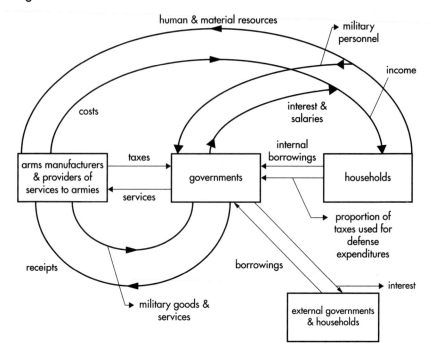

governmental interventions of the kind that Adam Smith thought necessary to avoid a dehumanization of the less favored sectors of society.[23] By the time World War II began, we were no longer living in a society in which, as Heilbroner and Galbraith say, "old-age retirement, medical expenses, and income during periods of unemployment are felt to be properly the sole responsibility of the individuals concerned."[24] This is the compassionate attitude that created the entitlements, so called because any individual or other entity that meets the requirements written into the respective laws is entitled to receive money from Social Security, Medicare, Medicaid, and similar programs. The debt now jumped from $42 billion in 1940 to $72 billion in 1942 and $158 billion in 1945.[25]

However, the worst was still to come. After the war, fear inspired policies of increased defense expenditures with an increasingly sophisticated, hence costly, technology. Then, in the 1980s, there was a decrease in taxes guided by the magical belief that lower taxes fuel the economy, and as the national product grows so do government revenues. Growth did happen: The national product grew from $1.6 trillion in 1975 to $7.5 trillion in 1996,[26] but the debt increased from $576 billion to $5.4 trillion: the outstanding public debt as of May 1, 1997.[27] Moreover, the increase in wealth was not shared equitably by the country's households, nor did those who benefited more from the economic growth increase their contributions to the government budget. The average family income among the 20 percent of the population with the lowest income decreased 15 percent between 1979 and 1994, while it grew 52 percent in the top 5 percent of the population.[28] Corporate income taxes represented 23 percent of the budget in 1967 but only 11 percent in 1994. Meanwhile, the contributions from individual income taxes and Social Security, which is also an individual contribution, grew in the same period from 63 percent to 80 percent.[29]

Besides the effect on the entitlements from demographics, the behavior of the beneficiaries, health-care professionals, and bureacracies that manage those much-needed programs all contributed to the huge deficits. Actually, problems start with some of the entitlement laws themselves. For instance, health-care programs are supposed to help in redressing market inequalities, coming in support of those who do not earn enough to cover medical expenses, but the law did not make dfferences between those who earn $10,000 or less per year and those who earn $100,000 or more. The bureaucracy kept increasing the cost of paperwork instead of promoting efforts to learn more about the people who really needed the programs and about how to correct vices in their use.

On the supply side of the health-care services, a virtual monopoly was created with no objection from the government. It was not a monopoly by one enterprise; it was a monopoly by one profession—or, more precisely, by professionals of one system of medicine. It became an oversophisticated, high-tech system that increased the cost of medical services to outrageous proportions, making it difficult for the country to ensure access to health care for all its inhabitants. Inspired by a scientific fundamentalism, the medical profession fought and destroyed other well-established and less costly medical approaches, like homeopathy and herbal medicine.[30] Moreover, it discouraged the educational system from teaching self-care and mutual care in those many cases in household life when safe and cheap natural products can solve minor problems without costly and dangerous drugs or medical interventions.

A full discussion of the debt situation in the United States—where demographics, mismanagement of entitlements, and excessive military expenditures all play a role—is out of the scope and purpose of this book. I only mention a few problems because they show once more the effect of government and market activities conducted by market operators and politicians whose rational consciousness, structured as it is into power control and wealth accumulation, is easily beset by fears, influenced by magic recipes of scientific and economic fundamentalism, and made insensitive to social and economic realities that do not fit the theoretical models of their advisors.

A similar slumberous rationality prevailed in the rest of the world during the cold war. It produced similar effects. The Soviet Union, incapable of borrowing because of the limitations of its own system, ended broken after the prolonged hand-wrestling. Its markets were in disarray, its peoples in despair, its lands polluted. The dependent nations, which were betting on one or the other hand, incurred heavy debts to buy arms not from local enterprises but from foreign military-industrial complexes. These arms were applied to vicious internal repression and crazy external adventures. Dependent nations also borrowed for often unproductive investments inspired by the *amour propre* of their leaders with their ideas of self-sufficiency, and their desire to leave for posterity prestigious works where their names could be engraved. Debts, and the fact that their armies were usually compulsorily drafted, compounded to impose a heavy burden on their households. They had to pay high taxes, suffer the lack of public services, and endure loss of income and often the loss of loved ones, whose labor and life were forcibly taken by the armies. The youngest had to confront a tragic reality: As civilians they were denied most of the things that make youth enjoyable, and as draftees they were submitted to all kinds of hardships and even required to sacrifice their germinating lives.

CUTTING MILITARY EXPENSES

One positive effect of the end of the cold war has been a reduction in military expenditures. In 1994, the world spent $840 billion for military purposes—the lowest level since 1969, and 35 percent below the all-time peak of $1.3 trillion in 1987 (all the figures are constant 1994 dollars). In the former Soviet Union, military investments fell nearly 70 percent in the period 1990 to 1994.[31] However, the burden on their economy, measured by the ratio of military expenditures over gross national product (ME/GNP), is still over 10 percent. For the United States it will not be easy, because "a cutback in defense spending is always felt very sharply in particular areas, where there may be no other jobs available, or among occupational groups who have no alternative employment at equivalent pay, or in companies that are 'captives' of the Department of Defense."[32]

Meanwhile, some countries kept investing heavily in the military, among them eleven East Asian countries, including China, Japan, Thailand, Burma, Malaysia, Singapore, and Taiwan.[33] In some cases, the figures are outrageous. Ethiopia's military expenditures, for instance, climbed from $447 million in 1985 to $1217 million in 1991, $725 million of the latter being for arms imports and representing 80 percent of the total imports by the country. In the same period, Saudi Arabia climbed from $17.7 billion to $35.4 billion. Other countries in Asia were still investing heavily in 1991. For India and Kuwait it was close to $8 billion; for South Korea, $6.3 billion; and for Iran and the United Arab Emirates, $4.2 billion; while Israel, Syria, and Pakistan were above the $3 billion mark. In Europe, the big spenders were Germany, France, and the United Kingdom, which ranged from $16 billion to $22 billion. Traditionally peaceful countries like the Netherlands, Norway, Sweden, and Belgium, and former satellites of the Soviet Union like former Czechoslovakia, Hungary, and Romania were still spending above $1 billion and some close to $4 billion. In South America, Argentina, Brazil, Colombia, Cuba, and Venezuela were each above the billion-dollar mark.[34]

These and other countries buy mainly from the United States. Although U.S. exports fell from $21 billion in 1987 to $12.4 billion in 1994, that still represented 56 percent of world arms exports that year. This is because for all other countries, except the United Kingdom, arms exports fell even more sharply than in the United States. For instance, while the Soviet Union's share of arms exports in 1987 was 37 percent, this dropped to only 6 percent for Russia in 1994. The combined exports of all European countries fell from 66 percent of total arms exports in 1984 to 35 percent in 1994. Developing countries are now joining the supply club. China, with $800 million in 1994 arms sales, tied with France as the world's fourth leading arms exporter. Qatar, Iran, Brazil, and Ukraine also were among the top twenty exporters that year.[35]

Need we wonder why there is so much guerilla fighting and there are so many terrorist attacks in the world? Need we wonder why new countries are testing atomic bombs? India had a GNP per capita of only $340 in 1995. That year 48 percent of India's adult population was illiterate and 52.5 percent was living on less than 1 international dollar a day. Nevertheless, that same year India was spending 14.5 percent of its total government expenditure on defense while devoting only 11.9 percent to social services.[36] Can we call these rational decisions? The reader should now find it easy to accept that the answer is yes—they are technically and financially rational, but they belittle a human condition that has evolved to the point of requiring a new consciousness. The clothes that we wore when we were infants, Jefferson would say, do not fit us anymore.

The risks that war financing entailed for the economies did not escape Adam Smith's shrewd perception:

> The ordinary expence of the greater part of modern governments in time of peace being equal or nearly equal to their ordinary revenue, when war comes, they are both unwilling and unable to increase their revenue in proportion to the increase of their expence. They are unwilling, for fear of offending the people, who by so great and so sudden an increase of taxes, would soon be disgusted with the war; and they are unable, from not well knowing what taxes would be sufficient to produce the revenue wanted. The facility of borrowing delivers them from the embarrassment which this fear and inability would otherwise occasion. By means of borrowing they are enabled, with a very moderate increase in taxes, to raise, from year to year, money sufficient for carrying on the war.[37]

Inspired by his predominant motive of promoting love harnessing and life enjoyment, Smith, after discussing the well-known principle that debts are seldom reduced after war's end, sought for measures to reduce the number and duration of wars. The rational structure of his consciousness led him to suggest that making taxes as high as necessary to defray all military expenditures would make wars shorter and periods of peace longer. Let us listen to him:

> Wars would in general be more speedily concluded, and less wantonly undertaken. The people feeling, during the continuance of the war, the complete burden of it, would soon grow weary of it, and government, in order to humour them, would not be under the necessity of carrying it on longer than it was necessary to do so. The foresight of the heavy and unavoidable burdens of war would hinder the people from wantonly calling for it when there was no real or solid interest to fight for.[38]

Smith's rationality and position among the elite of his time did not allow him to perceive that people call for war not in response to compelling instincts or intuitions but in response to programs that the governing elites write in their minds. In chapter 9, I will discuss potentially more humane and cost-effective ways of securing peace and order, and of protecting life and property, than wars as we know them. Meanwhile, I will describe other changes in the economies that took place while the superpowers were wrestling.

POPULATION EXPLOSION AND ENVIRONMENTAL THREATS

Since the pioneering *Silent Spring* by Rachel Carson, many books have been written that describe and discuss the increased damages inflicted by humankind on nature. The Worldwatch Institute publishes every year a report, *The State of the World,* in which the environmental trends are carefully described and the damages thoroughly surveyed. The 1998 report states:

> From 1950 to 1997, the use of lumber tripled, that of paper increased sixfold, the fish catch increased nearly fivefold, grain consumption nearly tripled, fossil fuel burning nearly quadrupled, and air and

water pollutants multiplied severalfold. The unfortunate reality is that the economy continues to expand, but the ecosystem on which it depends does not, creating an increasing stressed relationship. . . . Forests are shrinking, water tables are falling, soils are eroding, wetlands are disappearing, fisheries are collapsing, rangelands are deteriorating, rivers are running dry, temperatures are rising, coral reefs are dying, and plant and animal species are disappearing.[39]

The trend that drags all others, as a locomotive drags a train, is the explosive increase in world population. The numbers speak for themselves: With a global population of nearly 6 billion, there are twice as many people as there were in 1970. The next 35 years will add another 2.5 billion, 90 percent of them in developing countries.[40] Political and religious leaders have created this destructive trend by stubbornly refusing to allow people to separate reproduction from the satisfaction of relational and recreational energy-balancing needs, which are deeply anchored in our archaic consciousness. Rather than responding to our needs and the needs of the Earth, here again we foul our rationality with myths from our nomadic past. In this case, we do not even obey a strict technical and financial rationality—we work against it.

The tragedy of populations growing beyond the carrying capacity of the land and the income-providing capacity of the economy was discussed in a scholarly manner by Thomas Robert Malthus. In his *Essay on the Principle of Population,* published in 1798, he said this:

A man who is born into a world already possessed, if he cannot get subsistence from his parents on whom he has a just demand, and if the society do not want his labour, has no claim of right to the smallest portion of food, and, in fact, has no business to be where he is. At nature's mighty feast there is no vacant cover for him. She tells him to be gone, and will quickly execute her own orders, if he do not work upon the compassion of some of her guests. If these guests get up and make room for him, other intruders immediately appear demanding the same favour. The report of a provision for all that come, fills the hall with numerous claimants. The order and harmony of the feast is disturbed, the plenty that before reigned is changed into scarcity; and the happiness of the guests is destroyed by the spectacle of misery and dependence in every part of the hall, and by the clamorous importunity of those, who are justly enraged at not finding the provision which they had been taught to expect. The guests learn too late their error, in counteracting those strict orders to all intruders, issued by the great mistress of the feast, who, wishing that all her guests should have plenty, and knowing that she could not provide for unlimited numbers, humanely refused to admit fresh comers when her table was already full.[41]

It would be hard to find a better example of the kind of analysis and policy recommendations that can be expected from rational structures of consciousness. Mathus provided a clear perception and brilliant description of the problem and the proposal of rational solutions: Don't be compassionate with those excluded from the feast of life; if they are abandoned to their fate, nature will soon *humanely* dispose of them through famine and disease; if not, the state will do it *patriotically* by sending them to war for the enlargement of the hall where the feast takes place.

One might think that the natural solution suggested by Malthus was the only one possible, given the state of contraceptive technology in his time. False! People have known since ancient times how to control the number of their offspring and still satisfy their sexual drives. But with the formation of industrial states, the masses began to be purposely kept ignorant of contraceptive opportunities and were instilled with fears about the sinful effects of their use. Even now, when contraceptive technologies are well advanced and easy to use, they are still ignored. It is still a subject that we do not discuss or teach openly and freely. Instead of harmonizing our natural urges with the requirements of economies built on limited natural resources, we still follow mental attitudes that would piously save embryonic life only to kill it later at its peak of development in perverse markets and the evil fields of war.

Contraceptive technology, even so-called natural methods, indeed involve risks. But until we perfect and develop safer methods, the risks of overwhelming Mother Earth and being dismissed as a species should have higher priority in our concerns than individual risks. Perfection has always been the enemy of the good. While we discuss the few percentage points of failure in preventing pregnancy that are intrinsic to different contraceptive methods, the global population is growing fast and could double in a period not longer than the present average individual life span.

ANOTHER BY-PRODUCT OF THE MYTHS ABOUT SEX

In the field of sexuality, the rationality of economists and government decision makers is often beguiled by myths. These myths are really gaps between reality as it might be perceived by alert senses and an awakened reason, and reality as it is construed by ideologies and dogmas that veil rationality and numb the senses. For instance, we find policy-makers and religious leaders who mythically believe that young people can abstain from sex. Moreover, they think that providing information on sexual biology, psychology, sociology, and spirituality, and on how to perform safe sex, overexcites the sexuality of the young, making them unable to repress it.

These kinds of myths impede efficient grappling with the destructive human, social, and economic effects of AIDS and other sexually transmitted diseases. Sexually transmitted diseases "are as common as malaria—more than 250 million new cases each year, at least one million of which will be HIV infections."[42] If we look at reality without the veils of myths, we perceive that sexual forces are so powerful that fears of disease rarely contain them, and that, on the other hand, well-informed people reduce the spread of disease by learning how to enjoy their sexuality while minimizing the risks for themselves and their partners.

In some countries the financial costs to households from the AIDS epidemics are devastating. In Tanzania, where it is estimated that as much as 30 percent of the population may be infected, "the average rural family spends sixty dollars in treatment and funeral expenses. This is equivalent to the country's annual rural income per capita."[43] In Thailand, where one in fifty adults is HIV-positive, "a study shows that health care costs for an AIDS patient was 10 times more than is currently spent by families on health." In Mexico, "a study shows that the cost of treating one individual with AIDS is roughly $4,500, equivalent to a year's salary for a medical doctor and more than three times the average minimum wage. More than 65 percent of such costs are met by the patient."[44]

The economic costs to nations are equally alarming. "As many as 10 percent of the Uganda Railway Corporation's 5,600 employees have succumbed to AIDS over the past few years, which means a labor turnover of 15 percent per year. A study of Thailand estimates that, through the year 2000, the cost of replacing long-haul truck drivers lost to AIDS will be $8 million. Overall, up to 4.2 percent of Thailand's adult work force could be suffering from AIDS. If all the people in Rwanda infected with AIDS sought medical care, 66 percent of total health expenditures would go toward treating the illness."[45]

The human costs are dramatically expressed by Dr. Roland Msiska, the head of the National AIDS Control Program in Zambia, one of the countries most affected by HIV. In Zambia, he said, "our social life is now limited to visits to hospitals, funeral homes, and cemeteries."[46]

During the 1970s, the United States efficiently organized efforts toward a responsible sexuality in the developing countries through its Agency for International Development. In the 1980s, under strong influence of the myths, the United States tragically reversed this policy just at the onset of the AIDS epidemics.

Only by breaking with the myths will we manage to cope with this crippling situation. We should start talking the language of unveiled reality and say to people: Enjoy your sexuality, but enjoy it safely and responsibly. Then, people will listen and start participating in containing sexually transmitted diseases and unwanted pregnancies.

TECHNOLOGICAL PROGRESS AND GLOBALIZATION OF FINANCE AND TRADE

The accelerated technological progress that started after World War I and increased after World War II had three main effects on the economies. It decreased the amount of human energy required to produce goods and services, it increased the amount of capital needed for industrial investments, and it increased international exchanges of people, money, resources, goods, and services.

The circular flows that Smith and Marx had occasion to analyze were built within the boundaries of a nation-state and had few links with outside flows. Inputs from the colonies, and products and services sold to the colonies, were consolidated within the national flow of the colonial power.

In his book *The Death of Money,* Joel Kurtzman lucidly analyzes the evolution from these national economies, where the flow of money was linked to the production and circulation of material goods and tangible services, to a global economy of abstract financial transactions. He says:

> During the Victorian era . . . in Britain—the most advanced nation at the time—and in Belgium and the United States, where the statistics from that period are reliable, 80 percent of the population earned its living by working either as farmers, domestic servants, or skilled workers—tinkers, livery workers, cobblers, blacksmiths, construction workers, and, increasingly, manufacturing workers. The rest of the population was engaged in services such as retailing, teaching, government work, or transportation . . . a maximum of 7 percent to 10 percent of all transactions had a global component.[47]

After World War I, each national circular flow became increasingly linked to many others. This was the result of advances in transportation and communication, the demand of sophisticated materials for increasingly complex production technologies, and the indoctrination of engineers and economists into believing in the magic and myth of economies of scale that required ever-larger production units, whether in industry, agriculture, or mining.[48]

The process that took place afterward can best be summarized by quoting a few more key paragraphs from Kurtzman's work:

- By 1925, 40 percent of the American workforce was engaged in manufacturing; domestics became scarce (replaced by washing, sewing, and vacuuming machines), and farmers left the farms, also replaced by machines.
- Today, 60 percent or more of all economic transactions have an

international component to them [and these transactions] take place as a result of the global electronic economy.

- Since World War II the world has become very confusing, with companies competing in one market while cooperating in another. Joint ventures and alliances have created an intricate set of relationships that are a challenge even for the best business minds to follow.

- There are very few purely *national* products and very few purely national transactions left. . . . Banks today extend you a mortgage and then resell that mortgage to Japanese or European investors. American automobile lenders bundle up their installment loans and resell them to overseas investors. Insurance companies in England invest in American venture capital funds. German and Japanese pension funds buy Manhattan real estate, and Mexican industrialists build condominiums in Florida and take over American companies.

- When it comes to what Karl Marx called *the means of production,* there are no national entities left.[49]

At the international level, the circulation of money acquired a life of its own. It is now increasingly resistant to linkage with any national circular flow. This loop is even more alienated from real economies, nature, and humans than the military-industrial loop depicted in Figure 11. Moreover, unlike the latter, the loop of international financial transactions is independent of any government and is managed solely by enterprises, but it still uses money provided by households, enterprises and governments from all over the world.

Figure 12 pictures the difference between what Kurtzman calls the real economy, the economy of the national circular flows producing goods and services that households use and consume, and the financial economy, the economy of the international speculative financial flows. The first, as Kurtzman says, is where "products are made, trade is conducted, research is carried out, services are rendered, . . . factory workers toil, doctors tend the sick, teachers teach, [and] roads, bridges, harbors, airports, and railway systems are built."[50] However, it is the second that moves money at a much higher speed than in the real economy, where each country painfully builds its gross national product. Following estimates by

Figure 12. INTERNATIONAL FINANCIAL SPECULATION

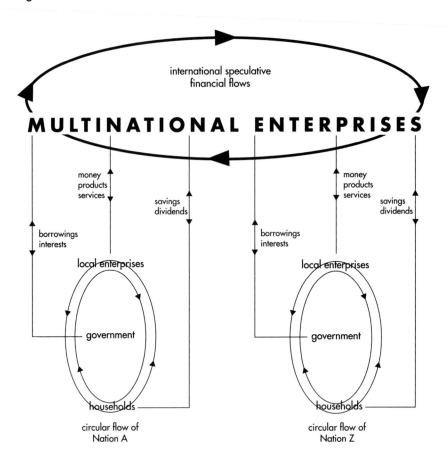

Citicorp's Paul F. Glaser, Kurtzman says that the financial economy is between thirty and fifty times bigger than the real economy. "That means that for every dollar spent on something 'real,' a hammer, scissors, screwdriver, car, or bottle of wine, $30 to $50 is spent on a stock, bond, futures contract, or insurance policy."[51]

The time horizon of the agents that generate the financial speculative flow is very short. If they invest in producing parts of a product with the cheap labor of country A, the investment should be recovered quickly so as to allow them to close and move it to country

B when this offers even cheaper labor, exacts less taxes, or is more careless with the health of its people and environment. Who cares if labor is the slave labor of children or political prisoners? Who cares if every move destabilizes thousands of households when the money leaves to beguile with illusions the households of the new place where it temporarily lands?

With the benediction of the academy, which provided them with the tools, brilliant professionals—who never saw a factory or a construction site; who never dealt with workers, handled materials, or operated machines; who never felt the scorching sun of an agricultural field, the overwhelming darkness of a mine, or the sticky wetness of a forest—move money through computers so fast that the flow, although intangible, is animated with enough power to crush humans and nature in its course.

Money seems to be dying as a symbol of the value of satisfiers of needs and desires. It is becoming a mythological ghost that dwells in the Mount Olympus of a global computer network created with no other aims than to feed the *amour propre* and satisfy the desire for power and wealth of the computer wizards and their bosses.

It is the peak adventure of a rationality guided by *amour propre*, power control, and wealth accumulation. After exiling the spirit, nature, and the body from the mind; after dividing the earth into warring nations; after separating humans by color of skin, gender, sexual preferences, and religious beliefs; rational structures of consciousness are now separating money from its material economic bases and creating an ever-increasing gap between the haves and the have-nots. The majority of people, who feed the speculative flow with hard-earned savings and onerous taxes, are becoming increasingly poor. The minority who manipulate the speculative flow are becoming increasingly rich. Will this gap create the social environment for the flourishing of another Marxist-like or Nazi-like nightmare?

The adventure is destabilizing households, businesses, the world, and the lives of the manipulators themselves. Despite their wealth and power, the manipulators do not find solutions for their own existential pain. The high speed of the speculative flow they have created may at some point centrifuge them to an abyss. But before this happens and they end by wrecking their own lives, they will leave too many miserable survivors, dead bodies, and dreary landscapes in their reckless trail. Will they be able to slow down, reintegrate what they have separated, and thus avoid catastrophe for themselves and the world?

In Part III, I explore this possibility, but first, we will take a look at the global order as it has become under the cumulative effects of past and present adventures of this misguided, divisive rationality.

6

INTERNATIONAL POWER AND WEALTH GAMES: THE OLD WORLD VIRTUOSOS ARE OUT OF TUNE

On Monday, July 6, 1992, the eighteenth annual economic summit of the Group of Seven opened in Munich, Germany. Reporting on this meeting, Carl Schoettler of the *Baltimore Sun* said: "The leaders of the world's seven richest nations arrived in Munich on Sunday like aging members of a rock band that hasn't yet learned to play music of the new age. Trouble is they haven't been playing the old tunes very well either. And they aren't very popular anymore."[1]

The old tunes are tunes written by the rational structure of consciousness. These tunes and their players are aging and are not finding many echoes among the young generations. New tunes written by an integrative, harmonizing structure of consciousness are starting to be heard, but there are no virtuoso players yet for these new tunes. The transition to a new international order is marked by the awkwardness of the new players and the sclerosis of the old.

THE NORTH COMPOSED THE OLD TUNES

For many centuries, European nations made use of their military power to open markets for their products, provide land for their growing populations, and find resources for their economies. They often fought among themselves to extend their possessions. Through military might and commercial rascality, the North dominated the South. It was a dominance full of greed and arrogance and, except for a few isolated individual cases, empty of a compassionate understanding of the diversity of human nature.

North American natives taught earlier explorers, like the French Jacques Cartier and the Plymouth pilgrims, how to survive harsh winters.[2] They were decimated by the next waves of English and French colonists. The advanced cultures of the Southern Andean mountains were organized, under the Inca Empire, into a tyrannical centrally planned and heavily controlled, but equitable, economy. They were destroyed by the Spanish conquerors. It was a fate shared by all South American indigenous establishments. On the other side of the ocean, the African genius was considered a manifestation of evil because it was so deeply in touch with nature.

The European dominators could not do otherwise. The repressive, dogmatic behavioral programs inserted into their subconscious minds, and their lack of understanding of the scientific knowledge already reached in their time, kept them from listening to their hearts' reason and their deep intuition. If they had listened, they would have heard their unconscious telling their minds that their rationalizations were wrong. They would have known intuitively that the people they were abusing and killing were as fully human as they were, and the cultures they were destroying could have taught them many productive lessons.

Had Columbus and his people taken off their ridiculously oppressive clothing, washed the stench of their confined bodies in the pristine waters of the Caribbean, and joined the beautiful naked natives in celebrating life, Latin America might have written a quite different history. Indeed, they did mix with natives and gave birth to new life, but they could not eliminate guilt and violence from their relationships. Instead of an open, peaceful feast of life on the sunny beaches, the torment of the flesh was satisfied in shameful and violent darkness.

It is often like this with rational consciousness: It is skilled in rationalizing irrational behavior and in repressing the rationality of the instinct. The greediness that *amour propre* generates, and the violence of power-controlling behavior, always spoil the chance that nature offers for banquets and feasts. Incapable of making use of these occasions for agape and spiritual celebration, *amour propre* and power control transform them into predatory events, where some gorge on food and carnal pleasure while the humanness of the others is violated and the spirituality of their beings is denied.

Many voices, such as those of Bishop Bartolomé de Las Casas in Mexico, anonymous Jesuits in South America, and well-intended European colonists and missionaries in Africa, and Asia, censured the atrocities of the conquest but could not modify the prevailing attitude among the conquerors toward the peoples of the South. They were generally considered to be deprived of soul, enslaved as beasts, and robbed of their resources. Alien cultures and religions were imposed on those who survived the treatment. Native survivors either feigned acceptance of the new culture and religion while secretly keeping their ancestral practices, or zealously adopted the new system of values and beliefs, becoming persecutors of the independent thinkers among their own people.

THE RHYTHM OF THE OLD TUNES CHANGED AFTER WORLD WAR II

World War II brought about a slight change in the structural arrangement of rationality. Competition, power control, and the pursuit of wealth still prevailed, but learning from previous mistakes engendered a more integrative approach to international relations than the victor/defeated approach taken after World War I. This time the victors decided to cooperate among themselves to rebuild their economies and help the defeated to do the same. Cooperation was facilitated by the fact that the victors and most of the defeated came essentially from the same cultural stock and shared a common historical evolution. When this was not the case, as with Japan, the changes in consciousness among Northern Westerners were enough to let them recognize that defeated nations should be allowed to keep their own traditional practices.

Once the reconstruction of Western Europe and Japan was quite advanced, international aid and cooperation turned South. Then, it was difficult for the Northerners to resist the temptation of telling the peoples of the South, who were behind in scientific and technological development, that they should imitate the North. The elites of the South, inclined to imitative behavior, made it even more difficult for the Northerners to fight against this temptation. Instead of imposing ideas and beliefs, and exacting resources by the power of guns and whips, ideas and beliefs were now transferred and resources were acquired by use of the power of money and knowledge.

The technologies and products sold to the South embodied patterns of values and behavior from the societies that had designed the products and developed and mastered the technologies. The North was still the boss, and although by and large the bosses behaved as rational managers of modern enterprises, the murdering thunder of guns occasionally reminded impulsive Southerners (or impetuous neighbors in the case of the communist East) who the bosses were.

There is nothing wrong with trying to sell others the comforts and amenities that technologically advanced societies produce and enjoy. Nor is it immoral to try to buy from others the resources required for one's own production. This is the usual game played in the markets. But, in order for it to be a fair game, sellers and buyers should both be well informed. However, no substantial efforts were made to empower Southern populations to make decisions about what and how to buy. International aid organizations only occasionally helped build local technological capacity to design investments that would respond to the opportunities, and be subjected to the constraints of local economic, physical, social, and financial environments.

Attempts by Northerners to understand the ways of life in the South, and the wisdom of their original cultures, were equally rare. International developers should have organized a two-way process in which North and South, working together at grass-roots levels, would both rediscover that original wisdom and blend it with modern science and technology. Instead, international developers trusted that local elites would act as relay agents between them and grass-roots communities, although it was evident in most cases that those elites were corrupt and greedy. Some international developers did this out of naiveness or political convenience. Most did it because it was the least stressful way to accomplish their tasks. Only a few fought hard to establish a direct dialogue with the people, circumventing the obstacles with which local elites tried to thwart their efforts.

SOUTHERN ELITES LIKE TO DANCE
TO THE TUNE OF THE OLD VIRTUOSOS

In almost every developing country, local elites have adopted the behavioral programs of elites in the advanced, industrialized countries. They obtain nutriment for their private economies by serving the private interests of the Northerners. In turn, elites of newly industrialized countries of the South nourish and benefit from elites of the less developed countries that are under their influence.

This symbiosis recalls the combination of the masters of which Adam Smith was so critical.[3] We can now say that business and land elites, being fewer, can combine much more easily; and international practice promotes or at least does not discourage these combinations, while it hinders a closer relationship among the dependents of those elites, the people at the bottom of the economies.

It is easy for a large enterprise of the South to get a loan for an investment whose technology and equipment will be supplied by a Northern concern. It is extremely difficult for a village-level enterprise to find money with which to finance technology and equipment that might increase production efficiency and improve product quality. I will give two examples that I witnessed. A new steel mill in a Latin American country received hundreds of millions of dollars to buy technology and equipment, mainly from Great Britain and Japan;[4] but a factory that produced soap in an Asian village for a chain of village-owned stores could not get a few tens of thousands of dollars to pay for the consulting visit of a small soap producer from the North. The Northern producer was willing to provide advice for no more compensation than his and a companion's airfare and travel expenses for a week of work and a week of enjoying the natural and cultural treasures of the host country. Additional money would have been required to buy one or two pieces of equipment that the visitor might have recommended to solve product quality problems the village factory was facing.[5]

THE TUNES TO WHICH
INTERNATIONAL ORGANIZATIONS DANCE

The international organizations that emerged from agreements reached at Bretton Woods by the victors of World War II are typical examples of the combinations of masters to which Adam Smith was referring. They are associations of elites from which the people are excluded. They are institutions created and managed by governments to vent the problems of the world's elites rather than the needs and aspirations of the masses. As is well-known, the governments of many developing countries are seldom civil servants of their constituencies. Often, they are military masters of terrorized populations.

Despite this structural birth defect, which excluded people's representation, international institutions have accomplished positive goals. The infrastructure of many countries has improved, literacy and life expectancy have increased, and trade and communications have been made easier. A few countries in Latin America and Asia have reached high levels of industrialization. India shifted from conditions of scarcity of food to having a surplus of agricultural production, although some of its population are still starving because of injustices in the distribution of income.

The narrow approach of a rational decision-making process, which relies on easy-to-manipulate cost-benefit analyses, blocked international developers and their counterparts in the local governments from bringing the usually unmeasurable concerns for humans and nature to their development projects. When they decided to consider at least some of these concerns, they engaged in considerable efforts to describe them mathematically. But mathematics, because it needs to simplify reality in order to make it fit an equation, often acts like the deer painted in the caves by our magic-believing ancestors. Sometimes this makes it easier to reach the goal; often it does nothing. Consequently, social and ecological problems have plagued infrastructural, industrial, and agricultural projects of a sound technical and financial rationality. Unfortunately, when international developers do manage to introduce human and ecological concerns into internationally financed projects, these concerns can still be thwarted, ignored, or betrayed by the local elites who are in charge of the implementation and management of the projects.

Under the leadership of Robert McNamara, the World Bank spearheaded an international attack on poverty. Before becoming the Bank's president, McNamara saw the irrationality of war from within the military-industrial complex that was supporting the crazy destruction of resources, people, and nature in Vietnam. He understood that the underlying cause of war and civil strife is poverty, and he knew by then that poverty results mainly from the combination of an unjust distribution of land and income with an explosive growth of population.

It took a considerable evolution in the structure of McNamara's consciousness—programmed as it was by academia to see the world through the distorting glasses of econometrics and sociometry—to reach the point, in 1970, at which he could say: "If we achieve the 'quantity' goals and neglect the 'quality' goals of development we will have failed. It is as simple as that. We will have failed."[6] In another speech at the United Nations Conference on Trade and Development, held in Santiago, Chile, in April 1972, he denounced the skewed income distribution patterns prevailing in the developing world and suggested that measures should be taken toward more equitable and comprehensive taxes, land reform, security in the tenancy of land, and increase in the productivity of small farms.[7] McNamara would not absolve the rich North from responsibility. In that same speech, he said:

> Just as we conclude that it is the responsibility of the political leaders of the developing nations to recognize the inequities that exist within their nations and to move to correct them, so we must likewise conclude that the wealthy nations of the world—possessing 25% of its people, but 80% of its wealth—should move now to provide the additional assistance, in the form of aid and trade, which the developing nations need to meet minimum national goals.[8]

In another speech, this time at the United Nations Conference on the Human Environment held in Stockholm in June, 1972, McNamara said that the leading edge of actions that aim at respecting humans and their habitat must be to protect them from poverty, which is the one hazard that can injure not only their habitat and health, but their spirit as well. He qualified poverty as cruel, senseless, and curable.[9]

Through his speeches, McNamara brought from his high position into the open a struggle that is common to many other business and political leaders, who wage it in a more subdued and shadowy way.[10] It is a struggle to move away from the rigidity, divisiveness, and excessive "mathematization" of the world created by a misprogrammed rational consciousness. It is a painful and tottery move toward integration, harmony, and an intuitively sensitive approach to the world. It is painful and tottery because it is not an easy task for anyone to delete the old programs that are still leading us to misperception and errors.

In the case of McNamara, the evolutionary effort he proposed to the World Bank was hindered from within and without. Inside the Bank, there was too much of *amour propre* and power games among the Bank's bureaucrats. McNamara did not share openly and candidly with them his own struggle. Hence, he could not create an internal network for mutual support and advice on the process of change. He asked the World Bank's staff to achieve quality, not only quantity, in the development process, but he stopped short of internalizing and communicating that quality is essentially love and life, while quantity speaks of power and wealth. He was bold in speaking of quality in an environment where econometrics reigned supreme, but shy in speaking of love and life in a temple where power and wealth are worshipped. In her biography of McNamara, Deborah Shapley quotes one of McNamara's assistants as saying, "He loves humanity more than he loves human beings."[11] McNamara had not reached the point of loving himself enough to feel his being part of all other beings, whether close or removed.

Outside the Bank, McNamara was constrained by the Bank's by-laws to work with governments. Those governments would press the Bank to attack poverty just by shooting money against it, refusing to change the structures of their societies and the consciousness of their people. When administered by governments, an influx of money from outside may even increase poverty. Poverty yields, instead, to loving work with the people, seeking to intensify their consciousness, thus developing their innate capacity to design and implement poverty-harnessing efforts by themselves. It is only through an awakened awareness that poor people begin to make decisions and transform their reality.[12]

This did not escape McNamara. He said, "Demography measures people. It cannot always measure their inner feelings. And yet understanding poor people—and the narrow range of options that poverty offers them—is the key to assisting them to broaden their choices."[13] This was an appealing new song for many within and outside the Bank, but many of the Bank's bureaucrats, as well as their colleagues at other institutions of the United Nations and at the bilateral aid organizations, and the government officials of developing countries with whom they were dealing, continued singing the old tunes. However, McNamara's music was so inviting that after a while, the old players at international organizations had to change their tunes somewhat. New songs started praising nongovernmental organizations, and their work with the poor became popular. Often, there were more words than deeds.

THE REQUIEM OF UNFULFILLED DREAMS

After more than forty consecutive years of international aid for and cooperation in social and economic development, Africa is in shambles, Latin America is in trouble, and, in Asia, islands of prosperity are enveloped in a sea of poverty and violence. Meanwhile, the gap between haves and have-nots has steadily increased. The gross national product for the five most affluent countries of the North is, on average, 315 times higher than for the five poorest countries of the South.[14]

A man in Norway can expect to live until he is 75. For a man in Niger, life expectancy is only 44 years. From every 1000 live births, 107 will die in Cambodia but only 4 in Japan. In Sweden there are 348 computers for every 1000 people; in Ghana, only 1.2. The United States produced in 1994 13,243 kilowatts hours of electricity for every man, woman, and child; Togo only 24.[15] These statistics reflect a number of broken, unfulfilled dreams that presage instability and revolt.

111

My personal experiences and my historical studies, on both of which I will comment in Part IV, have persuaded me that international aid institutions could have substantially prevented this situation, even if they could not totally avert it. They could have done so by complementing financial aid, technology transfer, and advice on fiscal, monetary, and economic policies with efforts to change the enculturation programs, thus building healthier structures of consciousness among the population. International organizations had the power and the knowledge to promote deep reforms in the educational systems, but the consciousness of their leaders and staff could not see that development problems were not in the populations' genes but rather in their minds. If the minds could be restructured, economies would follow. International organizations did exactly the reverse. They attempted to restructure the economies without ever attempting to restructure people's consciousness.

International organizations pretend not to see that people are being encultured with commands that are unfriendly to their nature and which ask submission to the power of other men and to particular man-made representations of the spirit. These commands make people resign themselves to denial of the fundamental needs lodged in the depth of their archaic ever-present origin, excite their mistrust of other cultures and societies, and burden them with anxiety about love. People encultured in this way can neither fully assume their role as citizens, even under the freest of constitutions, nor efficiently manage their economies, even when provided with sufficient funds and appropriate technology.

For large populations, life on Earth is worse than the valley of tears that some religions say it will always be. For these populations, life on Earth is not just a purgatory—it is hell. Despite the official recognition of human rights at the United Nations, "hundreds of millions of children worldwide toil in fields, factories and brothels." Even in the United States, "a report from the General Accounting Office found some 25,000 child labor violations in 1990." In India alone, "an estimated 1 million children work in bonded labor in brick kilns, stone quarries and construction;" they are virtual slaves who are paying their parents' debts. "Children in lightbulb factories in Indonesia work a 48-hour week for about $3 and child coffee-pickers in Zimbabwe earn the same for a 60-hour week."[16] In one of my visits to Thailand to study the ways that Thai people were transferring technology to small enterprises and villages, I saw children working in tile manufacturing whose fingers had been practically eaten away by the glaze they were applying.

After independence, African populations dreamed that they would simultaneously have more and be more. The dream never came true. *Amour propre*, power control, and wealth accumulation patterns were not strangers to native magical and mythical African societies. Academic studies abroad rationalized and reinforced these patterns among African leaders, who betrayed the hopes of their people. On the other hand, honest leaders, intending to improve the lot of their people, conferred uncritical allegiance to ideologies that were inoperable in the environments where they were applied. This was recognized by Julius Nyerere, the leader of Tanzania. He said, "There are certain things I would not do if I were to start again. One of them is the abolition of local government and the other is the disbanding of the cooperatives. We were impatient and ignorant."[17]

In Latin America, similar limitations in the perception of reality devastated countries that had already reached a high level of economic and social development, and handicapped the development of the others.[18] Narrow views of the global reality and lack of sensitivity toward the forces of love and life also misguided the decisions of Asian leaders. Narrowness and insensitivity are at the root of the dramas of Vietnam, Cambodia, the Philippines, and Indonesia, to name a few.

Progress in developing countries was further hindered by the either/or approach of the leaders of the advanced industrialized countries in the geopolitical power games that were part of the hand-wrestling between capitalism and Marxism described in the previous chapter. Small countries had to blindly follow the masters of their respective geographical areas under penalty of being considered either a dangerous capitalist pawn or an evil communist agency.

THE PATHETIC TUNES OF INDEBTEDNESS AND WAR

Meanwhile, commercial lenders were establishing the fast speculative financial flow described in the previous chapter. Developing
countries tapped from this flow to finance ineffective investments
and bloody military adventures. They ended with huge debts, the
payment of whose interests alone were already straining the internal economic flows. When they were about to stop paying because
the very existence of their economies was at risk, the international
financial and aid institutions had to come to their rescue and the
commercial lenders' rescue. While engaged in this task, which certainly diverted efforts from real development objectives, the international developers pretended not to see that expenditures in arms
and armies were often equaling, or surpassing, the amount of aid received. In other cases they overlooked the fact that the flight of capital from a country to foreign private accounts was on the same order
of magnitude as the debt. A few statistics illustrate the extent of
these flaws:

- "The capital flight in the period 1974–82, measured as percentage
  of gross external debt, was estimated as being 71.8% for Argentina, 21.8% for the Republic of Korea, 34.3% for Mexico, 32.3%
  for Peru, 36.1% for the Philippines, and 49.1% for Venezuela."[19]
- In 1989, India spent 8.6 billion dollars in defense while receiving
  only 1.8 billion dollars in official development assistance.[20]
- "In 1988, the U.S. proposed to increase the sales of arms to foreign
  countries by 28% as a way to reduce the deficit in the budget of
  the Pentagon. On the other hand, the International Monetary
  Fund was requesting countries that were buying those arms to
  end food subsidies."[21]

During the first decades of international aid for development, developing countries applied the money they received from international financial and aid institutions to investment projects. The use
of this money was controlled by tight procurement procedures and
primarily applied to the acquisition of fixed assets. Under those
conditions, although the infrastructural work and the productive

installations primarily benefited the local elites, they still trickled down some additional income to the poorest levels of the population.

In the 1980s, as a way of facing the debt crisis and helping commercial lenders get out of trouble, international financial organizations started lending for what they called structural adjustments. Structural adjustment loans, as described by the World Bank, "do not fund specific projects. They provide foreign exchange to help to meet the transitional costs of restructuring and policy reforms."[22] Structural adjustments promote changes in the patterns of public spending, tax systems, administration of state-owned enterprises, and government intervention in the markets. Money lent to the government can finance, for instance, the acquisition by private industrialists of imported raw and intermediate materials that are used to produce exports.

In this way, the possibilities of aid money ending in private accounts has increased. It is well known that local industrialists manage to keep foreign exchange earned from their international transactions outside their country by getting external suppliers to overbill them and by inducing external buyers to accept invoices that are lower than the real prices paid.

For instance, "Mexico said that its exports to the U.S. totaled $14 billion in 1984. The U.S. puts that total at $18 billion. The exporters apparently received more money than the amount reported at home."[23]

In 1978, McNamara started the yearly publication by the World Bank of a World Development Report. It usually analyzes the state of world development affairs and includes a detailed discussion of one particular subject, such as population growth, health, international debt, or environment. Only since 1981 has the valuable statistical section at the end of each report included data on defense expenditure by the central governments of the Bank's member countries. In 1988, the report not only provides statistical data but also analyzes in its text the meaning of military spending for the economy—and, cautious not to irritate its governmental constituency, the Bank presents two opposite viewpoints.[24]

On one hand, it cites a 1973 study that found that higher military spending was positively associated with economic growth. The Bank comments:

This and subsequent studies have argued that military spending can have positive spinoff effects, such as fostering technological innovation, training personnel who later move into civilian work, providing employment opportunities, building domestic institutions, stimulating a country's tax effort, and promoting more intensive use of existing resources. Furthermore, military industries can be a focus of industrialization activities. Although military spending in developing countries has traditionally been for personnel and imported weapons, in recent years several developing countries—including Argentina, Brazil, China, India, the Republic of Korea, and Pakistan—have developed arms export industries of their own. Brazil is now the world's sixth largest arms exporter.[25]

On the other hand, the Bank says:

These positive effects appear to be more than offset by the long-term negative impact of military spending. Research in the past decade, although not conclusive, points to a negative relation between military expenditure and economic growth. . . . although the controversy over the relation between military spending and economic growth is by no means resolved, evidence increasingly points to high military spending as contributing to fiscal and debt crises, complicating stabilization and adjustment, and negatively affecting economic growth and development. Whatever benefits might arise from such spending must be carefully weighed against these heavy costs.[26]

Studies, research, numbers, and more numbers—whose only purpose is to put reason to sleep and make it forget the dead, the wounded, the maimed, the orphans, the raped, the broken hearts, the scars on the land. What remains of McNamara's appeal to understand the *feelings* of people? What of his remarks on the need to care for quality and not only quantity?

The struggle between the body count of the military commander and the feelings of the international civil servant continue within the Bank. Under the strong pressure of its governmental audience, the Bank desperately seeks rationalizations for the irrationality of spending people's money on killing people instead of caring for their happiness. When correlations between military spending and economic growth become controversial, human nature will be blamed for the need to keep military spending. In the 1991 report, the Bank said: "If global military expenditure were reduced, the world would undoubtedly be a better place." However, right after this statement, the report asks, "But is this realistic?" and answers, "Humanity is no stranger to wars and conflicts—twentieth-century humanity least of all."[27]

Humanity, as the Bank report sees it, is not humanity as nature intended it to be but humanity as it was shaped by a rational structure of consciousness after being programmed for thousand of years into *amour propre*, power control, and wealth accumulation.

In the second half of the 1980s, developing countries spent on average 5 percent of their gross domestic product in supporting their military establishments. The Bank recognizes that this is "an enormous sum," a sum that "would be more than enough to double government spending on infrastructure or on health and education." It is further said that "aid and finance agencies are entitled to ask whether it makes sense to help governments whose first priority is not to develop but to add to their military strength."[28]

The struggle in the mind of the Bank's management and staff is clear. It is the same struggle that confronts each of us individually— a struggle between what nature tells us we should do and what society pressures us to do. It is a struggle from which nobody can claim to be immune because we all have been encultured in the same way. The higher the level of education we have attained, the more buttressed in our mind are the commands that tell us to invest in defending our societies from internal and external threats that our mind first creates and then seeks to destroy. Usually this happens in a more disadvantageous manner: The threats are created by the few who wield power and wealth, but the money and lives invested in fighting the threats are mostly contributed by the rest.

DANCING TO OLD TUNES HAS LEFT BODIES EXHAUSTED

The whole world, the poor and not so poor of the South, the rich of the North, the capitalists of the West, and the former Marxists of the East are all exhausted from dancing to the old tunes of *amour propre* and power control. Humankind has been left dizzy and without energy. It is now spinning and bumbling, incapable of finding a navigation route.

Sanguinary wars in the former Yugoslavia and in Rwanda. Deadly violence by gangs of all sorts in the streets of Los Angeles and Rio de Janeiro. Children and teenagers killing everywhere at a scary rate. The United States increasingly investing in building jails, seeking perhaps the dubious honor of being the country with the highest imprisoning capacity in the world. The countries of the former Soviet Union seeing racketeers paralyze their incipient privately originated economic flows. Neighbors patrolling the streets of Chinese and Iranian towns and villages to compel strict obedience to the rigid codes imposed by fundamentalist governments. People harassed and killed in the streets of all countries just because they are from another nation and are competing for scarce jobs, follow different rituals in worshipping the divinity, have a different skin color, or make love in a different way. We are back to spanking in schools, as if the Enlightenment had never happened. And the list could go on and on.

Rationality, which made us advance in so many aspects from the eighteenth century on, seems to have been left bewildered and scatterbrained by the shocks of two world wars and a protracted cold war. Incapable of recovering sound thoughts and clear perception of reality, rationality is reaching the twenty-first century in a soporific condition. And we have already seen that when reason sleeps, her dreams engender monsters.

The variations that an improperly enculturated rational mind can introduce in the music and songs that praise *amour propre*, power control, and wealth accumulation are almost infinite. We have been dancing with this music and tuning to these songs for so long that we are all worn out. We now need to learn dancing and singing to music that will invigorate the body, arouse the soul, and soothe the heart. The new music encompasses a great variety of melodies and rhythms. Let us see how we can play them.

118

PART III

A NEW CONSCIOUSNESS

By enculturing people into *amour de soi*, the mastery of the forces of love, and the enjoyment of life, our recent technical and financial rationality might be induced to integrate concern for humans and ecosystems into the decision-making process.

7

LIFE IN A JOYOUS ENVIRONMENT

We saw that each new structure of our consciousness is supported by previous structural arrangements but binds especially with the one immediately before it. Thus, the rational structure was built on the archaic, the magical, and the mythical structures, but it is the myths that emerged from the latter that are especially ingrained in our rationality.

The passage from the rational to the integrative, harmonizing structure is not different: It is reason that will provide the main foundation for building the new structure. However, the integrative, harmonizing structure will also be supported by strong footings going down from the rational layer through the mythical and the magical layers, to be solidly anchored in the archaic ever-present origin.

The evolutionary aim in developing an integrative harmonizing structure is neither to scorn nor to exalt reason. The purpose is to reduce the likelihood that particular interests might degrade reason to a slumberous state, inflicting new nightmares on humankind. The role of magic and myths in our lives will not be denied, but harmony and integration might prevent magic and myths from darkening and weakening the architecture of reason. The shift should be, above all, a shift from behavior inspired by *amour propre*, power control, and wealth accumulation to a behavior that is guided by *amour de soi* and attempts to master love and enjoy life.

To evolve to integration and harmony, we must identify the enculturation programs that hinder the mastery of love and the enjoyment of life. Once we recognize them, we must reprogram the subconscious hard disk of our minds with more user-friendly and nature-friendly behavioral commands. In chapter 4 (Table 1) we saw some of the commands that are used to enculture our minds into a sleepy, shortsighted, divisive rationality. Now I shall suggest an equally nonexhaustive list of commands, grouped according to the kinds of needs they satisfy, that could be used to stimulate an integrative, harmonizing view of ourselves and the world.

RECOVERING PLAYFULNESS

I should here remind readers of Jean Gebser's words quoted in the Introduction: By moving from the purely rational structure of our present consciousness to an integrative, harmonizing structure, we will not create a paradise on Earth. We will only make the world a little better by valuing the things that really matter. And one of those things is playfulness.

Through playfulness we discover the world as children and we relate to it as adults. If we lose playfulness in the process of growing up, life becomes a painfully heavy burden. It is not that being playful, loving ourselves, and mastering the forces of love will exempt us from pain. It is that by being playful, loving ourselves, and mastering the forces of love we will not create more pain than that which is an inevitable part of life.

Accidents and sickness are two of those inevitable painful components of life. However, it is our behavior, not life itself, that unnecessarily increases the opportunities for accidents to happen and for sickness to develop. Emotional and economic conflicts are also painful components of life, but the unnecessary complication of our legal systems, and our propensity to solve conflicts by force, often take pain to unbearable levels.

To recover playfulness we ought to reshape our societies. One of the first steps we should take in the transformation process is to modify unnecessarily repressive behavioral codes. Some of the rules have been unchanged since they were drawn by nomadic tribes in

Table 5.	STRUCTURING AN INTEGRATIVE AND HARMONIZING CONSCIOUSNESS
Needs	Commands for Structuring an Integrative, Harmonizing Consciousness
Biological	• The human body is the greatest achievement in the spiritually guided experiment of evolving the creation on planet Earth. Nothing related to it can be evil. There is nothing of it to hide or be ashamed of. The evolution of creation has made us rich sexual and sensual persons. • We can responsibly practice reproduction while enjoying the energy-balancing, relational, and recreational aspects of our sexuality and sensuality.
Biopsychological	• We can and should learn how to access knowledge for and take care of our bodies and our minds. We should become masters of our own physical, mental, emotional, and spiritual health. To maintain this health, we may seek help from professionals and technicians when necessary and convenient, but not surrender mastery to others, because nobody can tune into our bodily and spiritual messages better than ourselves. • The body and the mind respond better to gentleness and pleasure than to harshness and pain. Flexibility and playfulness are key to a harmonious development of both body and mind. • Nature is the source of food for nurturing our bodies, of beauty for making our minds happy, and of inspiration for reflecting on our relation with the spiritual forces that animate the universe. • The order of nature is built on chaos, and cruelty is not alien to her purpose of achieving balance between life and resources. We are not masters of nature, and we cannot shape a different order because we have yet to fully understand the chaos and the process that nature follows to create her order from it. However, having evolved from nature as conscious partners of the creative spirit on this planet, we should make every attempt to pacify nature's forces, especially the forces that shape the human community. This has aimlessly and unnecessarily increased chaos and cruelty within itself and in nature.
Psychological	• The creative spirit talks to us through the whole of our bodies, from beyond and within them. • Our existence can and should be a continuous surrender to the forces of love and life. This surrender includes the final peaceful surrender to death. However, throughout our life we should retain mastery of our health. • The material creations of the human mind can and should be used to increase life enjoyment, rejecting any excess that complicates life rather than increase happiness.
Sociocultural	• The fundamental glue that will keep the social tissue together is a clear and deeply internalized conviction that society and its governance have as their main objective to protect all its members and nature from violence. In our physical, intellectual, and emotional communications with others we may use persuasion, but brutality should never be tolerated. • Activities that affect ourselves and consensual partners are exempt from judgment by magistrates. These activities can only be judged by our internal, individual voices, which echo the cosmic voice. • The diversity of physical forms, behavioral patterns, cultural constructs, religious beliefs, sexual preferences, age demeanors, and gender manners are to be enjoyed. They should never become a motive for division and violence among humans. We should see life as a stew, taking delight in each different piece of it and celebrating the dish as a whole. We should never try to make of life a fondue where all the components finally take the same color, the same taste, the same smell. • Partnership in organizing and maintaining households requires constantly renewed romance, and a diversity of erotic fantasies to bring some of the polymorphic pleasures of our ever-present origin to enlighten, enliven, and lighten the rational constraints that are necessary to keep healthy social tissues. It is only the harmonization of instinctive drives and social requirements, of playfulness and responsibility, that will allow households to become strongly active social molecules. Their structural diversity cannot but strengthen the social tissue. • Households are participative undertakings to which not only active adult partners contribute. Children and the elderly also share responsibilities and opportunities. • The more vulnerable we become, openly sharing ideas, emotions, and feelings with others, the more we get support and advice for our lives. • We need to cooperate with others to reduce the damages on our lives from the struggle for survival. Moreover, it is through cooperation that we can reach beyond survival to a full development of our human condition.

transition from the mythical to the rational structure of consciousness—as if the evolution of the creation would have frozen then and
there, as if the advances in knowledge about ourselves and nature
would not have any effect on our lives, as if the technologies we create would not constantly modify the ways in which we organize our
lives.

Conventional attitudes are putting humankind into a straitjacket
that prevents the masses from thinking originally, loving tenderly,
and living zestfully. However, creative businesses, imaginative leaders, and ingenious thinkers are producing changes from within the
body of humankind despite the straitjacket. These changes are increasing pressure on the tightly knitted canvas of conventional attitudes and making it burst through all its seams. We have grown
enough to exercise self-control over our emotions, humble our desires, and balance the satisfaction of our instinctive personal needs
with the need to have a healthy, protective social tissue around us.

SEEKING EFFECTIVE WAYS OF DETERRING VIOLENCE

History tell us that the worst crimes—as measured by the number of
lives and property destroyed, and by the cruelty employed in destroying—have been committed not by individuals against other
individuals but by human communities against other human communities. These collective acts of violence and cruelty were motivated and guided by leaders and fanatics thirsty for power and
wealth.

Some individual crimes—in which people kill, maim, and torture
others, and steal or destroy property—are products of genetic and
metabolic errors, or neurological and hormonal deficiencies in the
criminal. Besides these errors from nature when the constitution of
some humans is molded, the main other causes of criminality are
poverty and minds programmed into *amour propre*, power control,
and wealth accumulation. What is a crime of passion if not a crime
of *amour propre*? Passion and pride result from enculturation into
amour propre, and sometimes the reaction to frustrated passion or
disappointed pride can be very violent, especially when the biology
of the individual is already prone to violent reactions. And what are

124

crimes ordered by Mafias and gangs if not crimes bred by greed and power? And do not the senseless crimes of well-to-do children and teenagers result from societies in which their subconscious receives daily messages that display, exalt, and condone violence? As the nineteenth-century English philosopher Henry Thomas Buckle said, "Society prepares the crime, the criminal commits it."[1]

Despondent, dispirited subjects kill, break into others' property, pickpocket, and rob at gunpoint either at their own initiative or in submission to the will of the excessively greedy. We cannot say that these people do not have a conscience. The fault is with a society that disables their internal communication channels with the spirit and does not empower them to become masters of their physical, mental, emotional, and spiritual health. When individuals pro-grammed in this way are either born in poverty or fall into poverty later in life, they usually either submit to fate and suffer in this val-ley of tears, waiting for a prize in the afterlife, or decide to forcibly snatch the satisfiers of their survival needs. Often, they also snatch superfluous material goods that society displays alluringly, and nowadays the money snatched increasingly buys not the means for survival but escape from pain through drugs. Only a few manage to lift themselves from poverty and abjection, and work their way up-ward, through whatever crevice they may find, until they occupy a position in mainstream society.

Whatever the nature and cause of crime, society must restrain criminals to prevent them from doing more harm. At the same time, society may benefit from studying them rather than harshly punish-ing them. If we secure criminals under decent living conditions in environments fit to promote progressive regeneration rather than abject retrogression, we may achieve two objectives. The first would be to develop and put to work the talents and skills they still retain. Thus, they would produce goods and services for their own mainte-nance, reducing the cost to society of securing and studying them. The other objective would be to learn more about the works of na-ture and society. We may learn how to repair the mistakes that na-ture makes in structuring individual constitutions, and we may learn how to correct the mistakes that society makes in structuring human consciousness. Some may argue that if these suggestions were implemented, many would commit crimes just to escape from abject poverty to the restricted and controlled but rather comfortable environments created for their rehabilitation. Indeed, this might happen for as long as society remains unhealthy and continues to create and exploit poverty, alienating the mind of the poor from body and spirit.

The evolution toward a new consciousness might produce deep transformations in our legal systems. Instead of settling a controversy by establishing who is the winner and who the loser, new legal institutions might seek win-win arrangements. From using punishment as the main deterrent of crime, policy-makers and legal agents might shift to a focus on preventive modification of individual biologies and mind-sets, and on changing social conditions that breed violence. Instead of privileging wealth and power, legal and political systems might prefer to protect individual freedom in households, streets, and markets, and to advance social justice in the latter.

Reason, when not handicapped by dogmas, prejudices, or interests, can find many humane, cost-effective ways of dealing with criminals. A sleepy reason forgets instead what Henry Ford's alert rationality, which allowed him to innovate and do good business, saw clearly.[2] He said, "Capital punishment is as fundamentally wrong as a cure for crime as charity is wrong as a cure for poverty."[3]

When making decisions under a new consciousness, judges, juries, lawyers, and lawmakers might ask themselves whether their rulings promote *amour de soi* or support *amour propre*; whether they encourage the accumulation of wealth or favor an equitable distribution of income; whether they condone abuse of power or favor participation; whether they tighten old repressive coats that hinder human development or cover human nature with just the minimum of clothes necessary to keep a warm, convivial society; whether they help protect nature as provider of inputs and cleaner of waste in our economies and source of beauty and health in our lives or acquit nature's destructive exploiters.

A DIVERSITY OF HOUSEHOLD ORGANIZATIONS

An important task that a new consciousness will face, and is already facing while humankind approaches it, is to fully integrate women in societies and economies by giving them all the rights men have and treating them in the same way men are treated. There is a need to harmonize, rather than deny, the biological and psychological differences between both genders and the enormous variety of constitutions, orientations, and behaviors within each gender.

Relationships should be transformed from bloody games motivated by *amour propre*—games in which there are always winners and losers—to partnerships in which love and life are simultaneously cultivated within each partner and shared among partners. Then, men and women will become naturally equal partners in the organization, management, and enjoyment of households, enterprises, and governments.

Marriage should never mean a loss of identity for women. Married women should have names and lives of their own; exercise full ownership of body, mind, and emotions; and be free to communicate with the spirit along channels of their own design and selection. For the new consciousness, marriage will not be the only option exercised by people in the establishment of households. We can already see a variety of forms among the latter, each form presenting particular constraints and opportunities.

SINGLE-MEMBER HOUSEHOLDS

Single-member households are the result of decisions to live alone, divorces, separations, or death of one of the partners. They may involve children, whether as a result of conscious decisions to have them despite a desire to live alone or because of divorces and separations. Single-member households without children favor autonomy, provide more opportunities for unhindered contacts with one's body and the spirit, and simplify the establishment of varied and uncompromising contacts with others. Leonardo da Vinci is quoted as saying that "if you are alone, you are all your own; with a companion you are half yourself; so you squander yourself according to the indiscretion of your company."[4]

However, single-member households also mean solitude, which, although it may not be the sad solitude of our present households, is still aloneness. We should remember that we really become full human beings when we have a he-Friday or a she-Friday with whom to share love and life,[5] rejoicing together when life invites us to have a cup of aromatic coffee, and supporting each other when life turns the coffee bitter.[6]

Single-member households that do include children, and where the single parent cannot afford to pay for child care at home, need support from society in the form of day-care centers at the workplace. A creative reshaping of the latter would allow male and female workers and employees to stay home and care for the children in case of a health crisis.

Facing suggestions of this kind, our rationality immediately thinks of abuses. Indeed, abuses will not disappear under an integrative, harmonizing consciousness. We can only expect that if people live playful and secure lives in playful and fair societies, having learned to appreciate the things that really matter to life and love, abuses will be reduced to a minimum.

NUCLEAR AND EXTENDED FAMILIES

I said in Chapter 4 that the monogamic family represents the most elaborate and sophisticated compromise between our archaic natural instincts and our social desire to have a solid base for the development of both partners and their offspring. Monogamous partnerships, whether heterosexual or homosexual, still offer the most possibilities for harmonizing enjoyment of oneself with responsibility toward the other and society. They provide opportunities for growing together, constantly recreating love and life while mastering the first and responding to the ebbs and flows of the second. For this to happen, both members ought to reach partnership with an already well-developed and healthy *amour de soi*. Their partnership covenant could read

> We promise to help each other become as fully human and alive autonomous beings as possible, developing together our capacity to play and produce; sharing ideas, emotions, feelings, needs, and desires; enjoying together the material, intellectual, and spiritual aspects of life; and caring together for children we may decide to include in our household by natural parenting or adoption.[7]

128

If love forces more powerful than those that bring us together emerge in the future, and we can neither integrate them in our life nor overcome them by strengthening our relationship, or if despite our harmonizing efforts our vision of the world and our lives start diverging considerably, we will part as friends, dividing what we earned together and continuing to care together for the physical, mental, emotional, and spiritual health of our children, if any.

Monogamous marriages can either organize nuclear households, with or without children, or coordinate extended families. In nuclear childless households, it is relatively easy for the partners to share housekeeping duties or pay for housekeeping services, depending on their level of income and the level of privacy they desire at home. Couples with children and a modest income, who want to open equally broad horizons for the life of both partners without handicapping the life of the children, will require from society supportive measures similar to those needed by single parents. In the case of couples, a reorganization of working practices and fair salaries might allow each member to work only half time, sharing household chores and marketplace possibilities. Advances in communication technologies might provide increased opportunities for work to be done from home, although this too involves constraints as well as opportunities.

Extended families could benefit from the experience of the elder members while providing them a loving, caring environment in their declining years. Unfortunately, the behavior of the elderly usually follows the patterns of *amour propre* and power control that they learned during their enculturation process. This irritates the younger generations, who have learned similar behavior. The irritation might reach even higher levels when those younger components of an extended household have managed to change their behavior toward respect for love and life, learning to value the things that really matter.

Integrating old and young under the same roof is not an easy task. It might require efforts to restructure consciousness from the young and old alike. This effort would be rewarded with new opportunities for life enjoyment and the sharing of love. By facilitating their integration

129

into the households of their offspring, the elders might find their self-esteem increased and their anxiety over money and death reduced. They might also find that through a convivial exchange with the economically and socially active members of the household, it is easier to keep pace with changes in society and economies.

Children benefit more than anybody else from extended families, because they can exchange love with more than one or two persons. At their age, they can absorb and release love as easily as a sponge absorbs and releases water. And when they grow to become teenagers, a playful, loving, and understanding dialogue with parents, grandparents, and older relatives enhances the life of all generations and reduces the chances of conflict. It prevents teenagers from tailoring for themselves a coat of values and beliefs that hides their real and beautiful humanness because it is too loose. The baggy constructs of those systems of values and beliefs are usually adopted from peers who, because they do not have a strong family base to support them in those difficult years, yield to despair, cynicism, escape, and the most bizarre ways of expressing their dissatisfaction with an oppressive, greedy, hypocritical, and short-sighted society. When teenagers are integrated into a healthy and open family dialogue, their stalwart freshness helps the older members to retailor their old coats of values and beliefs, adjusting to changes in social mores and thought-forms. This, in turn, adds enjoyment to old age.

Under a new consciousness, teenagers might be given full participation in the management of the household's finances, the maintenance of its physical assets, and the production of the services required to cope with life's needs. I have repeatedly witnessed that full participation of the youngsters increases both individual responsibility and communal conviviality, creating a playful, enjoyable family environment, quite in contrast to the sad solitude and conflicts in most present-day homes.

Advantages, however, should not mask frustrating situations with which nuclear families, and especially extended families, often grapple. For instance, if the household is so small that there is little privacy, dissatisfaction may soon dampen the spirits. Another situation that usually turns household life sour is when the older people become sick and the couple must take care of the old and the young at the same time. To ease the pain during these periods, many social attitudes might need to change, especially in the training and practice of medicine and in the organization of nursing and rehabilitation services.

Rather than fighting death, medicine practiced with an integrative, harmonizing consciousness might center on providing information and advice for the elderly to continue mastering their physical, mental, emotional, and spiritual health. When outside interventions become necessary, medicine might employ the gentlest and least intrusive healing practices. And when life decides that it will offer no more opportunities for a sick or injured person to enjoy with her a cup of coffee, medicine might seek to ease the psychological and physical pains of the transition for both the dying person and his or her family. A medicine impregnated by *amour de soi* might forsake the practice of keeping artificially vegetating a being whom nature claims back to her regenerative womb.

COMMUNITY ARRANGEMENTS

Still another household arrangement brings under the same roof, or under the same communal development, people who may or may not be related by marriage or blood but who have made the decision to live together, consensually sharing their economies, their emotions, their ideas, and sometimes also their bodies, and providing one another with the different services required to maintain a community. This arrangement has been tried already, although few experiments have been succesful.[8] It is an arrangement that usually produces more constraints on the participants than the household arrangements previously described. However, it also gives them new opportunities for a joyful life in solidarity.

Many past and present experiments of this kind have been organized around powerful ideological or spiritual leaders. Powerful leaders easily slip from grandiose cooperative constructs down and back to behavior inspired once more by power control and wealth accumulation. They obscure the perception of reality for their followers, mystifying their minds with beguiling words, soul-lifting songs, and captivating rituals. Communities, more than any other household arrangement, require an alert rationality illuminated by love. They are doomed to fail under a rationality obscured by myths or deluded by utopias.

An integrative approach may use the stories, traditions, and legends of our mythical past to bring poetry, beauty, and relaxation to the heavy task of being rational. The new consciousness should be able to recognize those myths as symbolic narratives of past realities rather than use them, or newly created myths, as paradigms for the interpretation of present reality.

Some of the community experiments were and are based on the already mentioned preanalytic vision of human nature that sees it as emerging from an original sin for which we should all, and forever, suffer punishment. This vision may even induce the leaders to ask the community members to abstain from any sexual activity and to mortify the body, which is seen as the seat of the devil.

An integrative, harmonizing consciousness, as we have already discussed, instead sees human nature as endowed by an original blessing with an amazing capacity to produce, create, re-create, and rejoice. When this is the vision of a community, it refuses to divide itself into leaders and followers. There, people simply explore together new paths to a more fulfilling life, trying to synergize their individual capacities for the task of playfully producing satisfiers of all their needs.

THE FUTURE OF WOMEN AND YOUTH

In the organization of modern households, we are reaching a turning point. Women are moving away irreversibly from their earlier exclusive roles of housekeepers and mothers, while men are moving away irreversibly from their earlier exclusive roles of breadwinners and social, political, religious, and scientific leaders. Each gender could do much for the progress of the other, especially men for women, who previously were barred from so many social, economic, political, and scientific domains.

Robert Salmon, vice-president in charge of the studies on the enterprise's future at L'Oreal, in a recent book on trends in entrepreneurial organizations and economies, maintains that enterprises should give women the status they deserve.[9] He says that every employer should arrange work schedules in consultation with women. He also points to the fact that on boards of directors of French enterprises, men still account for 95 percent of the members, and he comments that by convening meetings at 7 in the evening, or organizing discussion breakfasts and dinners, male staff do not take into account the stressful timetables that female executive staff must maintain when they also are heads of single households or when their husbands do not share housekeeping tasks. Salmon quotes women as saying, "We are allowed to do everything our fathers did as long as we keep doing everything our mothers did."[10] Salmon asks a poignant question: "How can we justify in the eyes of school-age children that they should return at four and a half to an empty house because their parents work, that they should still fulfill their homework despite feeling lonely and deserted, and that at the end of their sad schooling period they have yet to face a scarcity of jobs that affects particularly the young?"[11]

In social and household organization, any movement forward is charged with risks and pregnant with opportunities. We lose some precious things at home, and gain some attractive things outside the home. Frequently, the things we lose at home are related to life and love, to "being" time, while the things we gain are related to money, prestige, power, and more generally "survival" time.[12] We need knowledge and wisdom to attenuate the effects of the losses on our lives and not be made dizzy by the gains. We must care especially about the effects of losses and gains on the younger generation, who walk the new paths with us. There are no recipes on how to reach the best tradeoff between gains and losses. The only thing society can and should do is to avoid creating conditions in which survival needs push people to go for the gains without even a chance to count the losses.

TIME TO BE ONESELF AND TIME TO BE ONE FAMILY

The most important decision faced by a modern household with children is how a single householder or both members of a partnership can harmonize the time and energy invested in satisfying financial needs, career ambitions, parental responsibilities, sexual urges, and intellectual and recreational cravings. Because the energy available to each person is limited, those investments are not independent from one another: an overinvestment in one activity means reduced investment in the others. Without a decent income, it is difficult to help children develop fully the potential of their bodies and minds. Parents who are sexually, sensually, or intellectually unsatisfied slip easily into neurosis, which their children perceive. Children capture even the most subtle negativities in the words and deeds of their parents.

It is not easy to reach the optimal mix of energy investments. Moreover, the optimal point is different from one person to another, from one partnership to another. To approach the optimal requires a constant and open dialogue between partners, the task becoming even more complicated for a single parent without a permanent significant other with whom to face risks and enjoy opportunities. In both cases, it is a trial-and-error process for which the children themselves provide feedback.

In this delicate process of learning how to be simultaneously oneself and one family, we should try to avoid being deluded by magic beliefs of our creation. Here again we should be careful of the real effect of the magic paintings in the caverns of our rational structures. One of our latest art works is called quality time. It is a composite picture with many elements. Let us see how they look.

One element depicts children as benefiting from socializing with male and female peers of their own age. This is absolutely true. Before the time of big cities and small nuclear families, it was easily accomplished. Children would play with their siblings and neighbors of their age. Even an only child would not have difficulties in finding peers among the latter. Everything happened at, or near, homes that were abuzz with life—not always life of the best quality, but life nevertheless. Now, with homes that are deserted for most of the day, and neighborhoods that are unsafe, the socialization of children below kindergarten age has either been transferred to day-care centers or converted into the opposite of socialization: a passive restraint under the care of often inexperienced babysitters with neither the rich emotions and intuitive life of the old illiterate housekeepers of yesteryear, nor the rich culture of the tutors that high-income families could afford.

The magic picture then goes on to suggest that even under the best socializing environment, whether outside or inside the home, children still need close physical, emotional, and intellectual communications with their parents. Since this is also true, parents allocate some time each day to be with the children and—here comes the magic pass that will catch the deer!—have convinced themselves that because it is time devoted just to the children, it is superior to the time devoted to them in old-style household arrangements, where attention to children was always mixed with household chores.

From 9 to 5 it is work time, from 5 to 9 it is "high-quality" children's time. Are work problems instantly erased from the mind when we pick up the child from the day-care center or say good-bye to the babysitter? Even if household chores are shared between partners, do they have enough energy to prepare a zesty meal, listen to the thousand and one stories and questions of their infants, share the stories of their own life in the marketplace, put the children to bed, and still have a moment of intimate tenderness between themselves? Are weekends better when parents are transformed into taxi drivers who move the children to and from sports activities, parties, theme parks, museums, malls, and gyms? Could this flurry of activities compensate for the inactivity and dullness of the week? Not to speak of households where one parent has two jobs to collect a sizable income, or where one or both parents either are intrinsic workaholics or are pressured by insensitive bosses to work longer periods. Nor to speak of times when disease or emotional stress visits the household.

Is this really quality time for reaching out to the others, to investigate the wilderness in the child or partner who is sharing the car or the table, and explore the constellations locked up in their skulls?[13] And even if it is, do not we need also some quality time to be ourselves, to investigate our own wilderness, to explore the constellations in our own skulls? It is not with the magic of words that we will find answers to these crucial questions. Nor do they disappear when we move to an integrative, harmonizing consciousness, but we find easier to make trade-offs when we learn to appreciate the things that really matter to life and love. Only a decrease in individual greed and ambition, and a move of society toward increasingly blending human concerns in the technical and financial rationality of businesses and markets, will gradually allow us to be at one with ourselves and our families.

YOUTH AND A NEW ROMANTICISM

When children grow to become young adults, in addition to healthy homes they need safe streets and joyful markets. When I was growing up in a provincial town of Northern Argentina, I would get knowledge at school and learn values at school and home, but it was with my friends, in the streets and parks, that I acquired existential wisdom. This continued to be so even at the college level, because universities in Argentina were beehives hanging on the urban jungle rather than cocoons nestled in polished campuses.

Homes and schools certainly help us in acquiring the mastery of our physical, mental, emotional, and spiritual health that John Stuart Mill believed to be the key condition for building free societies. However, as young adults, we exercise this mastery in streets and markets, seeking our own health and well-being through our own particular way and without compelling one another to live as seems good to the rest.[14]

Youth is handicapped when life in the streets is both threatened by violent gangs and wild snipers and overcontrolled in the name of obsolete morals. When streets are dangerous and repressive places, it is difficult for people to honestly and openly exchange satisfiers of their physical, mental, and emotional needs. When hands hold guns and exchange drugs, they can't stretch forth to reach others in gestures of friendship and love. When minds hold fears of aggression and repression, they can neither recognize external messages of love and friendship nor interpret the messages of love from internal spiritual sources.

Youth brought up in more harmonious and joyful homes and streets than those of today may bring forth a new romantic movement. It will be a different romanticism than the one that swept Europe and reached North and South America during the nineteenth century. This previous romantic movement was brought forth by an emotional reaction against a rationality that flaunted the glory of increased scientific knowledge of nature and increased industrial production of material wealth while hiding its counterparts of human misery, neglect of the beauty of nature, and conflicts between nations and within people.

It was a romanticism tinged with sadness. Moreover, it was a romanticism that found satisfaction in sadness. René, the famous romantic hero of Chateaubriand's writings[15] watches a shepherd warm his hands by a humble brushwood fire in a corner of the woods and listens to the melancholic airs he is singing. The scene makes René reflect that "in every land the natural song of man is sad, even when it renders happiness." Our heart, René says, is a defective instrument, a lyre with several chords missing, which forces us to express our joyful moods in notes meant for lamentation.[16]

At another point in his life, René, facing a very conflictive situation with his sister, confesses: "I even felt a kind of unexpected satisfaction in the fullness of my anguish, and I became aware, with a sense of hidden joy, that sorrow is not a feeling which consumes itself like pleasure."[17]

Before Chateaubriand, Samuel Richardson in England, in *Clarissa* (1748), and Jean Jacques Rousseau in France, with *Julie, ou la nouvelle Héloîse* (1761), described female characters as romantic as Chateaubriand's René or Goethe's Werther. None of these characters is able to harmonize the tenderness of her feelings with the passions of her instincts, and society is always there to remind them that instinctive drives are sinful. Julie says to her tutor, who will eventually become her lover: "The very first day we met, I imbibed the poison which now infects my senses and my reason; I felt it instantly, and thine eyes, thy sentiments, thy discourse, thy guilty pen, daily increase its malignity."[18] When finally he deflowers her, she thinks all is lost: "One unguarded moment has betrayed me to endless misery. I am fallen into the abyss of infamy, from which there is no return; and if I am to live, it is only to be wretched."[19] Julie's mother dies of grief on learning the news.

I bet on a quite different new romantic wave. It will bring about a romanticism that will be essentially playful, accepting pleasure and sorrow as parts of life and love. My imagination puts on the lips of a René, or a Julia, of the twenty-first century the romantic manifesto drafted here:

A Romantic Manifesto

I find satisfaction in the pursuit of love, and a life that gives full expression to the powers of my mind and my body, while keeping open, uncensored, and unmediated lines of communication with the spirit that dwells inside me.

It is a satisfaction not free of sorrow, but I let neither melancholy fill all my moments, nor allow my heart to steep in ennui and misery.

It is playfulness that fills all my moments. I play with all parts of my body, all ideas in my mind, and all emotions of my heart.

It is playfulness that makes me accept sorrow and death as normal, inevitable parts of life. I accept sorrow and death when they are brought naturally into my life by accident, disease, and deception. I refuse to produce sorrow and death artificially through oppression, exploitation, conflict, and war. I also refuse to produce sadness and pain by fencing love and life with dogmas and prejudices.

The long evolutionary process of human consciousness has increased my abilities to work in partnership with the creator in further improving human love and life by integrating and harmonizing what rationality has separated and opposed. Love and life were blind necessities in our archaic origin. They became ruthless competitive sports under the rationality of my parents and grandparents. It is my task to help love and life to mature into playful cooperative games.

I do not feel sick of civilization. I feel sick from the physical and mental poisons created by a civilization whose social metabolism went out of balance while it was guided by a drowsy rationality. I do not feel that to find a cure for this sickness I should lose myself in the chaotic wilderness of nature, deluded by ideas of returning to an archaic past. Neither will I find a cure by giving up my individuality to become absorbed in the amorphous, ineflexible masses that political and religious leaders of the old consciousness still try to assemble for warring in defense of particular interests or for building repressive utopias.

I also reject the psychedelic delusions of intoxicants, which add misery and suffering to the misery and suffering from which they promise escape.

Aided by the inner push of the creative spirit, I want to pull myself into giving more careful consideration to those things that really matter to life. I will achieve this objective by transforming, as much as I can, painful labor to earn my life into joyful work to fulfill my life. My transformative instruments will be love, laughter, tears, knowledge, observation, intuitions, and instincts. I will free all of them from the restraints that ideologies, dogmas, and prejudices created in the minds of my parents and grandparents.

It is not just because I breathe and think that I am human and alive. I am human and alive when I breathe to make love, be in love, give, receive, and feel love. I feel human and alive when I think on how to wisely master the forces that arise from making, being, giving, receiving, and feeling love. I am human and alive when those forces help me to produce and create for myself, my beloved, my community, and the world. I am human and alive when I feel that I am still a part of nature, having grown from being one more of its submissive creatures to become her respectful and loving partner.

Advances in the structure of our consciousness, and the technology and organization of work at home and in businesses, might provide future youth with opportunities for expressing their diverse endowments of abilities while ensuring that their basic biological and biopsychological needs, and those of their children, are satisfied. To seize these chances, we will need to find answers to two crucial questions: Can we generate enough employment opportunities to integrate in the marketplace all women and men who desire to become part of it? Will the marketplace of the future distribute wealth and leisure time more equitably than it is doing now? These questions lead to the discussion of how an evolution toward integration and harmony might help us to build more joyful, sustainable, and equitable economies.

8

ECONOMIES ADJUSTED TO NATURE'S CAPACITY AND HUMAN NEEDS

B esides bringing sadness and solitude to our lives, our rational structure of consciousness, enculturated into *amour propre*, power control, and wealth accumulation, has also created joyless economies.[1] We learn to worship Mammon. We forget to praise Folly, as the old philosopher Erasmus of Rotterdam did. Folly, the goddess of vitality and happiness, has a group of loyal companions that help her "in bringing the whole world under sway, so that even great rulers have to bow to her rule." Among those companions are Philautia (self-love), Hedone (pleasure), Tryphe (sensuality), Comus (revelry), and Negretos Hypnos (sound sleep).[2]

A similar mythical cohort might help our rationality to change our economies from joyless to joyful by introducing playfulness in the marketplace. Too often, our rationality takes playfulness for amusement, distraction, and diversion, which all connote an escape from oneself, a way of numbing existential pain and restlessness. Under an integrative, harmonizing structure of consciousness, we might instead see playfulness as the mode in which we free ourselves of technological and social constraints and, guided by self-love, creatively explore all domains of life. Playfulness might then make us bask in pleasure, indulge in sensuality, celebrate revelry, and repose in sound sleep. And, because playfulness diverts human energy from greed and power games to recreational, relational, and creative activities, it might induce behavior that promotes equity in the distribution of wealth.

The French writer Albert Camus is quoted as saying that "without work, all life goes rotten— but when work is soulless, life stifles and dies." I would say that work becomes soulless when it is pure labor without any element of playfulness. When we quit being hunters and gatherers, we started designing processes for the production and marketing of goods and services that transformed almost all work into pure labor, and often made of labor a real curse.[3] We seldom introduce concerns for the human beings in the design of those production and marketing processes. A humane use of love-mastered technology might integrate playfulness into work, and free time for additionally practicing playfulness on its own. But let us not get deluded by utopias—playfulness cannot be sustained without work.

During the long period in which we lived under our archaic structure of consciousness, our survival was entirely supported by an economy of playfulness. Work is a social creation that started with our magical consciousness, and it became cursed labor when we started dividing ourselves between those who worked little and appropriated most of the wealth created by the work of the others, and those who labored to exhaustion and numbness, receiving in exchange only crumbs of the cake they produced. It was not the creative spirit that cursed its human creation by transforming work into labor, it was us humans who cursed one another.

An Economy of Playfulness Might Complement the Economy of Wealth

The economies that our rational structure of consciousness has developed are concerned with the production, distribution, use, and consumption of tradable goods and services. Harmonizing structures of consciousness might induce us to go beyond this narrow approach. We might create economies concerned with the production, distribution, use, and consumption of all kinds of satisfiers of human needs. These satisfiers would include new entities in addition to the traditional tradable goods and services. Among the new entities we would find inferential knowledge received through education; noninferential knowledge received through intuition; physical, emotional, spiritual, and intellectual relations among people and between people and nature; and physical, emotional, spiritual, and intellectual self-expression.

In the new economies, we would consider as productive activities those in which we invest our energy to produce tradable goods and services. We would call playful activities those in which we invest our energy just to satisfy our needs. Among the playful activities, we would further distinguish wealth-consuming activities from gratuitous activities. The first satisfy needs by consuming or using goods and services supplied by the productive system or traded among households. Gratuitous playful activities satisfy needs through self-expression, relations among individuals, and relations between individuals and nature.

When we playfully invest energy in satisfying our needs, we are being truly ourselves. Being time is also playing time. However, we must also invest energy in producing goods and services that we later buy in the marketplace for our subsistence. The time devoted to earn money with which to buy them is survival time. There is yet a third way of investing our energy: We can apply it to games of domination and accumulation, or to escape from reality. In this case, it is more appropriate to say that we are wasting, or "killing" time, and, as Gebser shrewdly observes, when we kill time, we also kill life.[4]

For instance, when we watch a television show that provides knowledge or recreation, we are using our being time, but when we look at messages that influence our bodily and mental processes negatively, we are "killing" life and time. Similarly, when we engage in a sport for the sake of playing, we respond to several needs: energy balancing, recreation, care and protection of the body, participation, and physical, emotional, and intellectual exchanges with others. Sports then provide a moment of intense being time. This is quite different from engaging in spectator sports as either players or spectators. For spectators, it is a socially induced way of satisfying recreational needs that wastes large blocks of vital time. For the players, it is mainly survival time, a way of earning a living. Opportunities to find, through the game, satisfaction of recreational needs, and emotional and intellectual exchanges with playmates, are minimized by pressures from the public, team-owners, and managers, who all push the players to compete crudely.

Many productive activities might be made simultaneously playful, blending being time into survival time. For most craftspeople and artists, the production process has always been as important as the final product. For them, the process provides playfulness, while the final product provides income. Industrial processes might also be designed to provide workers with playful elements while they accomplish their productive work. The reward for production would still be a salary; the reward for the playful part of the work would be just sensual pleasure, existential joy.

For instance, in large, automated, cheese-making factories, workers can command the process of producing cheese from a distant control panel. They are thus estranged from the materials under transformation, and they feel their task to be boring. In smaller plants, where cheese is produced in batches, workers remain in sensual contact with the milk and the curd, using mechanical means only to reduce the physical stress associated with certain tasks, like lifting the curd from the vats. Their closeness to the process allows them to gather playful rewards from feeling, smelling, tasting, and seeing the transformations they are effecting. To produce the same amount of cheese, the nonautomated procedure requires more labor but less capital investment. When comparing the total cost to society of both processes we should account for the increased social stability that is attained by creating additional employment and having a more satisfied population. Moreover, an increase in the direct cost of labor to the enterprise is often compensated by a decrease in indirect costs related to absenteeism, health care, conflict, and errors. Happy workers tend to work more steadily and in a more focused manner and to be healthier, and they do not need to compensate for their dissatisfaction about work by getting involved in often futile arguments and strifes. In the manual process, a mistake can send to waste only one or two thousand liters of milk. In the automated plant, a mistake can spoil tens of thousands of liters.

Fishing provides a good example of an activity that can be practiced according to different modalities. It is a playful wealth-consuming activity when performed only for pleasure, using goods, such as reels and boats, and consuming services such as the dredging of rivers and the publishing of meteorological information. Fishing becomes a productive activity when the catch is sold in the market. It is a playful gratuitous activity when people catch fish by using their bodies and elements obtained from nature, with the sole purpose of feeding themselves.[5] Similarly,we may play the piano to express our joys or sorrows, or to produce musical messages and distribute them to audiences. In the first case it is a playful wealth-consuming activity; in the second it becomes a productive activity. However, we can also make music just by whistling or snapping our fingers, and express feelings by singing, which both are playful gratuitous activities.

Sometimes, the introduction of an aesthetic factor into a productive job may be enough to bring some playfulness into work. There are many ways of introducing those aesthetic factors. We can provide opportunities to raise the view from one's job to contemplate a beautiful landscape, to accompany mechanical repetitive movements with appropriate music, to make the workplace itself enjoyable, to eat during lunch breaks in an inviting environment, to have a good fragrant shower at the end of the journey. When I was director of a large investment project, it took me some time to convince the investors to include plants, good light, and a cozy relaxing corner for a coffee break within the engine room. Engineers and managers were used to the idea of engine rooms slick with grease, a sort of shoddy sauna where fully clothed people could sweat for eight hours. I thought that engine rooms should not be designed to punish those working in them. When we deny workers the possibility of blending even small doses of being time into their survival time, the latter becomes a veritable torture time.

A harmonizing, integrative consciousness might reverse the present distressful paradox of our technical and financial rationality that eagerly provides a perfectly air-conditioned environment to a computer but refuses to invest in reducing risks and harshness for workers exposed to high temperatures, magnetic fields, absence of light, toxic chemicals, and other equally threatening conditions. Even in the economy of our households, we happily buy the best oil to protect our car's engine, but we haggle when buying food for our biological engines.

MARKET AND HOUSEHOLD BEHAVIOR

In their textbook on economics, Robert L. Heilbroner and James K. Galbraith ask: "What do economists see when they scrutinize the world of economic activity?" They answer:

> Two attributes of a market society attract their attention:
> 1. Individuals in such a society display a particular behavior pattern when they participate in economic activities, as consumers or businesspeople. They behave in acquisitive, money-searching, "maximizing" ways.
> 2. A series of obstacles or constraints stands between the acquisitive drive of marketers and their realization of economic gain. Some are the constraints of nature; some are the obstacles of social institutions."[6]

The authors remark that they "are talking about the kind of behavior that we find in a market society," and they further comment:

> Perhaps in a different society of the future, another hypothesis about behavior would have to serve as our starting point. People might then be driven by the desire to better the condition of others rather than of themselves. A story about heaven and hell is to the point. Hell has been described as a place where people sit at tables with sumptuous food, unable to eat because they have three-foot long forks and spoons strapped to their hands. Heaven is then described as the very same place. There, people feed one another.[7]

My studies on the evolution of the structure of our consciousness lead me to suggest some amendments to these statements.

First, behavior in present market societies fits Heilbroner's and Galbraith's description because their members have been programmed into *amour propre*, power control, and wealth accumulation. An enculturation into *amour de soi*, love mastering, and life enjoyment may produce a different behavior in our societies without altering their free-market structure.

Second, in our market societies, increasing numbers of people are already seeking to optimize their lives rather than maximize their income. These are people who are transiting from the rational to the integrative, harmonizing structure of consciousness without waiting for guidance from obsolete educational systems and social and political organizations.

Third, maximizers and optimizers both suffer from imperfect information. People receive incomplete and biased information on the options presented to them by markets. They are equally misinformed when facing political decisions, and they are denied information about the most important factor in their economic and political decision-making processes: knowledge about themselves.

Fourth, people are inclined to serve others only if they have learned to and been allowed to love themselves since their early childhood. The people of the story's hell are people full of *amour propre*. Instead, it is *amour de soi* that leads those in the story's heaven to rationally learn to use the long-handled spoons to feed one another.

Fifth, under a more evolved integrative structure of consciousness, we may prefer to never reach a situation that requires feeding by long handles, which maintains a distance between feeder and the fed. Instead, we may prefer to close all the gaps among ourselves, whether physical, mental, emotional, or spiritual, and help one another to find the means of always having something on one's plate. Then, we should let each eat with his or her own cutlery, at his or her own pace, responding to his or her own personal needs.

Sixth, an enculturation into *amour propre*, power control, and wealth accumulation makes market operators in our present market societies ignore the constraints of nature, and to fight tooth and nail against social institutions that try to achieve a more fair distribution of income by limiting wealth accumulation.

CONSTRAINING ECONOMIES TO WORK WITHIN NATURE'S LIMITATIONS

Guided by a harmonizing consciousness, we will notice not only that "the mind can be happy in itself"[8] but also that nature is our greatest source of satisfaction. Our survival and happiness depend on its nurturing and cleansing abilities. To this end, we might adjust the type and volume of our economic flows to the constraints and opportunities that nature presents us, at both the global and the local level of social and economic organization.

In Figure 13, I propose a design for the circular flow that may facilitate our understanding of those constraints and opportunities. It is a design inspired by Herman Daly,[9] who sees the circular flow of money, resources, goods, and services as taking place within an open system, the economy, which exchanges matter and energy with a much vaster closed system, the Earth environment.[10] The latter receives energy only from the sun, and it is this energy that sustains all human life on Earth.

Making use of the energy of the sun, nature constantly regenerates the stock of plants on which animals and humans feed, as well as the currents of water and air that nurture most forms of life. These stocks provide more than just nourishment. They are used also as material inputs for the production of artifacts.[11] The stock of plants, animals, and humans, and the currents of air and water, are renewed in relatively short periods of time. By contrast, it took millions of years for nature to build the stock of fossil fuels, which, for all practical purposes, should be considered nonrenewable. Minerals are also nonrenewable. They are the result of energies at play during the birth and early evolution of our universe. As with plants, animals, water, and air, the economic role of minerals is double: they nourish life, and they provide inputs to production.

These are just the services of nature as provider of resources to the economy and to life. But nature is also the cleanser of waste produced by economic activity and the biological phenomena of life. This waste is composed of material residues and of energy that flows back to the environment after having used up its potential to produce work in production and life processes. New life and production

147

Figure 13. THE SUSTAINABILITY OF THE CIRCULAR FLOW

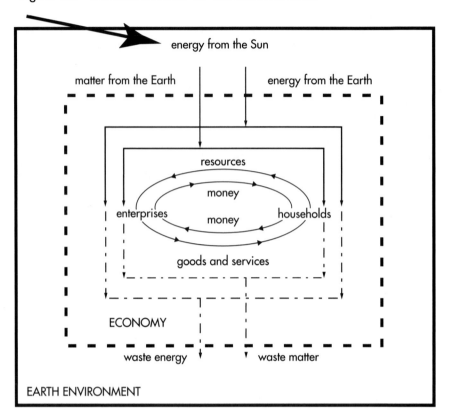

processes can reuse some of the building blocks of the waste materials, thanks to Nature's cleansing processes, which free them from the more complex forms that compose the waste streams.

Without these services from nature, it would be impossible to establish and maintain economic flows. Because the capacity of nature to cleanse waste and regenerate resources is limited, it imposes limits on the amount and type of economic activities that can be performed. When economic activities damage the soil and the currents of water and air, nature loses the basis from which she can regenerate the stock of plants and animals by making use of the energy of the sun. When the stocks of renewable resources are exploited at a faster pace than their rate of regeneration, as was the case with anchovies in the Peruvian seas, local economies are destroyed. When the stocks of nonrenewable resources are depleted too fast, the future of economies is threatened because nature might not be able to regenerate them. And if she can, it will certainly take her more than seven generations.[12] When the cleansing capacity of the environment is overtaxed, pollution threatens our lives and the lives of other species, and we have yet to know the effects on our lives and our economies from an indiscriminate extinction of these other species.

It was Herman Daly's keen-sighted observation that we cannot add indefinitely to the stock of either people or artifacts, whether in the global economy or in a particular local economy. At each level, the rate at which population grows and artifacts are produced should be adjusted to nature's rate of resource renewal and to its cleansing capacity.

EXPLOITING EACH ECONOMY'S
RESOURCES AT THEIR RENEWAL RATE

Traditionally, natural raw resources are traded and labor is mobile. Hence, many local and national economies produce beyond the limits of their own stock of natural resources. However, I suggest that in the future, under a harmonizing, integrative consciousness, rather than trading raw natural resources, we might prefer to trade intermediate and finished products, technology, and creative services that each local and national economy produces with its own natural resources and labor. Indeed, it may take a very long time for technologically advanced economies to reduce production to a level compatible with their own stock of resources. However, as they start moving in this direction, they also start opening opportunities for less favored economies to produce more wealth for their people by undertaking at least some steps in the processes by which their natural resources are transformed into capital goods and consumer products traded with those more advanced economies.

For instance, countries with rich mineral deposits may trade the corresponding metals rather than raw ores. Another example: A shift in consciousness may lead medicine to once again use herbs and their tinctures or dilutions rather than synthetic drugs. This would open possibilities for countries where those herbs grow naturally to cultivate and export them. They may even prepare and export the extracts rather than the dried or fresh herbs. Nowadays, rational scientific behavior leads chemical and pharmaceutical enterprises to screen plants, identify their active principles, and then produce the active principles synthetically in large quantities. The economies where those herbs are found do not benefit from this behavior, nor does human health.

Ideally, the capital for implementing the processes that add value to local products and services would also be locally recruited. However, many countries may need foreign inflows of capital to fulfill the value-adding purpose. In some cases it is paradoxical that local capital is invested elsewhere in a search for purely financial gains while foreign capital helps to develop the local economies.[13]

It is different with the cleansing services that nature provides to the economies. These cannot be traded. Pollution rights that are bought and sold are just one more invention of our divisive, slumberous rationality, which is purely concerned with money and technical efficiency but neglects concerns for humans and ecosystems. It is one more invention that disconnects financial movements from real economic flows. Local and national economies should not be allowed to produce goods or accumulate people beyond the cleansing capacity of the surrounding environment, just because they can buy pollution rights from other less polluting economies, not even if global pollution is kept within permissible limits by these means. People, property, and ecosystems in other economies, mostly those neighboring the purchasing economies, but in some cases also those distant, will be affected by this "bought" pollution. It is almost impossible to stop pollution from sneaking into other spaces.

Human creativity may help nature achieve a faster rate of regeneration of renewables and reach a higher cleansing capacity. Human creativity may also stimulate nature to unveil new sources of energy. However, until this happens, the rate at which artifacts and people are produced should never exceed nature's prevailing rates of resource regeneration and environmental cleansing. If we exceed these limits, the fragile ecological balances and the refined biological and psychological human balances can be damaged beyond repair, threatening the very existence of human life.[14]

Concern for ecosystems and their services is a necessary condition for economic sustainability and the survival of the human species, but it is not a sufficient condition. It must be complemented with equity. Otherwise, only those will survive who control power and wealth at the expense of many others, whose life may be reduced to a short, primitive, and wretched existence, even in the nicest and best protected natural environment.

CREATING SOCIAL CONSTRAINTS TO ASSURE EQUITY

I have already quoted Adam Smith as saying that the poor inevitably fall into despondency unless governments intervene to maintain a balance in the distribution of income.[15] Since the early 1980s, most governments in the free-market societies have been doing precisely the opposite. They have let the gap between rich and poor increase, and have allowed the market initiatives of a few to create oppression and poverty for the rest.

This has happened in developed and developing countries alike. It suffices to give two examples. In the United States, the 20 percent of the population with the lowest income shared 5.3 percent of the total income in 1980 and only 4.7 percent in 1985. At the other end, the share of the highest 20 percent went from 39.9 to 41.9 percent in the same period. In Sri Lanka, a bloody civil war was not an obstacle for the rich to become richer. They increased their share of the country's wealth from 43.4 percent in 1970 to 56.2 percent in 1986, while the poorest 20 percent went from 7.5 percent down to 4.9 percent in the same period.[16]

This situation reveals a slumberous rationality, strongly enculturated into power control and wealth accumulation. Leaders with a new consciousness might refuse to be either drugged by greedy entrepreneurs to the point of blinding themselves to the poverty of large sectors of the population, or excited by theoreticians who think that bureaucracies can solve all the people's problems. A new consciousness might convince leaders that the best thing to do is to help people expand their vision of the world and themselves. The task of educating people to become masters of their physical, mental, emotional, and spiritual health is one that governments should never forgo.

When the enculturation process is designed with this empowerment objective in mind, we might see government interventions reduced to four main tasks: to protect people against violence and oppression, to assure a fair distribution of income, to provide information and education, and to watch over the commons. Protection of people and nature against aggressive behavior might always be a necessity, because even when governments will finally decide to orient the enculturation process toward developing an integrative, harmonizing consciousness, some individuals will still display *amour propre* and suffer from metabolic errors.[17]

New political leaders might develop abilities to balance two apparently contradictory suggestions made by Adam Smith: one, that governments do more by doing less, and the other, that without government interventions the lot of the poor never improves. New leaders will need to integrate and harmonize these still valid proposals in a world that, sociologically and technologically, is light-years away from the transition from mercantilism to capitalism witnessed by Smith. To achieve this integration and harmonization, the new political and social leaders will need to work hand in hand with the emerging new brand of entrepreneurial and labor leaders, because business is, and is highly likely to continue being, the dominant institution of our time.

The unhealthy practice of tobacco smoking can provide a good example of what I mean by balanced government intervention. Banishing tobacco smoking from public places, and informing people about the risks associated with tobacco consumption, are typical government interventions that protect people. To make tobacco smoking illegal would be, instead, a typically unnecessary and counterproductive intervention, liable to produce violence and corruption. It would most likely bring about the organization of illegal markets controlled by racketeers, and fights among gangs for maintaining or increasing their respective market territories.

A similar harmonizing approach can be exercised in the promotion of a fair distribution of income and of time just for play. To this end, governments should cease repressing the exercise of playful gratuitous activities and start applying moral and tax suasion on those who accumulate excessive wealth. However, the brightest signs in the road to equity and freedom might be lighted not by the governments but by the entrepreneurs themselves. As we will see in chapter 11, some of them are already struggling with changes in the patterns of use of entrepreneurial profits, and in the distribution of time between productive and playful activities. These few are responding to a spiritual suasion from within, rather than to taxation and moral suasion from without.

THE ROLE OF LABOR UNIONS

It is amazing to see that many of Adam Smith's cultural criticisms, written at the end of the eighteenth century, are still applicable to our societies. Among them, I have already quoted one about the masters combining to grab the largest possible part of the total income generated in an economy while impeding workers from combining to improve their lot.[18] We had to wait until this century to see laws protecting the right of workers to free association, and outlawing unfair practices of employers. When workers started organizing their unions, they had to struggle hard to increase even slightly their participation in total wealth. They required, and still require, support from government in this struggle.

Were unions exempt from unfair practices? Certainly not. Workers and their union leaders did not escape the prevailing enculturation patterns. The consciousness structures of workers and entrepreneurs were similar. Power and wealth games were played within the unions as within enterprises. In the negotiations between both, few sought win-win solutions. Each party tried to prevail on the other. This confrontational relationship between capital owners and labor providers might change substantially when the new brand of businesspeople, who are rethinking the way they are doing business, becomes the majority.

Under a new structure of consciousness, labor unions may also

153

rethink their role in society. They may try to help workers not only to *have* more of the wealth they help create, but to *be* more, increasing their self-esteem and awareness of their social role. Workers can and shall constantly advance toward higher cultural levels, higher creativity, and improved mastery and enjoyment of the forces of love. Without renouncing their right to work, they might start asserting their right to playfulness, which, for a long time in the evolution of humankind, was a privilege of the elites.

An alliance of workers and entrepreneurs with a new consciousness might help us all find time to straighten up our backs and lift our eyes from the desks, the machines, the land, the materials on which we work. Thus, we would free ourselves for the task of looking deeper and wider at ourselves, and at nature around us, learning to play with all the elements to be found in both domains. Guided by a purely technical and financial rationality, those who control power and accumulate wealth fear that a reduction of working time will handicap our economies and destroy the social tissue. Instead, those who are intent on rationally mastering love and enjoying life know that when more time for playful activities is allowed, productivity, creativity, and happiness increase, nourishing healthy social tissues.

The main task of labor unions in the future might be to help their members become masters of their own physical, emotional, mental, and spiritual health, and to transform all labor into work. The latter would then embody the meaning that Khalil Gibran summed up so well.

You work to follow the rhythms of the Earth and its soul. Because to remain idle is to estrange oneself from the seasons and quit life's march towards infinitude that takes place in friendship and proud submission to the seasons.

When working you are really in love with life. And to love life through work is to come very close to the deepest mystery of life.

Life is darkness only when there is no impulse. And every impulse is blind when there is no knowledge. And every knowledge is vain when there is no work. And every work is empty when there is no love. And when you work with love you are united with yourselves, with the others, and with God.

And what is it to work with love? It is to weave the fabric with yarns spun from your heart, as if it would be a fabric that your lover will use. It is to build a house with affection, as if it would be one where your lover would live. It is to sow seeds with tenderness and harvest with joy, as if the fruits would be for your lover's delight. It is to infuse everything you do with the breath of your own spirit.

I have often overheard, as in a dream, "The one who works on marble and finds the shape of his own soul in the stone is more noble than the one who tills the land. The one who grabs the rainbow to place it on a canvas transformed in the picture of a man is more than one who makes sandals for our feet." But, I tell you, not in dreams, but in the wakefulness of midday, that the wind does not speak more sweetly to the gigantic oaks than to the smallest leaves of grass. And the only one who excels is the one who changes the voice of the wind into a song that his love makes sweeter.

Work is love made visible.

If you are apathetic when you bake bread, you are baking a bitter bread that will only half appease the hunger of people. And if you growl while mashing the grapes, your grumbling poisons the wine. And if you sing without loving your singing, even if you sing like the angels, you are deafening the ears of people to the voices of the day and the voices of the night.[19]

By asserting their rights to have more time for playful activities and to integrate playfulness into work, workers, managers, entrepreneurs, and professionals might contribute to the creation of more job opportunities, at a time when societies face the combined threats of a decrease in those opportunities due to technological progress, and an increase in competition for fewer jobs due to an explosive growth of population. To ward off these threats, we should simultaneously promote a redistribution of working time and playing time, adjust the Earth's population to its resources and cleansing capacity, temper if not cancel the morbid global search for cheap labor, and create an international order that could halt the number of economic and political refugees moving from one country to another.

The call to enter the twenty-first century with a new consciousness is not a battle cry of one sector of society against another sector. It is a call for us all to unite in learning to master love and life, appreciating the things that really matter, and relinking with the creative spirit at a level of evolution that outgrows our magical and mythical past and our present slumberous rationality. In one aspect or another of our lives, we are all workers and entrepreneurs in free-market democratic societies. Whether as workers or entrepreneurs, we have nothing to lose by evolving to a more advanced consciousness. The only things we may lose, and happily so, are our old stifling coats of values and beliefs. Remember Thomas Jefferson: They fitted us in our magic and mythical childhood; they are becoming unaesthetic, immodest, disfunctional. We have instead a world to gain: a world of love, bodily health, peace of mind, and spiritual joy. Let us wisely use the new broad electronic communication highways that are opening before us to enter united into this new world.

THE NET, THE WEB, AND THE NEW CONSCIOUSNESS

Nets and webs are usually used to catch something. This is not the case with the Internet and the World Wide Web. Although a few may use them to prey on others, these communication superhighways, as they are also called, bring together people from all corners of the world, and open access to knowledge at a scale hard to imagine twenty years ago.

In chapter 6 I discussed the alluring speed at which monetary values are electronically exchanged throughout the world. Equally alluring is the amount of information stored in, and exchanged through, the Net and the Web. A researcher in an isolated Antarctic laboratory can exchange information with a scientist in the French Centre National de la Recherche Scientifique (CNRS). They can see each other's faces on the computer screen, hear their voices through the computers' speakers, and exchange written and graphic data.

I have said repeatedly that establishing intellectual, emotional, and physical communication with other people is an unchangeable human need. It has been present since our archaic origin. Aside from physical communication, never has it been easier to exchange emotions and ideas than through the ever-increasing efficiency attained by combining computing, telecommunication, video, sound

156

synthesis, remote sensing, graphic scanning, and other technologies that are being used in the Net and the Web. These communicaton channels also satisfy, better than the old did, another ever-present need: the need for participation.

Those working with the Net and the Web have all the possibilities for transforming themselves from observers, viewers, and listeners into participants. By using appropriate software, we can change the dimensions, colors, and relative positions of different components of an art image received in the screen. A poem or literary piece can be edited and sent back to the poet or writer. A data sheet can be re-worked. On the Net and the Web we can be as creative as our abilities allow us to be. Moreover, in one way or another, all users of the Net and the Web are constantly recreating what they send and what they receive. On my computer screen I do not see the *Mona Lisa* in the dim light that the curators of the Louvre use to protect the painting. I see her with as much intensity of light and with as many color combinations as I decide my screen will have. I am no longer a passive viewer; I am interacting with Leonardo's work. I can irreverently re-create his wonderful creation.

Under the prevailing structures of consciousness, it still is difficult for us to reach out to those seated across our desks and dining tables, those sharing our beds and locker rooms, those travelling with us in cars, trains, and planes. It is equally difficult to reach deep inside ourselves. In many cases we are light-years away from the minds and hearts of others close to us and from our own selves. And now, almost suddenly, through the Net and the Web, we can reach at the speed of light the minds and hearts of people on the opposite side of the planet. By communicating with them, we learn more about ourselves. We are all becoming more transparent.

The electronic highways are also making the markets more transparent. Sitting at my computer, I can access the information I need to decide which car is the best buy for me. Once I make this decision, I can retrieve from the Net a list of all the dealers that sell that particular brand and model in a radius of 100 miles around my home. I also know the price those dealers pay for the car, the margin of revenues I can allow them in my negotiations, and all the equipment with which the car should be delivered to me for that price. I also know how much to expect for my old car if I trade it in as part of the deal. With all this information, I may even discuss the deal over the phone and fix a date to pick up my new car and trade my old one in.

Indeed, the gain in transparency is acquired at the cost of losing the playfulness that can be experienced by bargaining in a Tunisian bazaar or at a booth on a Florentine bridge. I suggest that under an integrative, harmonizing consciousness, both marketing forms will probably coexist.

The transparency brought about by the Net and the Web could make it easier for young creative entrepreneurs to enter the economic flows at a global scale. They can produce something in a village in Kentucky (U.S.A.) or Santiago del Estero (Argentina) and sell it through the Internet to the world. Thus, they contribute simultaneously to local flows and the global flow.

Artists can produce paintings, sculptures, ceramics, and the like in their households; feature their images and prices on a Web page; and sell them around the world without the need for expensive galleries and onerous intermediaries. Poets and writers can post their poems, novels, and essays for others to read directly from the screen or by printing them. As happens with any new technology, the electronic communication highways are pregnant with opportunities, but we do not know yet the full influence on society of the products and services it may deliver. For instance, will it further reduce employment in a world that is growing in population and shrinking in jobs?

CONTROL OVER THE NET AND THE WEB

It is said that we are in transit from the industrial to the information society. In the industrial society, productive activities were linked to a place, usually outside the households, within enterprises and organizations. They required a synchronization of tasks and involved the application of energy to some form of matter. In the information society, at least some of the productive activities will be linked to several places, some in households and some in enterprises and organizations. Some of the tasks involved in these activities will be desynchronized, and mental energy will flow through the electronic channels from one task to the other. This can facilitate, as we have

158

already discussed, the development of healthy local economies linked to the larger national and international markets, unless the use of the new channels ends by being centralized by the powerful groups that now dominate all markets.

By and large, the industrial society was governed by rational structures of consciousness enculturated into competing for power and wealth. Will the information society be governed by the new integrative, harmonizing consciousness whose rationality is enculturated into cooperating for love and life? If the latter happens, we may see ourselves transformed from anonymous consumers and users into full-grown individuals who receive full information about their decisions to buy mostly those things that really matter to life and love. We will also be able, if this happens, to link with as many others in the world as it pleases us, and freely exchange with them messages about any aspect of life and love.

A persistence of the old power-control, greedy mood of governance could mean instead that the electronic highways will be used to push us into an even higher frenzy of consumerism, and that our subjects of exchange will be limited to those approved by the governing orthodoxy.

The debate on these issues is opening just as this book is being published. Commenting on the challenges and opportunities presented by the information society, a European scholar, Joel de Rosnay, said recently that the very use of the term *highways* reveals the desire for controlling, because on highways it is possible to apply toll fees and to count and control circulation.[20] De Rosnay proposes to use instead the organic metaphor of a strongly ramified system of capillaries, arteries, and veins, irrigating as far as the last and smallest cell of society.

Under a new consciousness, the Net and the Web may assure the constant cultural regeneration and full intellectual, emotional, and spiritual flourishing of all the cells. Under the prevailing consciousness, the Net and the Web can end providing most of the cells with nutrition that is just sufficient to keep them as socially functioning units, but never enough to fully develop their humaneness.

The industrial society, on one hand, was a world of submissive people, who occasionally exploded in anger but fell again into submission, once their bottled energies had been released. On the other hand, there were a few dominant personalities in finance, politics, science, religion, arts, entertainment, sports, and other realms of human activity. The information society may instead become a world of PERSONS, all creating, all producing, all thinking, all playing, and all learning, each according to the potential of his or her natural endowment for creation, production, thought, play, and particular ways of organizing the household.

THE ECONOMY OF SEXUALITY

The relations between playfulness and productivity, between gratuitousness and wealth-consumption, and between time to be and time to escape from oneself, become particularly complex when we deal with sexual activity. As we saw in chapter 3, its exercise can simultaneously satisfy biological, psychological, and sociocultural needs, but it can also add an additional being to the stock of people in a given economy, thereby becoming a productive activity.

The economy of sexuality is an economy that pervades all other economies (Figure 14). When we study human activity in markets, households, enterprises, and governments, we find that sexuality is a powerful motivator of many different, sometimes opposed behaviors. It can induce higher creativity and increased productivity but also can cause laziness and dullness. It can fuel competition but also friendship and cooperation. It can stimulate power games but also conviviality. It may spur greed but also generosity.

The knowledge and mastery of the forces of love are among the less developed human abilities. Love does not always involve sex, and sex does not always involve love. Neither does sensual intimacy between bodies, and with one's own body, always involve a sexual experience. It can be just a moment of playing, feeling, and getting to know better the spirit that animates the bodies.

Sexuality is the human activity that has undeservedly originated more codes and laws than any other activity since our departure from the archaic paradise. Some of the regulations obeyed economic and environmental constraints. Others were inspired by the eagerness to control and possess. Until recently, humankind struggled

160

Figure 14. The Economy of Sexuality Pervades All Other Economies

Contributions to the economy of sexuality	Contributions from the economy of sexuality inspired by	
	Amour propre	Amour de soi
• Wealth to pay for recreational sexual services	• Motivation for speeding the speculative flow of money to increase personal wealth	• Motivation to reduce personal participation in the operation of the flow to free time for enjoying the gratuitous recreational and relational aspects of sex
• Goods and services to separate reproduction from recreation and relationship, and to free time from household chores	• Use of sexual relations to increase power and wealth • Denial to women of access to the marketplace • Increase of the stock of people without concern for nature's carrying capacity • Prolonged adolescence, hence delayed participation in the formation of households and in economic flows • Demand for products that hide damage to the body from unhealthy life and that reflect power and wealth	• Responsible parenthood that decreases the economic and ecological costs of overpopulation • Flexibility of gender roles that facilitate the entrance of women into the marketplace • Motivation to reduce working time • Demand fro products that protect the body and reflect its health and individual beauty
• Opportunities to relate to other people and nature • Increased creativity • Mastery and enjoyment of love forces	• Relationships treated like a sport, with losers and winners • Carelessness about acquiring sexually transmitted diseases and infecting partners	• Care for oneself and one's partners, reducing the suffering from and costs to society of sexually transmitted diseases • Intimacy with and improved knowledge of others and of nature

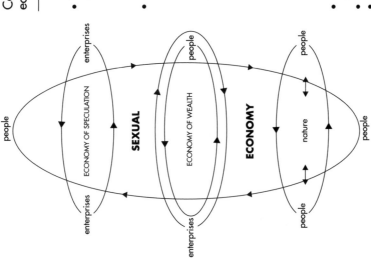

people — enterprises

ECONOMY OF SPECULATION

enterprises

SEXUAL

people

ECONOMY OF WEALTH

enterprises

ECONOMY

people

nature

people

people

with the difficulties in separating the recreational and relational aspects of this activity from its reproductive purposes. Hence, it is no wonder that we find such disparate approaches to the subject. Most Jewish, Christian, and Muslim cultures consider that the relief of sexual tension is an important part of the male sexual economy, although not necessary for the female sexual economy. Some traditions of ancient India, China, and Japan consider instead that it is beneficial for both economies to master, rather than discharge, sexual tensions. Some Westerners advocate using male seeds only to increase their numbers *(amour propre)*. Some Easterners try to save seeds to increase their physical and mental strength *(amour de soi)*. Some traditions see sexuality as a work of the Devil; other traditions perceive it as a gift of God.

Old dogmatic laws, codes, and regulations attempt to control—sometimes even suppress—our rich sexuality, handicapping creativity, originating hypocritical and often violent ways of bypassing the rules, and further alienating the spirit from the human mind and the human body. Instead, modern theologians, historians of religion, and psychologists agree with Ted McIlvenna and Laird Sutton that sexuality "is not something which is optional—it is a part of who and what we are."[21]

Historian of religion Mircea Eliade writes:

Sexuality . . . everywhere and always . . . is a polyvalent function whose primary and perhaps supreme valency is the cosmological function: so that to translate a psychic situation into sexual terms is by no means to belittle it; for, except in the modern world, sexuality has everywhere and always been a hierophany, and the sexual act an integral action and also a means of knowledge.[22]

Theologian Dorothee Soelle says:

Both religion and sexuality heal the split between ourselves and the universe. We discover that we are indeed 'part of everything' and one with the mystery of life. To talk about God in relation to our sexuality means to be aware of love moving in us, for 'in God we live and move and have our being.[23]

162

English psychologist Havelock Ellis states:

For until it is generally possible to acquire erotic personality and to master the art of loving, the development of the individual man or woman is marred, the acquirement of human happiness and harmony remains impossible.[24]

Sexuality influences our market behavior more strongly than any other natural need or socially acquired desire. Starving people still have sex, and the locus of population explosion is among the poor, not the rich countries. Sexuality shapes advertising messages and creates the demand for a variety of products and services. When this demand is not satisfied openly, sexuality pushes producers and consumers of the corresponding satisfiers to operate illegal markets.

When playful recreational and relational sexual needs are not fulfilled at home, rich people work harder than needed, sometimes exploiting humans and nature ruthlessly, to accumulate wealth. The process of accumulation becomes itself a substitute pleasure, and the accumulated wealth pays for the services of concubines, lovers, and sophisticated courtesans. Wealth also means potential power to sexually subdue those who work for them at their homes or in their enterprises.

Among poor people, an unfulfilled sexuality leads to the diversion of a good part of meager earnings from satisfying household needs to paying for the services of prostitutes, and for intoxicants that provide a escape from frustration and dissatisfaction.

Most present societies still "do not hesitate to falsify the truth and throw into darkness the leading protagonist of history, a protagonist that from the earthly paradise on never stopped shaking humankind's fate."[25] When dealing with sexual matters, political and social leaders, who profess to pursue and protect freedom in the marketplace, do not hesitate to coerce individual freedom in the households. Our rational science, perhaps following spiritual intuitions, put an end to the conflict between recreation, relationship and reproduction by making cheap contraceptives available. With them, deep changes occurred in the exercise of sexuality, in the relationship between genders, in the maturation process of youth, in demographics. It was an evolutionary mind change with all its fulfilled and unfulfilled expectations, its dark alleys and bright avenues, its potential for disorder and a higher, more humane order. However, many if not most of our political, social, and religious leaders seem impervious to this global mind change. Although their own sexuality is often brought viciously to the public arena, they are still awkward in dealing with it. These leaders are not following the evolution of our consciousness. Perhaps they lack appropriate indicators.

NEW POLITICAL LEADERS NEED NEW INDICATORS

Most business, political, and religious leaders are not yet tuning in to the signals that announce a new consciousness. It is difficult for them to wean themselves from the blinding and deafening prejudices and myths they imbibed during their enculturation, and they do not have appropriate guidelines that would translate the changes that are already happening into signs that they can capture.

Political leaders, especially, are in need of new, more comprehensive indicators for the task of driving our economies. The economic health and geopolitical power of a country have been, and to a large extent continue to be evaluated mainly through indicators that quantify the material aspects of its society. Some of these indicators are population, the area under the country's control, the size of the country's armies, gross national and domestic product (GNP and GDP), the rate of growth of production and consumption, the rate of inflation, and the balance of trade.

These oldest indicators often hide the true situation in a country's economy and its society. For instance, GNP and GDP do not tell us how the product is distributed among the country's population. It took some time to get figures on the distribution of income, and some countries do not yet produce reliable information on this social issue. Other indicators, such as illiteracy, enrollment at different levels of schooling, number of pupils per teacher, life expectancy, population per physician, infant and maternal mortality, birth and death rates, and contraceptive use, are also welcome additions to this primitive and often misleading picture, but they are not enough to enable an integrative decision-making process.

As Hazel Henderson suggests, a new set of indicators should include data on productive work performed within the households and on trade among households.[26] Besides exchanging goods, services, and money with enterprises, households also produce goods and services for their captive consumption and for monetary or barter trade with other households. The importance of these flows in the economy of the United States can be seen from the following figures:

- Some forty-one million Americans spend several hundred million hours each year on do-it-yourself home renovation, but only the material inputs used for this purpose are accounted for; labor is not. In 1980, the retail value of the material inputs was $28 billion; in 1985, it reached $43 billion, accounting for 56 percent of all expenditures on home alterations and repairs.
- Thirty-four million American families have vegetable gardens where they spend, on average, nearly 50 hours each summer seeding and hoeing. These gardens produce fruit and vegetables worth approximately $15 billion.
- Ten million people belong to mental and physical mutual-help health-care groups, ranging from Weight Watchers to Psychotics Anonymous. In 1980, their activities were valued at $60 billion, but they are never taken into account in the GNP.[27]

The figures given above show how insidious an economic analysis can be when it takes into account only the flows generated by formal enterprises and by governments. If economic analysis was to reflect production within households and exchanges among households, the GNP of some countries would be much larger than official figures show.

The most neglected contribution to economic welfare and individual well-being has always been the work of women at home as nursing mothers, educators, administrators, and housekeepers. In some developing countries, women are the main organizers and operators of household subsistence economies whose products are not counted in the GNP. However, these household economies, supplemented with barter trading among households and the selling of some surplus produce in local markets, are often considerably more important for the survival of the family than the salaries earned by the men of the family.

To give a full picture of a community, social indicators need to reflect also the degree of freedom allowed to households in exercising playful gratuitous activities, and in providing services to their members that households are often compelled to contract outside. For instance, endowed with freedom and information, households could do more and better than they do now to prevent disease and cure minor ailments. They can do this at a fraction of the cost of medical services by using gentle herbal and homeopathic remedies, by carefully combining the best available food with appropriate supplements, and by learning body therapies such as massage, acupressure, and energy balance.

Empowering people and giving them freedom to heal themselves and one another may produce two main effects, for which we should find indicators that can be included in the socioeconomic analyses. First, empowerment and freedom in healing would help in reducing the costs of health-care systems. Second, they would strengthen family bonds by promoting closer intellectual, emotional, and physical exchanges among family members. Neither contractual nor household-provided health services are free of mistakes. However, individual mistakes, even tragic ones, are less costly to society than the massive mistakes into which societies often plunge when governments protect a particular way of providing those services, denying the people information and access to the others and restricting their freedom to become their own health masters.

When parents become masters of their own physical, mental, emotional, and spiritual health, they can detect early signs of deficient physical and mental conditions in their offspring. These deficiencies can be often corrected with the nutritional, homeopathic, and other natural therapies already mentioned. Many troubled adolescents and impaired mature persons could have been saved if the debilitating conditions of their mental and physical constitutions had been gently modified in infancy.[28]

Sociopolitical leaders seem incapable of imagining the promises of a global mind-change for their societies and economies. They also seem incapable of appraising the accomplishments of those privately engaged in mind-change efforts. They urgently need indicators that reflect those promises and accomplishments until they develop the intuitive and rational capacity to imagine and appraise by themselves—or, in other words, until they start leading more by vision than by polls and statistics.

BUSINESS MANAGERS ALSO NEED NEW INDICATORS

To guide businesses, managers cannot rely anymore on purely material indicators, such as production capacity, market share, payroll size, total revenue, and profits. In their decision-making, they must now include criteria related to the psychological, environmental, and spiritual aspects of the enterprise's activities. Among other things, they should consider

- the flexibility of the enterprise to adapt to changing markets
- the degree of confidence it earns from consumers
- the level of integration of its personnel in the enterprise's vision
- the various interests of different functional groups within the enterprise
- the level of creativity within each of those different functional groups
- the degree of satisfaction of all needs among all personnel of the firm
- the contributions of the enterprise to the well-being of the communities where it operates, and to a harmonious global development
- the impact of the enterprise's activities on the local physical environment as well as possible repercussions in other environments

As Robert Salmon points out, even the support of artistic and literary activities is now of concern to entrepreneurs and managers.[29] Enterprises are slowly recognizing that to be productive, workers need to work in a healthy environment and to derive a decent living for themselves and their families from their work. For most entrepreneurs, "decent living" for their workers means that they and their families can satisfy biological and some biopsychological needs. For a few, the satisfaction of psychological and sociocultural needs is also becoming part of a decent living. These people understand that "the enterprise should not use people, but be useful to them."[30]

To produce products and services that will have market acceptance, enterprises must closely follow social changes. To avoid obsolescence, enterprises must watch technological changes attentively. And they need to observe changes in the structure of consciousness, because it is these changes in consciousness that affect all the others.

Moreover, to sustain and increase progress in their businesses, enterprises must promote change rather than react to it. Business initiatives are already preparing many of the changes in the coats of values and beliefs with which societies cover our naked ever-present origin as creatures of nature. Through the design of their products and services, their advertising, and their social and political involvement, enterprises influence our modes of thought and behavior. However, the process by which the structure of our consciousness evolves, once it is stimulated by a business initiative, may take unexpected directions and glow with an intensity of its own. This makes it necessary for enterprises to develop the capacity to gauge the process.

DETECTING CHANGES IN THE STRUCTURE OF OUR CONSCIOUSNESS

Political leaders are far behind entrepreneurs and managers in the development of this capacity to promote and assess changes in people's perception of reality. Socioeconomic policies fail to reflect the existential pain that pervades the lives of even successful entrepreneurs, the stress and fears of the future among workers, the hopelessness and anger among those left outside the economic flows, the weariness and boredom among the majority of people. Neither do political guidelines capture positive signs, such as the changes that pioneer enterprises are effecting in their way of thinking and doing

168

business. Most political leaders do not perceive that people are fed up with wearing stifling coats made of obsolete dogmas and beliefs, and with supporting, by their savings and taxes, the power games of old-style businesses and governments.

The mere inclusion in the driving dashboards of economies and enterprises of a gauge to measure those changes in people's perception of reality does not guarantee that many political leaders and entrepreneurial managers will start making the right decisions. The slumberous rationality of most of them might not be awakened fast enough by the alarm signals that the new gauge would trigger. Loud alarms may startle rather than awake them, and, still drowsy, they may decide to come down even more harshly on the discontented people and ignore the innovative businesspeople who are trying to change course. We might then expect more wars, more destruction of nature, more totalitarian repressive societies.

However, an unexpected brain wave might suddenly confront managers and political leaders with the horror of a life where survival requires the development of thick calluses within our consciousness to bar intuitions, emotions, instinct, and spirit from awakening reason. Managers and political leaders might then decide to accelerate the evolution of human consciousness. If this happens, humankind might avoid falling into what Hazel Henderson calls a "paedomorphosis," a regression to earlier stages of evolution because we have become too rigid and ill adapted to change.[31]

The options are between a world at war and a world at peace, between humans assaulting and destroying themselves and nature, and humans valuing life and love.

9

A WORLD AT PEACE: LEARNING FROM NATIVE AMERICANS

After a long period of warfare arising from intertribal blood feuds, five Native American nations—the Mohawk, Onondaga, Seneca, Oneida, and Cayuga, all settled in the general area of present New York State and environs—buried their weapons of war and bound themselves to what was called the Great Law of Peace. By the thirteenth century, these American "savages" had organized their societies around the idea that authority flows up from the people. At that time, "civilized" Europeans were still enculturated into believing that all authority flows down from the heights through kings and nobility. Moreover, for the Iroquois, *people* really meant all the people—women and children included. They all participated in the decision-making process that started at household or clan councils, from which representatives took proposals to a community or tribal council. The decisions of these tribal councils in turn informed the decisions made by the national councils and the Grand Council of the Confederacy.

The Great Law of Peace, and the social and political organizations that emerged from it, were studied with admiration by missionaries and scholars who visited North America after the establishment of the first European settlements. Later, some intellectuals of the British colonies, who later promoted the independence of the colonies from the British king, also became interested in Iroquois forms of governance and social organization. In the nineteenth century, the Iroquois perplexed anthropologists like Lewis Henry Morgan and worldly philosophers like Karl Marx and Friedrich Engels. Here is a list of some principles of the United States Constitution compared with Iroquois practice:[1]

Political patterns of the Iroquois Confederacy retained in the Constitution:
- federal union of semi-independent states
- checks and balances to avoid misuse of power
- referendum and recall (impeachment)

Political patterns of the Iroquois Confederacy included later in the Bill of Rights:
- freedom of religion
- freedom of speech
- freedom from unlawful search and seizure.

Political patterns found among the Iroquois and added to the U.S. Constitution under later amendments:
- universal suffrage despite race, color, or creed
- suffrage for women

Political patterns of the Iroquois Confederacy that are not yet in the U.S. Constitution
- women's rights
- children's rights
- responsibility for the environment (all decisions made with the impact on the Seventh Generation in mind)

The Iroquois did not base their incipient rational structures of consciousness on highly cemented mythical and magical layers. They let these layers remain soft and permeable to the archaic structures. Thus, they could still receive intuitive and instinctive wisdom. The Iroquois had long since lost the paradise of the archaic consciousness. But the spirit was not exiled from the mind, as it was in the rational structures of the Europeans who would end up persecuting them.[2] While the Iroquois culture of peace, participation, and concern for humans and nature was blooming in America (twelfth to eighteenth centuries), Europeans went through the tragic delusions of the Crusades, the horrors of religious and dynastic wars, the atrocities of the inquisition, and the killing of natives when they opened new continents to their conquests.

The voice of the spirit was familiar to the Iroquois from childhood on. They could interpret this voice according to their different perceptions at different ages, and while exercising different occupations in their societies. By bringing these different interpretations to their council circles, they enriched the decision-making process that was based on consensus-building. The Iroquois described their councils as circles of people who came together for wisdom to identify the decision or decisions with which everyone could live. They felt that the understanding of self and of one's relationship to one's community is a process of continuing learning.[3]

For the Iroquois, playfulness and beauty were part of their relationships among themselves and with nature. It is striking to learn about their efforts to eradicate violence from all those relationships. For instance, killing a deer or an elk was a sacred ritual in which the hunter gave thanks for the food. He would promise that the bones of his people would later nurture the land that was supporting the family to which the victim belonged. After the task, the hunter cleaned himself thoroughly and shared the meat with the whole community. We can well imagine how bewildered the Iroquois must have felt when they saw "civilized people" killing indiscriminately elks and deer in Iroquois territory, and learned from the Sioux about the masive killing of buffaloes in the plains.

How Peace Was Enforced

Iroquois elders knew that the natural penchant of some youngsters is toward a calm approach to the variability of life. This penchant argued well for their potential to resolve disputes; hence, from them would emerge the administrators of the Iroquois society. But elders would look also for youngsters with a quick eye and a strong hand, an easy stance and a firm grip, to train them as warriors. These would always be ready to respond to calls from the Confederacy's Grand Council.

Representatives of the Council would first go to any neighbor nation that was making war and invite their people to join the League of Peace, giving fair warning that if they did not cease hostilities, the Iroquois would be back. If hostilities continued, the offending neighbors were invited again to join the League and carefully warned that if they did not cease hostilities the Iroquois would be back in force. If, despite these two warnings, the neighbors continued or restarted hostilities, a third warning was required by the Great Law. A negative response to this last warning would cause the Iroquois warriors to descend on the offenders and decisively end hostilities.

The offending nation was not really conquered, but rather subdued toward peace and integration with the confederacy. The defeated nation kept its own government, rituals, and traditions. Many of its men were taken to Iroquois country and adopted as new sons by Iroquois women, as all Iroquois polity sprang from the hearth of the mothers, where all political voices from men, women, and children were heard. The purpose of this enforced tour of Iroquois homes was to give new members of the League some very hands-on experience with the nature of Iroquois self-government. After enough months to enable this learning had passed, the men from the previously hostile nation returned home.

APPLYING IROQUOIS WISDOM TO THE UNITED NATIONS SYSTEM

The United Nations system created after World War II is increasingly perceived as a myth because of the gap in our minds between the real possibility of organizing the nations of the world around a Great Law of Peace, and the monstrous reality of a world divided by power games of greedy interests.

World peace and progress require that the UN system be strengthened. It should be endowed with a powerful, independent military force, and the voice of the peoples of the Earth should be brought to its decision-making bodies. Peace requires a rapid response from the international community to threats from one country to another, or to a violation of human rights within a nation by ideological, religious, or economic groups that aim at establishing a dictatorship over the remainder of the country's population. Peace also requires early help to nations engaged in a peaceful and democratic evolution from old economic, social, and mental structures.

REACTING TO EARLY WARNINGS

Illuminated minds always give advanced warning to the world of budding tragedies. They see the dangers that lurk on the horizon and cry: "The wolf is coming!" The Spanish poet Leon Felipe did just that from the hills of Madrid when Hitler, Mussolini, and Stalin chose the fields of Spain to test their arms for the battles that would come.[4]

Political leaders of powerful countries often ignore those warnings. Sometimes they even sharpen and strengthen the teeth of the wolf, and even open the henhouses of other societies to his predatory actions. They seek two objectives that are equally deceptive: one, to make quick profits by selling arms; the other, to use aggressive power to plunder a country perceived as a dangerous competitor, or whose innovative social organizations threaten the status quo. What the leaders of the powerful nations do not perceive is that the beast, once primed by the blood of his first victims, usually turns to the henhouses of the societies that supported his initial adventures.

Independent institutions may develop the ability to issue well-documented early warnings, in addition to always listening to the cries of poets and writers.[5] Yet, to respond to the early warnings, the UN should be endowed with an international independent military force that could act promptly and efficiently. By establishing a UN security force, the global community would be prepared to heed the warnings, eradicating violence and repression when it buds anywhere in the world, rather than when it has already developed and is spreading. The mission of the UN security force might also include natural disaster preparedness and relief work.

All members of the UN system would contribute to the organization and maintenance of the international force. Their contributions would be proportionate to their GNP, or some other appropriate indicator of the country's wealth. Taxpayers of all countries would soon realize that they pay much less for supporting these services collectively than for maintaining national defense organizations.

The rather small but very well-equipped and well-trained army, the factories to supply it with the latest weapons, and the research laboratories to develop new weapons that can paralyze the offenders without killing too many or doing too much harm to their land and property might all be based on territories, most likely Pacific and Atlantic islands, surrendered by different nations to the administrative control of the UN. Simultaneously, the manufacture of arms and their possession in civilian hands ought to be banished in all countries. Small national and local police forces would be supplied with the least offensive arms by the UN-controlled factories.

As under the Iroquois Great Law of Peace, the UN Security Council might appeal three times to the common sense of the violators of peace or human rights. If the third appeal is disregarded, the UN army would act to decisively evict aggressive dictators, callous military juntas, heartless caudillos, ruthless destroyers of nature, and merciless religious leaders before they could consolidate their power.

After descending on the offenders of humankind, nature, or both with all their mighty force, the UN commanders would be required to organize free elections under the surveillance of the same private, independent institutions that sounded the early warnings.[6] The commanders, with the help of these organizations, would also promote exchanges among households of the country in question and households of countries with well-established democratic institutions and a decent record of respect for human rights. It would be equally effective to expose teachers of the intervened country to enculturation programs that awaken reason and foster integration and harmony. Thus, future generations of the country in question would be enculturated into a more evolved structure of consciousness.

These activities would follow not only the example of the Iroquois but also the more recent example of the Marshall Plan, which opened enterprises of the Western victors of World War II to entrepreneurs and managers of the defeated, helping them rebuild and update their industrial base. Similarly, the proposed actions might help rebuild and update the thought forms, the structure of consciousness, of the people on whose behalf the UN intervened.

Helping people advance toward more developed structures of consciousness should never be confused with imposing ideologies or systems of beliefs and behavior. It is, instead, an effort to help people in investigating the wilderness in the minds of the sociopolitical managers who originated so much suffering for their own and other nations. It is an effort to help people in exploring the constellations locked up in their own skulls. It is because these constellations were not allowed to shine that those obnoxious characters could rise to the top managerial positions of their societies.[7] It is an effort to help people free their minds from constraints, broaden their horizons, intensify their links with their bodies and inner spiritual sources, and let them decide what to believe and how to behave. There is no full guarantee that after the effort, people may not fall back into authoritarian forms of governance, but the likelihood is considerably decreased.

PROVIDING EARLY HELP

Lives, money, and suffering might also be spared by providing early help to honest, but inexperienced, reformist leaders elected by popular vote. Intent on lifting their people out of misery, despondency, ignorance, and oppression, if not sheer terror, these leaders often face strong opposition from combined external and internal forces whose patterns of thought and behavior created the situation the leaders want to reform. Without early help and appropriate advice, inexperienced reformist leaders tend to become the prey of "protectors" with their own set of ideological and commercial interests. Inexperienced leaders also tend to handle the economy in such a way that instead of producing more wealth to distribute, the economy discourages its creation.

Several institutions within the UN system have the resources required to provide this early help, among them the World Bank, the International Monetary Fund (IMF), and the United Nations Education, Science, and Culture Organization (UNESCO).

After World War II humankind longed for actions that would

uplift spirits and help everyone build more peaceful, humane societies. There was a strongly felt need to change patterns of thought and behavior. Intuitively, the peoples of the world felt that "problems cannot be solved by the same consciousness that created them."[8] UNESCO could have taken up the challenge of promoting an evolution in the structure of our consciousness, but it did not. Trapped in the usual games of *amour propre* and power control, UNESCO frustrated hopes entertained by humankind following the suffering and devastation of the war.

Soon after its creation, UNESCO was dominated by political managers of education, science, and culture rather than being governed by wise educational, scientific, and cultural leaders.[9] Those managers made no efforts to expand and intensify their own consciousness. Hence, they could not help the peoples of the world to do the same. They were preoccupied by rubbing shoulders with Nobel Prize winners and laureate writers and artists at sophisticated and costly meetings. Inspired by their advanced and well-adorned rational structure of consciousness, most of the scientific and cultural fundamentalists who staffed UNESCO thought that their task, at best, was to take the hard science and sophisticated culture of the North and West to the South and East. Life within UNESCO was not easy for the few progressive minds, the true leaders, who saw their task differently and tried to help developing countries build their local scientific capacity and promote local cultural activities. Often, UNESCO was one more battlefield in the struggle between the two economic systems discussed in chapter 5.

UNESCO might still be rescued and transformed into a UN agency that helps people to reach one another over and beyond borders, overcoming the chasm created by mistrust, mistakes, and nationalistic and religious wars, which all are products of an enculturation into competiton for power and wealth. There is clamor in the world for a global effort that by helping to restructure minds will make easier the task of creating peace and bringing progress to underdeveloped populations and mismanaged societies.

The World Bank's Economic Development Institute (EDI), which was created in 1955 as a sort of college to help member countries design and implement better policies, might join a renewed UNESCO in organizing those efforts. In the 1960s the EDI started spreading vigorously the gospel of planning and management, which helped most developing countries to put order into their finances. In the 1980s, EDI shifted its efforts to preaching, with equal fervor and efficiency, the gospel of trade liberalization and privatization. It might now use its resources and experience to promote with equal vigor a global mind change. As we will see in the last part of this book, experiments in transforming consciousness in different parts of the world show that short exposures to low-cost consciousness-expanding work elicit effective changes in the way people perceive reality and act on it, as well as in local business and political practices.

OTHER WAYS OF FUNDING GLOBAL PEACE EFFORTS

It would be unrealistic to think that a transformation of the UN system along the directions suggested here could be achieved in a short time. Among political and social managers there is still too much *amour propre*, power ambition, and greed, and the educational systems continue enculturating people into those patterns of belief and behavior. The transition toward more humane local, national, and global institutions cannot go faster than the process by which the structure of our consciousness is evolving.

The Global Commission to Fund the United Nations—a private initiative by people who are well advanced on the way to integration and harmony—suggests intermediate steps that may prepare us for the more ambitious future outlined above. Moreover, some of the steps they propose might well be integrated into the final stage of transformation. Their main suggestion involves the creation of a United Nations Security Insurance Agency (UNSIA), which would provide the UN with a substantial source of revenue for peacekeeping by selling insurance policies against aggression to member states. The key incentive for member states to buy this insurance is that they can obtain more security for less money. The key objective of the proponents is to slowly reduce hostility, military spending, and warfare in the world.[10] The proposal still relies on national military forces, but these would be special units of volunteers for whose military equipment and training the UN would pay. Retired colonel

Daniel M. Smith from the Center for Defense Information assesses the UNSIA proposal as feasible.[11]

As an example, the authors of the initiative forecast that a country that now spends $10 billion on defense might like to save $3 billion by cutting total military expenditures to $5 billion and buying a $2-billion insurance package that promises swift UN intervention in case of aggression. The magnitude and nature of this intervention would be clearly spelled out in the policy agreement. The risks the Agency would face, and therefore the premium it should charge to the insured country, would be assessed by multilateral, multidisciplinary teams of experts. A reduction in premium when neighboring countries also buy security insurance would provide additional incentives for a global reduction of military expenses.[12]

The Global Commission to Fund the United Nations is also studying other means of making the UN less dependent on member countries' dues, which are usually in arrears and do not keep pace with the UN's increased responsibilities. The commission suggests, for instance, a tax on international sales and transfers of arms; on the international trade of money, which is described in chapter 5; and on the use of the global commons, such as oceans, space, and electromagnetic spectra.[13]

The implementation of these suggestions could pave the way to the final desirable stage in which nations bury their arms and support, fully and willingly, a small but powerful army under the command of the UN. However, to reach this final objective, consciousness-restructuring efforts should parallel demilitarization, peacekeeping, and peacemaking efforts. We must never forget that our socioeconomic problems are not products of the scarcity of resources or the perversity of nature; they are products of a deficient state of mind.

DEMOCRATIZING AND REJUVENATING THE UNITED NATIONS

To progress in thought forms and action patterns, the peoples of the world should have an opportunity to voice their concerns within the UN system and participate in the policy-making process. We might

add a council of the peoples and a youth council to the present structure of the system.

The council of the peoples might be formed by two adult representatives from each country. These representatives might beelected
in a nonpartisan election whose logistics can be arranged by the UN
office in each country with the participation of UN-recognized nongovernmental organizations. Only those countries where a popular
vote can be freely cast should be accepted in the council. To decide
which those countries are, the UN might trust information received
from private organizations, like those suggested earlier in the discussion of early warnings.[14]

Similarly the youth council might be composed of two young representatives (ages 15 to 21) from each country that is accepted into
the people's council. We might trust the United Nations Children's
Fund (UNICEF) with the logistics of organizing and running this
council.

The relation of these two new councils to existing UN political
bodies and UN management might be better understood by comparing the works of the UN with the process of chartering a ship. Crew,
technicians, and staff can discuss with the representatives of the
charter enterprise the schedule, itinerary, periodicity of the trips,
length of each leg, working and living conditions on board, salaries,
and other compensations. Once all this is agreed upon, and the ship
is at sea, the captain can still ask the crew and technicians to participate in the making of everyday decisions, but in situations of risk
the captain must decisively assume the command. There may not be
time for consultations. The final decisions are his or her full responsibility. I see the General Assembly as the representative of the charter nations, the councils of the peoples and of youth as the crew and
technicians who labor on the spaceship Earth, and the Security
Council as the collective captainship.

The council of the peoples might establish guidelines for peacekeeping and the use of the global commons. Before passing them to
the General Assembly, these guidelines would be approved by the
youth council. In turn, policy resolutions passed by the General
Assembly might need approval by a majority of the members of
both new councils before being enforced. The enforcer would be

the Security Council, which, in case of emergencies, would apply guidelines and policies of its own accord.

We should not continue making decisions at a global level that ignore the world's youth. They are those who suffer most from social disorientation, economic crisis, and adult mismanagement. They are also those who can contribute most to the solution of those problems, because neither education nor economic survival have yet fully programmed their minds. They can bring to the UN healthy instincts and deep intuitions to balance the slumberous rationality of the governments represented at the UN political bodies.

We need young people to speak for the millions of child laborers worldwide. We need young people to speak for the increasing number of teenagers who commit suicide or are killed in the streets. We need young people to speak for the adolescents that see a decrease in employment opportunities and social solidarity.[15]

Awakened youth should speak for the millions of young people left to face a harsh life in markets, streets, and households with their divine nature fully clothed in absurd mental programs. They might have fared much better if left in their naked nature, which would know how to protect them. The social programs written in the hard disk of their subconscious introduce confusion rather than providing help in managing their powerful internal forces, some of which will never again be as strong as they are in youth.

The councils of the peoples and of youth might also speak more sincerely for Mother Earth than governments do. For instance, they might not try to hide, as some governments do, the reality that environmental destruction in many locations is a product of a population explosion that governments do nothing to control. The new councils might expose governments that sign the World Bank's loan agreements with no intention of enforcing covenants that require the adoption of environmental protective and regenerative measures.

Crimes Against Nature

For these reasons, I suggest that UN security forces should be ready to act not only against crimes affecting humanity but also against crimes affecting nature. In all likelihood, even under an integrative,

harmonizing consciousness, there will be political and business leaders who, guided by a destructive *amour propre* with its lust for power
and wealth, might severely damage people and nature. In such
cases, the use of an international force might be the most cost-effective way of subduing the leaders and submitting them to an international criminal court.

An international force and an international criminal court that
would enforce environmental regulations would save money and
suffering for people in all countries. Chlorofluorocarbons (CFCs),
which used to be standard in aerosols and air conditioning equipment, provide a good example. It has been established that CFCs deplete the ozone layer that protects Earth from excessive solar
radiation. Ozone depletion may cause some 300,000 additional cases
of skin cancer a year worldwide, and 1.7 million cases of cataracts.[16]
The use of CFCs in aerosols was banned by the U.S. Congress in
1977, and in 1987 an international protocol to control consumption
of CFCs and related substances that deplete ozone was signed in
Montreal. To comply with these decisions, advanced industrialized
countries are investing large sums of money to retrofit industry and
household equipment, but simultaneously an illegal market of the
old CFCs has emerged in those countries as well as in less developed
countries. The latter are being encouraged to continue using those
old products, which can be sold at attractive prices because they are
produced in amortized installations. Thus, the taxpayers of the advanced countries will pay the bill for both the retrofitting of their industrial and household equipment that was designed to use the old
CFCs, and the medical costs of the increased number of cancers and
cataracts caused by a continued deterioration of the ozone layer by
emissions of old CFCs from countries that ignore the international
protocols. A government that does this to its own citizens, and to its
close and distant neighbors, is as aggressive as one that allows its
military or paramilitary forces to cross borders and harass neighboring towns and villages. In the latter case, we see blood, death and disease immediately. With pollution, killings have a cleaner look. We do
not see bloody bodies lying on streets and fields; the coffins appear
much later at polished funeral homes.

INTEGRATING LOCAL, NATIONAL, AND GLOBAL ECONOMIC FLOWS

For each economy, whether of a village, a large city, a region, a nation, a group of nations, or the world, we can picture a circular flow[17] operating within the constraints and opportunities offered by its immediate environment and the whole Earth. We see in Figure 15 that the flows are always interrelated. The global flow encompasses all others and is supported by all others. There is an active exchange of materials, people, and money among them, and changes in either the production patterns or the natural environment at one level of flow affect all others.

Recent technological developments, although quite sophisticated and not specifically oriented toward small-scale production, are nevertheless enabling small local companies to claim a share in markets previously reserved for national and multinational monopolies or oligopolies. For instance, modern technologies for telephone communication allow small-scale undertakings in villages and small towns to provide local services at competitive costs. These local undertakings can be owned by people from the community and tie into national and international networks. Likewise, we can expect that advances in the technology of solar-powered and wind-powered devices, microhydropower, and superconductors will facilitate similar combinations of local production connected to larger distribution networks in the energy field. When, because of their efficient and ecologically sound use of energy, railway systems make a comeback, small-scale operations will take care of transportation needs among small communities near the train stations.

Let me give two more examples from production sectors with which I have had direct experience. In regions where a given fruit tree can be efficiently cultivated, local communities can use small-scale, first-rate technologies to produce juice concentrate, a safe way of storing the seasonal harvest for year-round use. Surplus juice can be sold to large corporations that mix different juices and produce an appealing variety of products for national and even international distribution. Some of these mixed juices may even return to the communities that produced the different individual juices in the mix,

183

there to be sold at local grocery stores, restaurants, and supermarkets. Small-scale multiuse abattoirs can similarly benefit communities established in areas where it is easy to raise livestock and fowl. Hamburger, sausage, and beefsteak do not need to come from outside those communities. Instead, their surplus production can be marketed through large corporations in areas whose environment is not conducive to producing fowl and livestock.

We should neglect neither the economies of scale that can be achieved through national and international large concerns nor the human, social, and ecological advantages of efficient small-scale local undertakings. We might benefit from both economies of scale and technologies

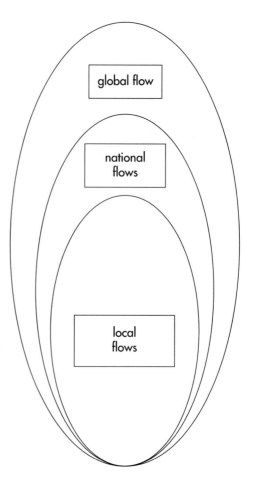

Figure 15. INTERDEPENDENCE OF ECONOMIC FLOWS

adjusted to smaller, more socially and ecologically convenient scales.

Large and small can both be beautiful. They can work together in integrating and harmonizing local, national, and global economic and financial flows. It is not the size of the tools that counts. It is much more important to consider how well they respond to the task of harmonizing technical and financial rationality with concern for humans and ecosystems.

At each level, natural renewable resources should be used at a rate that is below their rate of regeneration, while the amount of waste generated should never overtax the cleansing capacity of the environment. The diversity of environments, and therefore of resources and cleansing capacities, should further promote exchanges between communities, regions, and nations. The interdependence of flows in relation to ecological and environmental aspects ought to be emphasized. Whatever happens at one level impacts the other levels. An excess of waste from a local economic flow that cannot be cleansed by the immediate environment pollutes not only that particular locality but also the environments that sustain other local or national flows. Social and political conflicts, economic inequalities, or denial of human rights in one society generates migration to other societies, which then must either face the costs of assimilating this inflow of additional people, or adopt severe, often inhuman measures to stop the inflow. Poverty in one economy brings about violence and disease that then spread to other economies, even remote ones.

INTERNATIONAL FREE-TRADE AGREEMENTS

Fairness to humans and nature in international trade requires deep changes in the thought and behavior of all trade agents. Free-trade agreements, especially, are doomed to produce more troubles than benefits when they are not accompanied—or, even better preceded— by efforts to transform consciousness at all levels of the populations involved. Otherwise, free-trade agreements can easily be used by the rich to make them richer at the expense of the rest of the population and of nature, which are both overexploited.

In her book *Paradigms in Progress,* Hazel Henderson maintains that for free trade to produce the results that some politicians claim, it should be practiced on a level playing field,[18] meaning that the degree to which workers can both satisfy their needs and protect nature should be similar in all participating countries. When this is not the case, greedy entrepreneurs and managers attempt to increase their wealth by shifting their activities to those nations where wages are cheaper and the costs of compliance with environmental regulations are lower.

Usually, those are the nations whose population is growing well beyond the carrying capacity of their land, generating masses of poor unemployed and unlanded people who are at the mercy of the combination of masters denounced by Adam Smith. This time, it is a combination of local masters with international masters—a combination that often produces the following effects: both masters increase their wealth, the poor to whom they offer jobs shift from misery to poverty, and workers from the country where the product was once produced move from decent survival to despair. The latter then have to rely on shrinking social security systems and promises of new types of jobs that often prove to be illusory.

There are still many entrepreneurs and managers who do not mind selling products produced by underpaid workers and children. As long as they think and do business in this way, exchanges at the global level will not be fair. Additionally, there are consumers who happily buy more for less. By disregarding where and by whom the products were made, they do not realize that their decisions may throw a neighbor family into the streets, and decrease the possibilities for their own children to enter the markets as entrepreneurs or workers.

Robert Salmon says that French consumers are awakening to this reality. He gives the example of a retail chain of household electric equipment, Boulanger, whose owners, allied with manufacturers of the equipment, have succeeded in selling equipment made in France. The tags attached to each piece of equipment distinguish the place were the equipment was manufactured as if it were a bottle of very special wine. And the consumers have responded well: 56 percent said they are ready to pay up to 10 percent more for a French product because in this way they feel they contribute to maintaining the standards of living of the country's workers, and therefore their own.[19] A decision to buy locally or nationally that comes from the buyers themselves is more cost-effective to the economy than when it is imposed by decree. For one thing, it does without costly bureaucracies to enforce it.

Salmon complains that French government decision-makers, entrepreneurs, and managers are less conscious than French consumers of their responsibility in keeping a healthy economy. Quoting from a report prepared by a French senator, Jean Arthuis, he mentions the case of a bidding to provide the French army with ninety thousand overcoats. The bid was won by a French enterprise, which by manufacturing them in Mauritius could sell them at 107 francs, against 113 francs requested by the two other bidders, whose products were manufactured in France. In this way, the Ministry of Defense saved 540 thousand francs, but the French economy lost 6.2 million francs because of the unemployment induced by shifting the manufacture outside the country. The net loss for the latter is therefore 5.7 million francs.[20] A typical case of rational shortsightedness.

The situation cannot be changed by interventions from some supranational authority. Interventions may only increase market chaos and never bring relief to the poor. Only by a change of consciousness can the field be leveled. Instead of relying on external bulldozers to level the field on which the globetrotters play their competitive games, we can rely on the power of new thought-forms and a spiritual reconnection that can make those globetrotters walk hills and valleys with respect for the human and natural ecology of both. Then, hills and valleys might both be allowed to flourish. Instead of transplanting flowers from the hills to the valleys, water from reservoirs in the hills may irrigate the valleys, allowing them to produce their own ecologically well-adapted flowers.

BALANCING THE SWIFT FLOW OF MONEY AT THE TOP WITH A SUSTAINED FLOW OF AID TO THE BOTTOM

We saw in chapter 5 the alluring speed at which money circulates among global corporations and governments. The fast flow is ultimately sustained by savings of those households that can generate a surplus income, and by profits of enterprises. Many households, however, are excluded from local and national economies. Then, they not only cannot afford to save but do not have enough to survive.

Almost all present societies can be pictured as icebergs (see Figure 16). The affluent at the top are soaring on the winds of technological progress and enjoying the light of culture. A larger number of families are either at the water line, struggling to keep afloat with the ebbs and flows of the economy, or well below it, barely surviving.

Figure 16. THE SOCIOECONOMIC ICEBERG

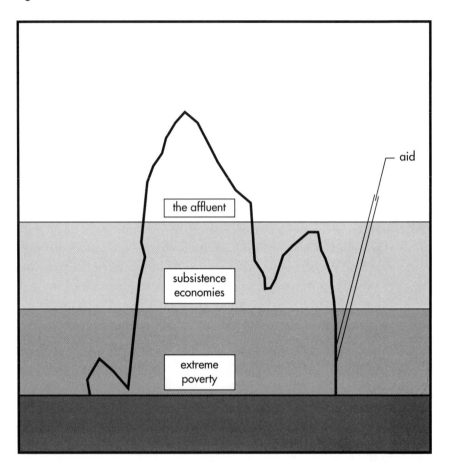

The winds of technological change often chill their efforts to emerge, and the light of culture reaches them quite dimly. Well down into the bottom, we find the despondent poor, unemployed, unlanded, and homeless. These are chastised by the winds of technological change, deprived of all cultural lights, and often excluded from social security systems. They barely survive by receiving oxygen through charity and aid.

International and bilateral financial and aid organizations are already trying to reach small farmers and entrepreneurs with money and knowledge. However, development efforts should not stop there. They should reach much further down and rescue the poorest of the poor from drowning in the cold, dark waters of the bottom.

Global sustainability requires the adoption of international policies aimed at two main objectives. One objective is to awaken the entrepreneurial talent that lies dormant in the submerged part of the icebergs. The other objective is to adjust the number of people in each economy to the carrying capacity of the land. Most countries whose average annual growth of population for the period 1980–1991 was above 3 percent could not afford to increase their economic flows at the same pace. Hence, their average income per capita constantly decreased. This was the case in Benin, Cote d'Ivoire, El Salvador, Ethiopia, Gabon, Ghana, Honduras, Iran, Jordan, Madagascar, Malawi, Namibia, Niger, Nigeria, Paraguay, Rwanda, Saudi Arabia, Syria, Tanzania, Togo, Zambia, and Zimbabwe.[21] When population grows faster than production, those who are well below the average income per capita are pushed further down in the bottom of the iceberg.

Those who are struggling to emerge from the deep layers of the socioeconomic icebergs do not usually know how and where to find the knowledge and financial aid that entrepreneurial initiatives require. They rely on the few empirical skills they have inherited or learned while struggling for survival, and they fear the risks associated with technological change. When a family is at those deep levels, failure often means more than just a loss of revenues or capital. Failure can then mean a sharp descent to the bottom—a fall into starvation.

To encourage entrepreneurship among poor households, it is necessary first to awaken their members to the causes of their poverty and to their potential for progressive changes. Only when their consciousness has intensified and expanded can technology and money be successfully transferred to them. Otherwise, money and equipment are misused, the latter being often left to decay at the first difficulty encountered in its operation.

Many nongovernmental organizations (NGOs) are involved in this task of consciousness expansion and intensification. Often these organizations also provide the technical assistance and venture and loan capital required to start enterprises. As we will see in chapter

11, the most succesful NGOs are those that channel knowledge and money only after the awakening has taken place.

In some countries, governments do not interfere with the NGOs in their attempts to awaken the capacity of the poor to develop by themselves. In other countries, governments are hostile to the NGOs, which they perceive as a threat. In extreme cases, governments allied to powerful local business groups organize violent repression of the NGOs to prevent them from promoting changes in the socioeconomic conditions from which those powerful interests are benefiting.

The NGOs themselves are sometimes guided by a limiting mindset. They often lack financial discipline and understanding of market behavior. Some try to organize poor people at the bottom of the economies without previously empowering them for full participation in decisions that must be made, and in the operations that result from those decisions. Others, romantically committed to saving nature, do not pay any attention to economic efficiency. By contrast, others, in their eagerness to save the poor, ignore the fact that no economy can be established on a sound basis when the regenerative powers of nature are impaired. Among NGOs we often find the same divisiveness and narrowness that exist among governmental and business organizations. We see this divisiveness and narrowness prevailing over integration and harmony. *Amour propre* and power control pervade the whole iceberg, but *amour de soi*, the mastery of love, and the enjoyment of life are also slowly permeating all levels.

CHANGING FROM DIVISIVENESS TO COOPERATION

Cost-effective work at the bottom of the icebergs requires the development of partnership between multilateral financial institutions, international and bilateral aid organizations, and NGOs. This cooperation might help to bypass inefficiencies of local bureaucracies and overcome entrenched local interests opposed to an increase in equity.

As early as July 1956, the World Bank established an affiliate, the International Finance Corporation (IFC), whose objective was to provide equity and loans to private enterprises without governmental guarantees. This was a way of circumventing the bylaws that do not allow the International Bank for Reconstruction and Development, the initial and core institution of the World Bank group, to operate directly in the private sector. The IFC has made important contributions to the mobilization of the private sector in developing countries, but its efforts can only reach the tips of the icebergs and go a few inches below the water line at the most. Mechanisms similar to the IFC are now necessary to increase efficiency in channeling financial and technical resources to the people who are well below the water line. However, these mechanisms should not limit themselves to increasing technical and financial efficiency. They also need to lead people to the mastery of their own development.

It is extremely difficult for financial and aid institutions, whether bilateral or multilateral, to deal directly with the millions of existing and potential small entrepreneurs at the bottom of the economies. They need to work with grass-roots organizations.[22] In turn, the latter need the financial resources, and technological and market expertise, possessed by the large financial and aid organizations. An integrative, harmonizing consciousness could bring them together. For this to happen, the sometimes arrogant staff of the large aid and financial institutions ought to stop selling to themselves and the world the myth of a textbook reality that is not really there. Similarly, the NGOs ought to stop believing in the magic of a development achieved neither with contributions from advanced science and technology nor financial discipline.

When leaders of international organizations, NGOs, and governments enlist themselves in efforts to awaken to reality, expand their vision, and intensify their analyses, they will be able to help people do the same. We cannot continue living under illusions, such as the belief that it is possible to increase defense budgets without paying taxes, increase population without harassing the land, or develop as healthy and full human beings when our education keeps us ignorant of ourselves and petrifies us with fears.

PART IV

THE TRANSFORMATIONAL PROCESS

The shift toward a new consciousness is already

happening in small circles of entrepreneurs,

village developers, community builders, educators,

religious leaders, artists, and scientists. The

process could be accelerated by transforming

the educational systems.

10

THE ROLE OF EDUCATION

The foundation of every state is the education of its youth, said the Greek philosopher Diogenes in the fourth century B.C.E. Twenty-two centuries later, Thomas Jefferson argued that public education is the foundation of democracy. In a letter to George Wythe on the revisal of the code of laws by the assembly of Virginia, written from Paris on August 13, 1786, Jefferson says:

> By far the most important bill in our whole code is that for the diffusion of knowledge among the people. No other sure foundation can be devised for the preservation of freedom, and happiness. If anybody thinks that kings, nobles, or priests are good conservators of the public happiness, send them here [that is to France, where] people, surrounded by so many blessings from nature, are yet loaded with misery by kings, nobles and priests, and by them alone.

And addressing Wythe directly, Jefferson continues:

> Preach, my dear Sir, a crusade against ignorance, establish and improve the law for educating the common people. Let our countrymen know that the people alone can protect us against these evils, and that the tax which will be paid for this purpose is not more than the thousandth part of what will be paid to kings, priests and nobles who will rise up among us if we leave the people in ignorance.[1]

Evolution has taken most countries away from the mighty power of kings, nobles, and priests as it was exercised in prerevolutionary France. However, paraphrasing Jefferson we may now say that taxes paid for free public education are not more than the thousandth part of what is paid in any country of the world to the merchants of war, robber barons, fundamentalist preachers, demagogues, and swindlers who rise up even among literate people because they are still kept ignorant of life and love.

To keep those characters from threatening the health of modern societies, alert people—the modern Diogenes, Jeffersons, and Wythes—will need to push national policy-makers and international organizations toward undertaking a deep reform of educational systems. Education should empower people to listen to their spiritual intuitions and instinctive drives, learning to develop the first and satisfy the latter without damaging the social tissue. From the basic enculturation period of childhood and adolescence, people should emerge with a mastery of their physical, emotional, mental, and spiritual health.

In the dry language of econometrics, the World Bank upholds the idea that the provision of an updated education is an unrenounceable duty of governments. The Bank finds that three years of elementary schooling, compared with none increases the GDP by 27 percent. Each additional year of schooling increases the GDP by about 4 percent a year—or a total of 12 percent for the next three years.[2]

In less dry language, the Bank makes this statement:

By improving people's ability to acquire and use information, education deepens their understanding of themselves and the world, enriches their minds by broadening their experiences, and improves the choices they make as consumers, producers, and citizens. Education increases their ability to meet their wants and those of their family by increasing their productivity, and their potential to achieve a higher standard of living. By improving people's confidence and their ability to create and innovate, it multiplies their opportunities for personal and social achievement.[3]

The Bank's report even uses poetry to make its point about the importance for governments to sustain public education. It quotes K'uan Tzu saying: "If you plan for a year, plant a seed. If for ten years, plant a tree. If for a hundred years, teach the people. When you sow a seed once, you will reap a single harvest. When you teach the people, you will reap a hundred harvests."[4]

However, under the prevailing structures of consciousness, education has produced too many bad harvests. The people it produces enter markets and societies accepting violence as a normal, inevitable part of life. Most of them feel pride in their possessions, and all too few are humbly happy just to be alive, productive, creative, and playful.

EDUCATION: A PROCESS TO SHAPE THE STRUCTURE OF OUR CONSCIOUSNESS

We saw that each child reproduces the different stages of the long evolutionary process of human consciousness while developing from infancy to adulthood. Infants come from the womb with a structure that corresponds to the archaic consciousness of our ever-present origin as creatures of nature. Immediately, their parents start the social process that will build on that basement the structure that prevails in the society where they live. Only children who are born within isolated tribes of a predominantly magical or mythical structure will remain at those stages. In most other societies of today, children will speed through the magical and mythical stages (talking to their toys as to live beings, believing that Santa Claus comes down the chimney to stuff their Christmas stockings, delighting in fairy tales, etc.) to an adult architecture where more elaborate myths and rationality mix in different proportions.

Schools speed up the process that parents initiate. That is when society uses education either as a tool to help students master the forces of life and love or as "a weapon whose effect depends on who holds it in his hands and at whom it is aimed."[5] The latter words were spoken by Stalin in an interview with H. G. Wells, the British historian and writer, held on July 23, 1934. Stalin was echoing Lenin,

197

who told another writer and journalist, Walter Duranty, "Give me four years to teach the children and the seed I have sown will never be uprooted."[6]

When dogmatic, authoritarian masters get hold of education, it becomes a weapon that destroys children's natural humanness by structuring their consciousness around rigid ideologies and dogmas and by giving them only technological information for their insertion as automatons into rigidly planned economies.

Education also becomes a weapon when it is denied to the masses, or to some sectors of society such as women or the poor and unlanded. Antonio de Oliveira Salazar, who reigned over Portugal for many decades, considered "education and undesirable literature" as his enemies.[7] Hitler said that "universal education is the most corroding and disintegrating poison that liberalism has ever invented for its own destruction."[8]

For democratic governments in free-market societies, there is no choice but to educate the whole of society. The choice they face is whether to organize education into developing a rationality inspired by *amour de soi* that seeks love and enjoys life, or into promoting a rationality that thrives under competion for power and money.

CONFLICTS BETWEEN PUBLIC AND PRIVATE EDUCATION

At the end of the last century, enlightened parents forced the educational system of France to restrain its authoritarian tendencies, respect the child's autonomy, and proclaim the superiority of the principle of affection.[9] An awakened reason could no longer be deluded into believing that violence was necessary to education. Unfortunately, those French parents did not go so far as to demand education to make violence unacceptable to the mind.

In school life, the trend toward respecting children's personalities, replacing authoritarian control with loving relationships, accelerated between the two world wars and especially after the second. We now seem to be facing an attempt to reverse this trend. Many parents are frightened by the violent reaction of children and teenagers against a society that makes it difficult, if not impossible, for them to satisfy their needs as creatures of nature while demanding obedience to obsolete lifestyles and organizations. Fear and insecurity lead those parents to fall prey again to dogmas and prejudices, pressuring governments to regress to damaging practices of the past.

Schools are censoring books, reintroducing divisive teachings on the superiority of one system of values and beliefs over the others, and shunning a scientific exploration of human behavior. Schools and parents are asking to be allowed to apply harsh punishments, blaming Eros, the spiritually animated forces of love and life, for vices that—rather than emerging from nature's perversity—are products of demoralizing societies, whose organization and management are usually under the control of dogmatic, prejudiced, power-ambitious personalities.

Governments lack leaders with a vision; they are run by managers who react to polls. Unqualified to light oracular, cheerful fires that illuminate new avenues, governments are unable to lead parents and students to and through the new roads that might improve private, social, and economic life. History and experience tell us that only true visionary leaders can fuel those fires and guide societies through new evolutionary paths. After some time on the new roads, people start to share the vision of the torch bearers and to recognize them as their leaders.[10]

The task of visionary leaders is not easy. Initially, they must adjust the speed with which the vision is implemented to the inertial fears of populations enculturated in the old paradigms of thought and behavior. Fires that visionary leaders light should be bright and clear, but not too intense, because they may then blind, scorch, and produce angry reactions from those who, after long hesitation, unsteadily venture on to the new roads.

To allay fears and reduce resistance to change, compromises might be worked out between the rights of parents to enculturate their offspring into particular patterns, the right of children and youth to refuse an education that they feel handicaps their development, and the right of societies, exercised through their governments, to orient the evolution of the structure of consciousness of their members. The enculturation process has always been a social process, whether undertaken by a nation or performed within a ghetto that either segregates itself from the surrounding society or is segregated by the latter.

Problems arise when the ghetto culture teaches mythologies of the past not as steps in the long path trod by humankind in its evolution but as dogmas that block our path toward the future.[11] We should bear in mind that the mythical layers of our consciousness are as resistant to being razed by progress as the arcane ever-present origin is. Myths, when reason understands them as such, neither handicap present life nor block our path to the future, unless religious instruction, as Adam Smith warned, becomes "a species of instruction of which the object is not so much to render the people good citizens in this world, as to prepare them for another and a better world in a life to come."[12]

Adam Smith reminds us:

> In the ancient philosophy, whatever was taught concerning the nature either of the human mind or of the Deity, made a part of the system of physics. Those beings, in whatever their essence might be supposed to consist, were parts of the great system of the universe, and parts too productive of the most important effects. . . . In that philosophy the duties of human life were treated of as subservient to the happiness and perfection of human life. But when moral, as well as natural philosophy, came to be taught only as subservient to theology, the duties of human life were treated of as chiefly subservient to the happiness of a life to come. . . . heaven was to be earned only by penance and mortification, by the austerities and abasement of a monk; not by the liberal, generous, and spirited conduct of a man. Casuistry and an ascetic morality made up, in most cases, the greater part of the moral philosophy of the schools.[13]

If Adam Smith considered traditional religious instruction not an adequate preparation for the societies and the economies of the end of the eighteenth century, they are even less suited to the societies and economies of the end of the twentieth century. Moreover, we see private instruction by ghetto cultures again "employing all the terrors of religion in order to oblige the people to transfer their allegiance to some more orthodox and obedient prince."[14] Although we do not have princes now, Smith's observation is still applicable to pressures suffered by governments in Argentina, the United States, Egypt, and Algeria, to name only a few countries. And are not these terrors of religion being used to thwart peace efforts between Palestinians and Israelis?

The ways to remedy these problems depend on whether the ghetto cultures limit themselves to putting reason to sleep in the minds of their members, or attempt to impose their views with violence on the whole social body. In the first case, again in the words of Adam Smith, "the public can impose upon almost the whole body of the people the necessity of acquiring those most essential parts of education, by obliging every man to undergo an examination or probation in them before he can obtain the freedom in any corporation, or be allowed to set up any trade either in a village or town corporate."[15] This statement still fits the conditions of even our most advanced societies, but it should now be addressed to every man and woman.

Quite different should be the attitude of society when the education of a ghetto culture promotes violence and incites its members to exercise violence on the whole social body. Then, the risks at stake are too high to allow that education to continue. This last situation reminds us once more of the fable of the wolf and the henhouses,[16] or the words of the American art critic Bernard Berenson, who said: "How small would have been the cost in lives and property and every kind of cultural value, if Mussolini had been nipped in the bud long before he played the part of the ape that opened the cage for the tiger Hitler."[17]

Once a public school system starts advancing integrative, harmonizing, *amour-de-soi*–imbued structures of consciousness among a population, the dialogue between public schools and private schools, between students and teachers, between parents and children becomes progressively easier. At some point, the whole society starts moving in the direction of harmony and integration, using *amour de soi* as its main behavioral guide. Initially, the movement might be loaded with problems and contradictions, but as it proceeds, internal resistances should decrease and change become smoother.

Concern for people's lives, and technical and financial rationality, both lead to the affirmation that governments cannot renounce their role as organizers and managers of free compulsory public school systems. Governments need to assume leadership because most parents are badly prepared to guide their children to a new consciousness. Moreover, parents themselves need to be guided to the new consciousness, and efforts to transform education will need to design new methodologies especially targeted to reach mature people and the elderly. Mass media and the new communication technologies can be creatively applied to this purpose.

Main Characteristics of Present Educational Systems

Educational systems are a set of interrelated institutions that contribute to the enculturation process. The main components of the set are households, day-care centers, kindergartens, primary and secondary schools, universities, colleges, churches, mass media, adult education organizations, arcade games, computer networks, and a variety of social organizations such as Alcoholics Anonymous and Weight Watchers.

In present free-market democracies, educational systems manifest two main characteristics. One is that fitting students for a future in the marketplace is the predominant concern of their schooling. The other characteristic is the abusive deployment of violence by the informal elements of the system: TV, movies, periodicals, arcade games, and the like. We scarcely find components of these educational systems that are concerned with preparing people for mastering life and love.

Schooling structures consciousness according to the idea that reality can be fully apprehended through the intellect alone and reduced to mathematical forms. The schooling process also remains faithful to the belief that humans are situated above and outside nature; therefore, the latter can be used as it pleases the former. Because the human body is seen as part of nature, the human mind should control it as well, making it serve mainly productive purposes. These widely held views have negatively influenced the enculturation process. They have led to assigning privileged socioeconomic status to intellectual tasks, to rejecting emotions and sensorial experiences from educational activities, and to reducing knowledge about nature and society to mathematical expressions.

THE PRIVILEGED STATUS OF INTELLECTUAL TASKS

Although more poorly paid than managerial and entrepreneurial tasks, intellectual tasks are much better rewarded than manual labor. The salary gap is clearly excessive either when the relative scarcities of the two are considered, or their respective contributions to productivity are taken into account.

As a consequence, education is looked on as a means of achieving success without the need to do physical labor. This attitude is reinforced by the fact that students seldom contribute work to build their school's physical assets, maintain them, and conduct the many different services that the educational process and daily school life require. Everything is done by hired labor without the participation of either students or teachers. All costs are covered by governments, by students' households, or by some combination of both.

REPRESSION OF EMOTIONS AND SENSORY EXPERIENCE

Feelings are considered alien to education. Even schooling in arts and literature is seen as an opportunity to capture techniques, rather than as a process of nurturing the capacity to feel, sense, and intuit, and to freely express feelings, sensations, and intuitions.

When studying history, children learn facts and figures. They are seldom allowed to bring out the emotions provoked by recorded events, and their own interpretations of those events. The lives of great heroes are seldom discussed. All those people who in the past did something that went into the records are almost regarded as non-human. Most teachers hesitate to respond to questions about the private life of historical characters, or about the feelings of military leaders on a battlefield full of corpses. Conquerors are to be praised by their descendants and blamed by the descendants of the conquered, when the latter recover their independence.

History could provide instead the means by which students become acquainted with the works of philosophers, artists, writers, poets, great performers, musicians, and scientists of each period.

203

Students should follow historical events in the socioeconomic, cultural, technological, and physical environment in which they took place. Students should also understand each period's patterns of household, economic, and sociopolitical behavior, and their interaction. The French historian Guy Breton says:

> Because the solemn historians who write the school texts do away with love, they make of French history a boring chronicle. For them, the events that have shaken France in the course of time must be the result of serious causes. They would feel embarrassed to recognize that a king declared war just because he was inebriated with joy after a night of love, or that a famous conquest was decided following the vagaries of a favorite.[18]

The shortsighted vision of education reveals itself again in the music class. There, students are seldom encouraged to develop their capacity to tune to the sound of great composers, to enjoy the folk music that is all around them, or to give expression to sounds that spring up from inside them.

The situation is no better in a physical education class. Children are often asked to do a certain number of push-ups and flex to touch the floor without bending their knees. They may begin or end physical education with military marches. There may be some time for sports, such as soccer, basketball, or volleyball, but with little fun or concern for increasing the coordination between mind and body. It will probably be a tough competition, with winners and losers. Nobody is asked what he or she would like to do, or which are the particular aches, pains, or weaknesses that he or she needs to work out? In all societies, if a boy complains when facing a difficult exercise or cannot do it, or shies away from a competitive sport, he will be ridiculed and sometimes even persecuted and ostracized. In some societies, if a girl enjoys competition and athletics, she may be equally ridiculed.

In all fields of learning, formality, solemnity, ceremoniousness, and rigid gender roles are privileged over playfulness, conviviality, creativity, laughter, and sprightliness. The trend toward alienation from nature, separation of mind from body, and separation of emotions and intuitions from thoughts is reinforced as children advance to secondary and college levels of education. The higher up the educational ladder, the more a certificate or degree is granted as a reward for the capacity to gather, store, and recall data and to adjust to social rules and regulations at the cost of denying our natural being. Only a few receive rewards for creating new scientific knowledge and new technologies. These few usually manage to keep strong connections with their inner source of intuitions and to freely express their feelings. After fighting the scientific establishment, they sometimes get a Nobel Prize, although increasingly Nobel Prizes reward mathematical wizards rather than creative geniuses.

MATHEMATICAL REDUCTIONISM

There is usually a wide gap between broad and complex reality, which is out there, and the forcibly limited reality expressed by a mathematical formula or the often distorted reality of a statistical analysis. By being obsessed with establishing mathematical correlations among data, we often miss things that are in reality, or see things that are not really there. This happens whether we are trying to increase our knowledge of nature or of society.

For instance, many social and economic decisions are based on polling people's views. In these polls, questions are often phrased in a way that attempts to elicit particular answers, and they are addressed to people who are uninformed, or at best partially informed, about the subject under study. Moreover, questions are prepared by, and answers elicited from, people who have been similarly programmed into *amour propre*, power control, and wealth accumulation. Hence, the possibilities of voicing, inducing, or promoting change toward a new consciousness are minimized.

An excessive reliance on mathematics in the attempt to understand reality further prevents the conscious mind from tuning in to intuitions and developing a creative vision. Mathematical reductionism makes the conscious mind even more dependent on the conventional voices of the scientific and social status quo, which fear change. A critique by John Maynard Keynes of a decision taken in 1925 by Winston Churchill as Chancellor of the Exchequer is to the point. Churchill took the British pound back to the values in gold and dollars that it had had before World War I. This measure contributed to social unrest and inflation in Britain, and Keynes reacted saying that Churchill did "such a silly thing because he had no instinctive judgment to prevent him from making mistakes. Lacking this instinctive judgment, he was deafened by the clamorous voices of conventional finance."[19]

CHILDREN'S RIGHTS

It will be impossible to eradicate violence from society if we allow that violence be exercised on children and youth in schools and households. Sometimes it is not overt physical abuse but just harsh treatment. At other times, violence is intrinsic to certain cultural practices, as when boys are circumcised, girls suffer genital mutilation,[20] and youth below the age of consent are tattooed.

Some parents and teachers still indulge in the magical belief that corporal punishment will reduce violence. This idea of using violence to fight violence responds to a complex mix of motivations. Sometimes it is a deviant form that allows the punisher to satisfy a repressed eroticism. In other cases, it obeys commands from age-old programs that tell parents and educators that children ought to be tamed through physical violence. To some people, violence is an inherent part of virility; for them, playfulness is totally alien to the educational process, while harshness is its ally.[21]

Corporal punishment leaves indelible marks on the body and mind of those who are punished and further cuts their links with the spirit. It makes them rebel against even the most necessary forms of social constraint. Anarchists at the end of the nineteenth century and the beginnings of the twentieth century "claimed to have derived their hatred of authority from the crushing experience of beatings."[22]

Future societies, permeated with *amour de soi*, might not tolerate any form of violence practiced on individuals who are below the age of consent. Societies might decide instead to extricate themselves from controlling masochistic individual behavior, or sadomasochistic relationships between consenting adults. However, an education that exposes the potential risks of those behaviors and promotes *amour de soi* might certainly reduce their incidence in society.

Those future societies will protect children from any kind of violence. It will be a child's right to be helped in developing *amour de soi*, mastering the forces of love, and enjoying life. Counseling and conciliation services could be devised to allow students to vent grievances with their teachers and parents. Students should be protected in their freedom to disagree with any education that they feel is damaging to their bodies and minds. An open discussion of those grievances, under the mediation of well-trained counselors, might help students build trade-offs between their disheveled instincts and their role as productive, creative, and playful members of society.[23] It might also help parents and teachers to clearly see weaknesses in their task of guiding the young toward those trade-offs. Parents and teachers might discover shadows in their own consciousness that they unwittingly project onto the young who are under their guidance.

A NEW PHENOMENON: FEARFUL TEACHERS

The profession of teaching, which once was the most respected and, in some countries, the best-paid social task, is now beset by fears, poor social recognition, and underpayment. Teachers fear the violence of juvenile gangs and even of toddlers who, imitating TV characters, appear brandishing kitchen knives. Teachers must face irritable parents who, full of *amour propre*, demand an A+ for their kids—these, of course, being always brilliant to their parents! Teachers must confront politicized school boards where parents are mostly concerned with making ideological points and are anxious to protect their narrow-mindedness. These parents try to prevent schools from bringing to children's attention issues that may shake the parent's prejudices and authoritarianism. As if all these were not more than enough to discourage young people with a vocation for teaching, teachers have now one more thing to fear: false accusations of misconduct and harassment.

Undeniably, there have always been teachers, both secular and religious, who have manipulated their students to make of them their sexual objects. If the students are at or above the age of consent, it should be nobody else's business. But if they do this with children, they have stepped over the limit of nonintervention by society, because they must have used deceit and violence of one kind or another.

Often, the deviant ways used by those teachers to satisfy their sexual needs is a product of social repression and socially created ignorance of sexual matters. It is highly likely that their enculturation prevented a close contact with their bodies and their inner spiritual selves. They do not know who they really are, and if they do, they do not accept themselves as they are. If their misbehavior were to be punished following the suggestions made in chapter 7,[24] society would be able to help them evolve and regain a healthy life. At the same time, society would receive feedback to help it redress its inappropriate enculturating procedures. To throw the culprits in prisons, as these are now organized, can only increase their chance of becoming even more deviant and violent.

This dark alley of reality apart, society has created a new threat to honest, dedicated teachers. They now fear false accusations emerging mainly from two kinds of children and teenagers: those infatuated with their teachers and those who are made mischievous by their families who attempt to obtain economic gain through lawsuits.

All those who have been or are teachers know of boys and girls who send languorous looks to their teachers. They seek every opportunity to be close to them, to be singularly addressed by them, to be of service to them in menial errands, to make gifts to them. Honest teachers of fulfilled sexuality and deep spiritual roots understand such an infatuation as a temporary step in the evolution of the student. Those teachers neither chastise the infatuated nor abet the inexpertly played seduction game. In the past, these episodes would pass, leaving only sweet memories to be taken to more mature stages of life. Grown men and women would often come back to visit their teachers with their spouses and children to acknowledge what their teachers did for their personal growth by just being human and understanding.

Nowadays, some of these infatuated students, feeling frustrated by not being able to win the seduction game, can find a greedy parent, with his or her friendly but equally greedy lawyer, and accuse the teacher of doing what they would like the teacher to do and the teacher did not. Even when justice swiftly uncovers the falsehood, the teacher suffers so many aggravations that his or her spirit sours and a disgust for teaching settles deep.

Fears and deception pervade our educational systems. Undeniably, it is necessary today to tell children to distrust strangers in the real world of the streets they travel, the markets where they shop, and the places of recreation to which they are attracted. However, from a prudent attitude that warns children of real dangers, it is easy and tempting to step to an attitude that extends distrust of strangers to teachers, classmates, and even siblings and older members of the family. We should make every effort not to advance those steps, even knowing that child abusers may be found among all of the latter.

Until our consciousness evolves and the real world improves, we ought to find ways of harmonizing distrust that protects children with trust in the love of those who care for them. We should never put bloody games in which adults involve children for their own satisfaction in the same category as sensual games that children have always played—games that barns, attics, forests, and river banks have witnessed and which are healthy for their development. We should carefully avoid constantly drawing for children a somber societal picture, just because red abnormal dots are shown on the huge canvas of reality. Apprehension and suspicion reinforce prejudices, hampering a grasp of the unity of the human race and the intrinsic physical and moral beauty of most of its members.

When informing children of risks such as those associated with crossing streets, using stairs, approaching courses of water, lighting fires, and being abused by adults, we should try to simultaneously breed self-confidence by helping them to develop their own instinctive intuitive detectors of danger. Our aim should be to preserve their survival without annulling their natural curiosity to explore their physical and social surroundings.

Informed, confident consumers make efficient market operators. Similarly, informed, confident children make joyful household and school members. Children should be tenderly protected to avoid, as much as possible, terrifying situations that can become engraved in their subconscious and destroy self-assurance and self-esteem. But if they are severely policed and trained into becoming suspicious and fearful of all expressions of tenderness and love, they will never develop self-assurance and self-esteem. We must bend every effort to not make children color-blind, seeing green lights where there is danger, while mistaking for red lights the signs that love and life light green, inviting them to explore new avenues.

Headmasters and teachers were terrifying to children and teenagers of the past. Now, headmasters and teachers are terrified by their students. We want neither one situation nor the other. We want to develop an integrative, participative, harmonizing society where healthy forces of life and love are not perceived as threats, and where we learn to recognize and avert real dangers from nature and society. For this purpose, our educational systems will need to undergo a profound transformation.

TRANSFORMING EDUCATION

Many believe that improvements in social and economic conditions are a prerequisite for progressive changes in the patterns of thought and behavior. Others maintain, instead, that changes in frame of mind should precede and prepare social and economic transformations. It is not an either/or situation. Changes in the structure of consciousness facilitate and give stability to changes in the structure of a society and an economy. Both are necessary conditions for our evolution. Neither in isolation is sufficient to promote it.

While at the World Bank, I invited Mr. A. T. Ariyaratne, founder and leader of the Sri Lankan Sarvodaya Movement, to give a lecture on his developmental experiment to staff members of the institution.[25] In the questions-and-answer period, an economist on education asked Ariyaratne what was education to him. The answer was swift: "If I take a person to a desert island, leave him there with only a few tools, and come back two weeks later to find him alive and well, that person I would say is an educated person."

Indeed, this is a mythical metaphor, in the sense that the reality of the desert island in the speaker's mind may not be the reality of a particular desert island where not only the education of the individual, but also his or her biology and the ecology of the place, will determine the chances of survival. Leaving aside this weakness, what Ariyaratne was trying to say is that education should essentially be an education for life. For John Dewey it is more than that; for him "education is a social process . . . education is growth . . . education is not preparation for life; education is life itself."[26] For Krishnamurti, "it is only when we face experience as it comes and do not avoid disturbance that we keep intelligence highly awakened; and intelligence highly awakened is intuition, which is the only true guide in life."[27] But for intuition to become our guide we need to understand ourselves, "for it is within each one of us that the whole of existence is gathered."[28]

With degrees of success that vary from country to country and sometimes from school to school, educational systems fulfill the task of transferring the technological knowledge already accumulated by humankind to the new generations. But they fail to help those generations learn about themselves and develop as full physical, emotional, and spiritual beings. Our education is mainly an education for market and social fitness, seldom an education for life—for physical, emotional, intellectual, and spiritual mastery.

Learning Who We Are

Krishnamurti said that schools should never teach what to think, but how to think. I consider that we should go one step further and teach how to integrate thoughts, feelings, emotions, intuitions, instinctive messages, and sensory experiences in the process by which we shape ideas and guide our conduct. Schools should ease the task of knowing and loving that which we are. We are all born with an innate ability to know who we are, but education often diminishes, and sometimes even destroys, this ability. It prefers to engrave in our subconscious rigid models of what we should be and what society wants us to become, telling us that anything else is dangerous and must be suppressed.

By increasing our ability to consciously recognize, integrate, and harmonize intuitions, emotions, feelings, sensory perceptions, instinctive drives, and social commands, we also develop improved skills to access the pool of knowledge that humankind has accumulated. In a transformed education, formation might become more important than information. It is much easier to get the latter than it is to achieve the former. Computers, CD-ROMs, TV, and electronic networks all make it increasingly easier to access knowledge about nature, technologies, historical and social data, and humankind's creations in the arts and literature.

We should avoid, however, falling into the mythical belief that the new technological means of accessing information might allow us to educate ourselves and our children in the privacy of our homes. For our formation as full human beings, nothing can yet replace the guidance of a well-prepared wise teacher and the enriching experience of sharing part of our lives with classmates of our age who are not our siblings. Technological means can give us information about the outside world and our biology. Teachers and classmates help us to increase our knowledge of ourselves. In schools that cultivate freedom and trust, teachers and classmates help us reach "beyond the face across our tables, learn to investigate the wilderness in the seat next to us, and explore the constellations locked up in our skulls."[29]

We explore and litter with our artifacts the vast expanses of the universe; we dig into the innermost spaces of the atom; we dangerously toy with genes, cells, and molecules; but we continue to ignore ourselves. It will be crucial for a transformed education to reverse this trend, helping students unfold the splendor of life that is within them.

SPIRITUAL ASPECTS

Education should help new generations reconnect the conscious mind with the spiritual sources of our arcane ever-present origin. Students should perceive the creation and evolution of life on Earth as an experiment. It is an experiment in which we are all involved, and from which we all, in partnership with the great experimenter, might learn to avoid repeating in the future mistakes made during progress to the present. Frederick Franck asks, "Could the Meaning of being born human be to become Human?"[30]

212

For this purpose, future education will need to overcome the narrow-mindedness of agnostics, atheists, and religious establishments alike. Public schools should not teach the rituals and credos of any particular religion but should expose students to the rituals and teachings of all. Students should perceive them as particular languages developed by humankind at different stages in its permanent quest for its spiritual sources.[31] Nor should schools hide the divisiveness that some of these languages have created, saying that the god (or gods) to which one group has given a name, perhaps a figure or form, is better than some other group's god(s). This practice has led to schizophrenic behavior that speaks of peace, justice, and the rule of the spirit on Earth while practicing horrible wars, holocausts, and genocides.

A few examples will suffice to show the atrocities produced when religious establishments enter the competition for power and wealth. There are countless others.

- In order to increase royal power, the queen mother of France, Catherine de Medici, played the French Catholic faction led by the house of Guise against the Huguenot faction led by the house of Condé, with the result that the former killed some 100,000 Huguenots on Saint Bartholomew's Day, August 24, 1572.
- A crusade ordered by Pope Innocent III against the Albigenses, a religious sect that was active during the twelfth and thirteenth centuries in the south of France, was used by northern nobles to invade the region, seizing and sacking the land and killing its inhabitants. By the end of the fourteenth century, the Albigenses had been wiped out.
- Soon after the declaration of India's independence from British rule, hoodlums of traditionalist Hindu organizations like the RSS (Rashtriya Swayamsevak Sangh) and the Mahasabha started killing Muslims. This led Gandhi, at age seventy-eight, to enter into his sixteenth hunger strike, this time on behalf of India's Muslims. He was soon killed by one of the fanatic Hindus.
- Buddhists and Hindus have been at each other's throats in Sri Lanka for several decades.

- Christian Serbs and Bosnian Muslims are engaged in mutual killings, rapes, and destruction of property.

Students should be reminded of these sorrowful, tragic events. The purpose of these reminders is not to blame the past, the path already followed, but to learn how to open a better path to the future. Students should discover that despite these crimes against the spirit made in its very name, our development as full human beings cannot ignore its constant voice within each of us.

The great religious leaders—Moses, Christ, Mohammed, Buddha, Lao-tsu—tried to reconcile Earthly creatures still impregnated with magic and myths with rational representations of their spiritual creator. Modern philosophers—Erasmus, Kant, Spinoza, and Hegel, among many others—tried to rationally understand the role of the spirit in the world. Students should learn to appreciate the beauty of the rituals developed by religious leaders and the charm of the ideas elaborated by philosophers. It should be a joyful experience for believers of all denominations and nonbelievers to join Jews in lighting a menorah at Hanukkah, eat appetizing latkes,[32] sing contagious Jewish songs, and learn about the revolt of the Maccabees. Believers and nonbelievers can rejoice with Christians in feeling, or just imagining, the incarnation of the spirit through the bread and the wine of the Eucharist, a reminder of Jesus' powerful message that the creative spirit dwells in each of us. We can all rejoice in telling and acting out stories from the Sufi tradition, and accompanying Muslims in chanting their Arabic litanies.[33]

The marvelous mythical heroes of the Mahabharata have already been brought to life in a three-hour film of the same name that atheists and peoples from all religions are celebrating.[34] It could be a similarly playful experience for all to compare the political thoughts of the Buddha with modern politics, and examine Buddhist psychology in the light of Freudian, Jungian, and other modern psychological schools of thought.[35] And wouldn't atheists, Christians, Jews, Moslems, Buddhist, and Hindus learn more respect for the wisdom of indigenous populations if they were to read, comment on, and perhaps enact stories like "Who Speaks for Wolf" from the North American Iroquois,[36] or "The Little Decameron" from the Paraguayan Nivacle?[37]

214

To really learn how to think rather than what to think, students must have their minds opened to different views and interpretations of the spiritual traditions. To exclude from schools either the traditional forms and content of different religions or the sometimes irreverent, playful ways in which creative minds see them would defeat the purpose of building an integrative, harmonizing structure of consciousness. Students should see and discuss a film like *King David,* in which the cruelty of some of the prophets and kings of Israel is revealed, and use a film like *The Last Temptation of Christ*[38] as a springboard to introspective thought about contrasting internal voices, and as a tool for understanding a historical moment that deeply marked humankind's subsequent evolution.

Quite a different attitude forces students into mechanically mumbling prayers or simulating a state of meditation when their minds are full of pranks and laughter—not to speak of the violence that is done to children and teenagers when the prayers and religious teachings enforced on them are alien to their own beliefs and their ethical and aesthetic views of the world. It is somewhat less violent, although more hypocritical, when students can refuse to attend the classes where the majority are saying those prayers or being instructed on those teachings. It is dangerously hypocritical because it singles out those who leave as different and therefore potential prey of another game of *amour propre* in environments where "oddballs" are not respected but are seen as inferiors, perhaps even dangerous.

An anecdote from my youth is to the point. It shows how the inherent playful wisdom of healthy youth in a free environment can overcome the ideological narrow-mindedness of adults and their shortsighted power games. During one of my high school years, the minister of education of one of the fraudulent and regressive administrations suffered by Argentina between 1930 and 1946 ordered all schools to teach the Catholic doctrine. Non-Catholics were given the option to receive moral education instead. I was the only agnostic teenager of Jewish ancestry in the whole class, and when faced with the dilemma, I consulted first with my parents, who gave me the freedom to choose whatever would feel more comfortable for me. I then turned to my friends, all Catholics, who convinced me that I would inflict pain on myself if I chose to leave the classroom and be alone with another teacher, who would end up teaching me the same doctrine under the disguise of moral education. They promised that if I stayed with them we would always find opportunities for merriment, it being more difficult for teachers to control thirty pestiferous youth than one single boy. I was surprised in my agnosticism when I saw the promise of merriment being carried out to scatological extremes that are not fit to be printed in this book. The ephemeral minister was soon gone, more moderate administrations reestablished the tradition of secularism that had made Argentine schools the pivot of the country's impressive development from 1860 to 1930,[39] and the episode remained as one more learning experience of my youth, thanks to my understanding agnostic parents and my free-spirited Catholic friends.

The main task of education is to open our minds, not close them with rigid scientific, philosophical, political, or religious dogmas. Schools should teach students to look at humankind and its habitat as from an Earth satellite, rather than as from a cave. To know ourselves is not an easy task in our societies, and we have not yet learned to let our humaneness develop toward the spiritual beings that we really are, free from unnecessary constraints. Hence, we all—rich and poor, young and old, men and women—are suffering existential pains. These pains vary in kind and intensity from one being to another, but they spread a discontent that pervades all cultures.

TRANSFORMING DISCONTENT WITH CIVILIZATION INTO ENJOYMENT OF CIVILIZATION

Freud said that "it is impossible to overlook the extent to which civilization is built up upon a renunciation of instinct, how much it presupposes precisely the non-satisfaction (by suppression, repression, or some other means?) of powerful instincts. This 'cultural privation' dominates the large field of social relationships between human beings." He adds: "It is not easy to understand how it can become possible to deprive an instinct of satisfaction. Nor is doing so without danger."[40]

Studies on the structure of our consciousness may help us to understand how it became possible to deprive an instinct of satisfaction, while history allows us to clearly see the dangers. The study of present societies reminds us that we still remain in danger. When we emerged from the archaic consciousness, we and our partner, the great experimenter, had to learn how to build societies. Intuitively we knew that to weave any kind of social tissue, we had to program the hard disk of our subconscious with commands that would introduce some order in the often chaotic, polymorphic instinctual urges that nature sends through the unconscious. We went too far and tried to suppress our origin, ignoring that it is ever-present.

We failed to bring playfulness to the tasks of producing goods and services, organizing families, and operating markets and societies. Within each of these tasks, we could have found different ways of simultaneously mastering and satisfying our erotic, libidinal impulses.[41] Instead, we repressed those impulses and learned to channel the repressed energies into power control and wealth accumulation among the elites, and into a painful, sometimes violent struggle for survival among the poor. But instinct can never be suppressed. It finds spurious, coarse, and often violent ways of bypassing severe repressive social commands. This creates tension, and tension originates the existential uneasiness and restlessness that we all suffer, whatever our position in society may be.

A deep transformation of education might assuage that uneasiness among future generations by attempting to integrate their erotic personalities and their social personalities, because "for until it is generally possible to acquire erotic personality and to master the art of loving, the development of the individual man or woman is marred, the acquirement of human happiness and harmony remains impossible."[42]

Theologians of a deep spirituality are becoming aware of this need to not only avoid repression but help people master the forces of love. These, under different circumstances, can express themselves as sex, as an aesthetic and playful eroticism, as pure spirituality, and as all of these together, as when "the love of one being for another shows itself powerful enough to fuse (without confusing) into a single impression the multitude of our perceptions and our emotions."[43] The last words are quoted from one of those theologians, Pierre Teilhard de Chardin. He perceives love as "a primitive and universal psychic energy which gives significance to everything around us . . . a sacred reserve of energy and the very blood stream of spiritual evolution," and thinks that "love is tending, in its fully hominized form, to fulfill a much larger function than the mere call to reproduction."[44]

Science and religion are converging in considering love as a powerful spiritual force in all its multifarious forms, which include and transcend sex. However, education still turns away from helping students master these forces. Students join markets and form households without full information on how the spirit has organized their bodies, how to respond through sex to love, and how bodies and minds can unite in pure relation and recreation without intercourse. They are awkward in giving pleasure to one another, and inept in bringing spiritual aspects to their interplay. They are not prepared to assume their responsibility toward their mates, their offspring, and the Earth by separating their recreational sexual activities and relationships from procreation. Trained into *amour propre* and competition, youth transform relationships into another competitive sport where love affairs are counted as points in a game, and if one partner loses by becoming pregnant or diseased, that is part of the game too.

Feelings of guilt, shame, and fear make students miss opportunities to experiment with channeling the forces of love into productive and creative work, or into contemplation and meditation, without destroying the erotic nature of those forces. Students are seldom aware that the mastery of the forces of love involves the search for balance and harmony among its different manifestations. If repressed, the forces of love either erupt as somatization or transmute into aggression to oneself, others, and nature. If abused by overindulgence in any of their forms of expression—whether sex, work, creation, or contemplation—our organic sensations shift from feelings of health and vigor to an impression of physical weakness and mental lethargy. The harmonious satisfaction of the forces of love leads to homeostasis; their repression or abuse subverts instead the subtle metabolic, mental, and spiritual processes on which our health is based.

It is tantamount to criminal behavior by the adults who organize the educational systems to send young people into market operation and household organization with neither full knowledge of the role and the intensity of the forces of love nor the skills to master them. As Freud said: "In sending the young out into life with such a false psychological orientation, education is behaving as though one were to equip people starting on a Polar expedition with summer clothings and maps of the Italian Lakes."[45]

Sex education is more than just providing information on contraceptives, the mechanics of intercourse, and the biology, psychology, and pathology of sexuality. An education designed to advance the structure of consciousness of the students toward integration, harmony, *amour de soi*, mastery of the forces of love, and enjoyment of life should not have sex education as a separate matter in its curriculum. Sexuality is to be learned from all subjects and all experiences. In schools less ridden by guilt and shame than our present schools, discussions on sex and sexuality will emerge during the study of history, anthropology, ecology, biology, arts, literature, music, and almost any subject, because sexuality pervades them all.

We have yet to catch up with Erasmus of Rotterdam, who, in 1522, wrote the *Colloquia Familiaria*. In his own words, the aim of the book was to teach his six-year-old godson good Latin and to educate him for the world.

> The text therefore deals with all sorts of everyday experiences and problems, including sexual ones. There are detailed and very frank discussions of sexual desire, sexual pleasure, and sexual intercourse, conception, pregnancy, birth, marriage, divorce, prostitution, and venereal disease. The language is straightforward and sometime humorous. Sex appears as a natural and pleasant part of life which must be approached with understanding and common sense.[46]

Learning about sex is learning about being free, happy, and at peace with ourselves and others. It is learning how to enjoy our own nature and nature at large. It is learning about preserving our health and well-being without hurting others. It is about developing as fully human and fully alive beings, with the help of many others but without dependence on any other.

In 1967 I had the opportunity to converse on these issues with university students in Stockholm. Swedish youth were then being given full information on sex and the freedom to practice it. More-over, the economic situation allowed young people an easy entrance into the marketplace. Nevertheless, I could not see much happiness and laughter around me. On weekends, the number of young people drunk in the streets amazed me. I asked my party why this was so. Their answer: "We have been given freedom and information, true, but we have not changed our mind-set; in many aspects we are still middle-aged Vikings, although now we are wealthy Vikings." Once more I must quote Teilhard de Chardin, who, as if he had listened to this conversation, says in his *Building the Earth*: "We are ready to boast of living in a century of enlightenment and science. And yet the truth is quite the reverse; we are still lingering among rudimentary and infantile forms of intellectual conquest."[47]

11

ONGOING EXPERIMENTS

We saw earlier how rational enculturating programs often block communication between the conscious mind and the unconscious. When our observations of socioeconomic reality and our socioeconomic decisions are guided by those programs, we lack feedback from our internal spiritual sources. In our decision-making process, we must then rely on feedback from external sources.[1] This feedback is usually provided by statistics based on the opinions and behaviors of other equally conditioned and restricted beings, who are also alienated from nature, and who also perceive the manifestations of their instinctive intuitive capacity as threats to rationality and efficiency. A purely technical and financial rationality then overshadows any concerns for humans and ecosystems.

Instead, when the conscious mind develops the skill to constantly compare the commands from the enculturating programs with the suggestions received from the unconscious, an internal feedback loop is established. Individuals then reach deeper and broader levels of perception, which enable them to integrate those human and ecological concerns into the decision-making process.

An integrative, harmonizing consciousness makes use of both feedback loops: the internal and the external. People are increasingly engaging in efforts to reach this more advanced level in the evolution of consciousness. They are trying to develop the ability to recognize and remove obsolete, handicapping programs of behavior and belief from their subconscious. They want to listen more carefully for the messages from their inner spiritual source, and interpret them more clearly. They like to enhance their perception of external facts, displaying meaningful interrelationships in the multidimensional space of reality rather than in a linear perspective, on a flat plane, whose sole axes are power and wealth. I shall briefly discuss some of these ongoing efforts.

EXPERIMENTS AMONG BUSINESSPEOPLE

John Maynard Keynes tells us that one of his teachers at King's College, the philosopher G. E. Moore, taught him that "the appropriate subjects of passionate contemplation and communion were a beloved person, beauty and truth, and one's prime objects in life were love, the creation and enjoyment of aesthetic experience and the pursuit of knowledge. Of these, love came a long way first."[2]

Nowadays, it is not just a lone economist and his teacher who speak of mastering love and enjoying aesthetic experiences. Businesspeople are increasingly using the same language. They feel the lack of love in their lives because of a lack of time to commune with their beloved, create and enjoy aesthetic experiences, and pursue deeper knowledge of the world and themselves. Hence, they feel a tremendous desire for change. They recognize that our culture has transformed entrepreneurship from an instrument for survival and enjoyment into an instrument for repressing our true beings and oppressing our fellow beings. By deciding that entrepreneurship should keep us constantly busy, we developed busy-ness.[3] By deciding that business should be guided by *amour propre* rather than *amour de soi*, we encouraged cutthroat competition with its predatory practices and restraint of trade.

On the other hand, many businesspersons are realizing that they succeeded in business because they are intuitive. They have not allowed the enculturation process to bar them access to their deep instinctive and intuitive unconscious sources. However, it does not escape them that they have usually applied intuition and instinct to increase the technical and financial rationality of their businesses, but seldom to improve their lives.

I received my first lesson on the role that intuitions and feelings could play in business from an Argentine entrepreneur, José Trivisonno. I was a young chemical engineer who had just graduated with honors from an Argentine university by writing a dissertation on the dairy industry. Trivisonno was the owner of a dairy enterprise that processed more than 100,000 liters of milk daily in ten factories scattered throughout the Argentine prairies, within a radius of fifty miles from the enterprise's headquarters. It was a milk empire built on sheer intuition and family efforts. At the time he hired me as his first and only technically and scientifically trained person, he was building new facilities at headquarters. Products from the rural plants, mostly cheese and butter, would be stored there, aged when necessary, and distributed from this central point to the whole country.

I thought that this project could provide an excellent opportunity to further expand and modernize Trivisonno's businesses by introducing economies of scale. The rural sites could be transformed into milk-collecting places, and the new headquarters could be enlarged to process all the collected milk in just one place. Armed with investment figures, flow charts, and break-even-point analyses, I suggested this transformation to Trivisonno. His response, the response of a businessman who had not even completed high school, was simply this: "I have carefully reviewed your study. Your figures clearly show that I could decrease costs, increase profits, and pay off the investments in a few years. To this end, I would need to fire most of the workers in each of the rural plants. What will then happen to the tiny villages whose life revolves around the milk plant? I come myself from one of these villages and cannot do this to them. I am happy with the success of my enterprise. I earn enough. I don't need to have more at the expenses of my fellows."

A few years later, I left my job with Trivisonno to climb another step up on the entrepreneurial ladder at another quite different enterprise, but his words never left my memory. Now, I hear similar words among a new breed of businesspeople.

BUSINESSPEOPLE'S VOICES

In 1989, I had the privilege of organizing and participating in an international meeting convened in Mendoza, Argentina, by a group of Argentine entrepreneurs to discuss the human and ecological bases of business and the economy.[4] At this meeting, an American entre-preneur, Arman Simone, stated that "business leaders are becoming aware of the fact that money and power do not provide meaning for life. They know that if they strive for genuine meaning, they must live not for power but for love. But on the other hand, they under-stand the world of money and power, and hence can be especially ef-fective when their assistance is needed in those realms."

Luiz D. Villares, of Brazil, said this to the audience:

> The world is changing, the speed of change keeps increasing and the very mechanics and dynamic of change is also changing. In this process the enterprise is the dominant institution, and within the enterprise we see that a transition is taking place. This transition is taking us from specific roles and distinct positions to a shared respon-sibility; from a competitive, hierarchically dependent behavior to an interdependent, cooperative attitude; from considering work as a means, by which some earn their living and others accumulate wealth, to envision work as an instrument for self-realization and per-sonal growth; from managing workers as resources to dealing with them as beings in constant evolution and co-creators of well-being and wealth; from tradition and experimentation as the leading guides of entrepreneurial behavior to vision as the main influence on entrepre-neurial decision-making and action.

In the same vein, an Argentine food industry entrepreneur, Ri-cardo Gandolfo, confessed to the participants that he was handi-capped by educational patterns that tried to separate his spiritual life from his business activities, confining the first to the weekly visit to the church and reducing the second to the achievement of huge prof-its. He described his enterprise as a place where spirituality and business are integrated. He and his employees are committed to offer healthy products to the community. They perceive competitors as sources of help, because through them they discover marketing mistakes. For Ricardo Gandolfo, friendly communion with the spirit requires a deep and unprejudiced exploration of inner life and a ca-pacity to give and receive love.

These entrepreneurial attitudes and perceptions led the late Willis Harman,[5] then Chairman of the World Business Academy, to assert in a message to the Argentine encounter that "the pragmatic world of business has moved out and planted its flag in territory which will eventually be more thoroughly explored through an extended scientific paradigm."

There are echoes from France, a country where, according to Robert Salmon, vice-president of future studies at L'Oreal, "Cartesianism seldom recognizes intuition's worth."[6] In the preface to Salmon's book *Tous Les Chemins Mènent á l'Homme,* Lindsay Owen-Jones, chief executive officer of the same enterprise, writes:

> Enterprises should welcome visionary people. Although these can be often annoying, enterprises should listen to them with curiosity and understanding . . . . When evolution speeds up, we cannot elude it allowing short-term concerns to mask swaying mutations. Paradoxically, we lack visionary people just when the opacity of the future is increasing.[7]

James Liebig, a former entrepreneur and business manager, has researched and written about new trends in business. Between 1990 and 1993, Liebig interviewed ninety businesspersons in seventy organizations from fourteen countries. Approximately half of the people interviewed are profiled in his book *Merchants Of Vision.*[8] This is what some of those businesspersons have to say:[9]

> One thing apparent today is that there is a major shift going on. Power in governments that were under central control is being devolved down to the people. And we're also seeing that in corporations. It's the same phenomenon, and I don't think it can ever reverse itself.
>   *Joseph Jaworski, Head, Business Environment Section,*
>   *Shell International, London*

> The real change is that human beings are changing right now. We are in the midst of a stretch of the human mind, of human consciousness. We are completely changing our way of thinking.
>   *Rolf Österberg, Swedish author, lecturer, business consultant*

> What do we really want? We really want evolution to continue! We have to take care of the future. We have to take care of our children.

And for that there will have to be an evolution of human consciousness.
Helmut Volkmann, Senior Director, Application Research Center,
Siemens AG

When I went into business in 1949, I made a commitment to my family that I was going to spend twenty-five percent of my time trying to do things I thought were important in the world other than making money.
Cabell Brand, President, Recovery Systems, Inc., Salem, Virginia

Openness is the action manifestation of trust. If the system isn't open, don't talk about trust.
Jacques Chaize, Managing Director, SOCLA, Chalone Sur Saône,
France

We don't have power and we don't have wealth. We are power and we are wealth. Authentic power and wealth are not acquired as quantities outside ourselves. They are qualities which are already in us, but which we must discover, appreciate, nurture, and enjoy.
María A. Palcos, Founder and Director, Rio Abierto, Buenos Aires,
Argentina

Business should be a means to an end. That end is something which energizes the human spirit
Jacqueline Cambata, President, Phoenix Chemical Ltd, Herndon,
Virginia

The assumption that one must be successful to be happy is like chasing one's tail. Worry only about how to better enjoy your creative life, using your own joy as your reliable and personal yardstick.
Sergio Lub, CEO, Sergio Lub, Inc., Walnut Creek, California

Many other books and periodicals portray similar outstanding examples of transformation of consciousness among entrepreneurs.[10]

HOW THE ENTREPRENEURIAL EVOLUTION IS TAKING PLACE
Entrepreneurs and business administrators are feeling existential uneasiness if not sheer pain. They feel intoxicated by the competi-

tive paradigm that they follow. They perceive that they are deceiving and neglecting their own beings, their family life, and their children. To allay their pain and calm their uneasiness, they are looking for places where they can feel safe to bare their souls to their peers, and exchange support and advice on how to get rid of the obnoxious mental programs that are handicapping their existence. To accomplish this last objective might prove to be more difficult than to overcome drug addiction or alcoholism. Businesspeople feel the need to discuss their problems within organizations that recall the fire councils of the old Iroquois: small local councils feeding into larger national and international networks. Modern communication technology might facilitate this process.

In the United States, sparks from diverse institutions, such as Esalen, Omega, the New York Open Center, the Institute of Noetic Sciences, and the World Business Academy, kindled the first fires around which entrepreneurs and managers began to meet. As I have witnessed, the hearts and minds of businesspeople become inspired with new ideas and new feelings when they sit in those circles. Newcomers easily yield to the warmth that spreads from the inner circle to the outer circles. Students and professionals also enjoy this invigorating warmth, which thaws the frozen frames in which academia has often enclosed their minds.

Each local group seems to develop its own procedures, its own ways of inviting others to join the circle, and its own communication patterns with other circles. When participating in those circles, one can perceive remnants of old programs still at work. *Amour propre* and power control still lead to personality clashes and intrigue, but slowly hierarchies abate, masks crack, and roles fade away.

Once people engage in the transformational process, the effects are felt first at a personal level and subsequently at the level of their families, their enterprises, and their communities. Within the groups, stories are exchanged about the steps that each is taking toward a more developed structure of consciousness, and the effects they feel while walking toward the future.

Some cross-fertilization is taking place among the circles through private networks and specialized publications. Contacts are being established with universities and political and religious leaders. The movement has already grown to the point where it has deserved a six-page article in *Fortune,* a magazine of mainstream business. This article traces the origins of the movement back to the 1940s, with the emergence of systems theory and social psychology.[11]

The contact of new entrepreneurs with political, religious, and academic leaders deserves special consideration. Working under the old paradigm, businesspeople often use the power that money can buy to manipulate those leaders. We may hope that the new breed of businesspeople might instead use their economic leverage to promote new ways of thinking and doing politics, of providing spiritual guidance, and of supplying and creating knowledge.

Most political leaders are motivated by *amour propre,* and exercise power for the sake of powerful interests. The new business leaders might induce instead an amour-de-soi–motivated attitude of service to the community. Entrepreneurs and managers with a new consciousness might also support a progressive transformation of their diverse religious congregations from fundamentalist beliefs that reduce the spirit to the role of controller of human behavior to a true relinking of the human mind with the body, nature, and the creative spirit that dwells in both. The evolution that businesspeople may promote would not destroy any organization; it would just promote the *aggiornamento* of them all. Each would maintain its rituals and traditions but would make them more responsive to the new consciousness that demands fewer terrestrial bonds, fewer heavenly dreams, and a more intense connection with our spiritual source in the here and now.

New business leaders could use their influence on university boards to bring to academia a better understanding of the role that intuition plays in the advancement of science, and to free scientific inquiry from rigid academic bonds.[12] Entrepreneurs and managers are becoming increasingly disappointed with the way in which schools, colleges, and universities are forming the people that will contribute their energies at all levels of enterprise. The business environment encourages an open-minded education and mistrusts a mind-closing schooling. At a meeting on the contributions of science and technology to Argentine industry, I heard a woman entrepreneur say that she had told her two teenage boys that if they want to participate actively in the family-owned business, they should do this immediately after high school, and not undertake further academic studies. She was convinced that college education handicaps creativity and blocks contact with deep intuition, thus killing entrepreneurship.

Along the same lines, a British entrepreneur, Anita Roddick, said: "We have a training school, which is not so much a training school as a centre of education. I am not interested in training staff—you can train dogs—I am interested in developing their human potential, their empowerment as individuals, and their sense of joy."[13]

Businesspeople understand that a redeeming economy of playfulness should replace our present profligate joyless economy. The exercise of responsibility for the whole—a motto of the World Business Academy—cannot be based on sacrifice and neglect of the self. On the contrary, it requires abundance of *amour de soi*; it demands responsibility for the self. Businesspeople feel that "killing" time[14] to earn our livelihood is as dangerous to ourselves, our families, and other living beings as all other killings are—even more so, if we kill time to accumulate money and power well above our needs.

EXPERIMENTS WITH THE NET AND THE WEB

In chapter 8, I discussed how the Net and the Web may increase market transparency and favor healthy local economic flows. People are already experimenting with doing business through the Internet, but they are also experimenting on how to use the Web and the Net to enhance their perception of reality and extricate themselves from the limitations imposed by old enculturation processes on the functioning of our consciousness. Willis Harman maintains that by deliberately changing their image of reality, by not accepting the limitations imposed by society on the functioning of our consciousness, people are changing the world.[15] The Net and the Web are facilitating the task.

The Net and the Web are providing channels to explore our wilderness and the cosmic wilderness, the constellations under our skin and skulls and the constellations of the universe. Through the Web and the Net, people from all over the world are finally getting an opportunity to participate in the sacred and profane dances of the whole Earth while maintaining their autonomy and their local roots. Silently, on their own, by themselves and for themselves, without revolutionary leaders, they are introducing deep changes in their lives and our human society.

They are the workers who, after a confining journey at the office, the factory, the workshop, the field, or the service organization, perhaps after some moments of tenderness with partners and offspring, want also a few minutes of dreaming a wider world through the Web and the Net.

They are the adolescents who feel their minds assaulted by a thousand and one strange feelings and have nobody at home, at work, or at school with whom to share the fears, anxieties, hopes, and desires that those feelings awaken, but can do it through the Web and the Net.

They are the women who, without losing touch with their offspring in the labile years of their development, also want to be part of the marketplace, the social organizations, the political fora, the poetry groups, the art guilds, and the women's discussion groups, to all of which they can now link through the Net and the Web.

They are the elderly whom society has "retired" from the marketplace, the fora, and the social organizations, whom their families have "retired" from participation in family affairs, whom their partners have "retired" from sexual activity, and who nevertheless long to remain active in all those fields. Fantasies lived in the virtual world can enhance their lives in the real world.

They are the ill and diseased, who do not want any longer to be patients of an impatient physician or an impersonal hospital ward, and who like to investigate, on their own, solutions for their health problems that others may have found in remote places on the planet. They are already doing this through the Web and the Net.

They are the oppressed sexual minorities, who can now communicate among themselves from Australia to Canada, from Mauritius to China, surmounting the bigotry, shortsightedness, and ancestral fears of their surroundings.

230

Indeed, these are people who have access to the technology that allows all those communications to take place. This access is not fairly distributed yet, but it is spreading, thanks to the progress that is constantly taking place in the electronics industry, and thanks to the way the users themselves are organizing the access. For now, it looks like the beginning of a true evolutionary movement toward bringing together the diversity of human products and natural environments. Thus, the noosphere may become at the same time a biosphere, an anthroposphere, and a spiritual sphere. Teilhard de Chardin's dream would then be accomplished: "A boundless field of evolution would open up before us; the field of collective creations, associations, representations, and emotions."[16]

All these fertile promises should not hide potential risks. One risk is that an excess of information may again rob our lives of time to be ourselves, to look and listen inside us and around us, not only to screens and speakers, and to guide our mind to be content with itself. The other risk is that the exposure of our intimacy through rather transparent means of communication can be used by new exploiters and abusers.

Most of the people communicating through the Web and the Net seem to be doing it of their free will, following independent decisions. Let us hope that the experiment will continue in this way and that the educational influence of the electronic networks themselves, and a reform of the enculturation patterns in the society at large, will decrease the number of people who—either lured by monetary rewards, or pushed by desperate necessity—rather than using the Web and the Net for connecting with the noosphere are being used by new masters for new games of power and wealth.

Let us also hope that governments will resist the *amour-propre-*inspired temptation to interfere in the peaceful evolution that the nets and the webs could bring about. Governmental interference may transform this evolution into another revolution, with its electronic guerrillas, its victims, its heroes, and its chaos, which can only increase the number of abusers and exploiters.

The electronic networks can ease our surfing on the emerging wave of a new consciousness, and free a Promethean humankind from some additional bonds of the many that it forged for itself. Paraphrasing Teilhard de Chardin once more, we may ask with him: "How can we lay down any limits to the effects of expansion, penetration, and spiritual fusion which would flow from the coherent ordering of our human multitude?"[17]

EXPERIMENTS IN EDUCATION

Experiments in education are essentially experiments in enculturation. Hence, they date back to when we moved away from the archaic consciousness and started building the first magical societies. In Western Europe, since the fifteenth century, there have been many attempts to change the enculturation patterns that prevailed during the Middle Ages. From Erasmus (1466–1536) with his *Colloquia Familiaria*,[18] to Bertrand Russell (1872–1970) with his Beacon Hill School, to the anthroposophy of Rudolf Steiner (1861–1925), to name just a few, these experiments have been aimed at freeing reason from the delusions of myths and magic. Some also attempted to free the mind from intoxication with *amour propre*.

More recently, after World War II, some of the experiments have been aimed at developing structures of consciousness that would go beyond pure rationality and start making inroads into the new integrative, harmonizing consciousness. I will discuss here only two of them, with which I have had firsthand experience during the late 1970s and the 1980s.

PAMPEDIE

Pampedie[19] is an enculturative instrument that can either provide a broad humanist complement to specialized technicians or open opportunities for awakening to inner and outer reality to those who have been excluded from any organized form of education. *Pampedie* consists of a set of 480 cards. Each $19 \times 10\frac{1}{2}$ cm card contains a drawing and a brief text. The set condenses the minimum knowledge that people should have in order to understand the natural and social world around them, develop the capacity to analyze their inner lives, and start building the skills to harmonize their needs as creatures of nature and cultural beings.

These cards can be used in several ways. The choice of a particular method depends on several factors: the purpose of the instruction, the ability of the teacher, the level of experience and exposure to scientific knowledge of the participants in the experiment, their particular interests, and the environment in which the experiment takes place. One card can serve as the basis for instruction for one hour, for a day, or for a whole week.

I had occasion to discuss the application of *Pampedie* in two contexts: an adult education program for villagers in Sri Lanka, and a cultural integration program for university students in Thailand.

In 1979, when I visited Sri Lanka, the Sarvodaya Movement was engaged in an adult education program for villagers as part of its rural development efforts.[20] I was favorably impressed by their efforts and the results obtained. Hence, some years later, after becoming acquainted with *Pampedie,* I thought it could provide them with an excellent tool to improve on those efforts. *Pampedie* could help their teachers bring the world to the village. In conversations with Savordaya's leaders, we outlined a possible scenario for the use of *Pampedie*'s cards in their adult education programs. To develop our example, we chose the card on basic colors, which is number 10 in volume 14 of *Pampedie.* This volume deals with the reason for art's existence, and its history. The main objective of the twenty-four cards in this volume is to show that everybody can be an artist. In just three paragraphs, card 10 describes the basic colors, the effects of their combinations, the materials that humankind has used to produce colors for use in art, and the significance that different cultures assign to different colors.

The adult illiterate people of the rural communities to whom this card is read, and its colorful picture shown, are then encouraged by the teacher to relate the information they receive to materials found in their environment, which they use as dyes for batiks, baskets, and yarns. Next, a video or a slide show exposes the villagers for the first time to the work of great European Medieval and Renaissance painters. Paintings of the pleasure palace of an early Buddhist King on the Sigiriya rock of their native Sri Lanka are also presented to the villagers, most of whom might never have had an occasion to visit the place. The teacher tells the villagers how those European and

233

local painters obtained painting materials. The sight of these particular pieces of art elicits interest in how people lived in Middle Age and Renaissance Europe, and in their own country under the ancient rulers (from the sixth century B.C.E. until the beginning of the the European conquests in the sixteenth century). The villagers discuss the difference between Middle Age and Renaissance painters in subjects chosen for their art, and the similarities in sensuality between the painters of Renaissance Europe and those who adorned the pleasure palaces of Sri Lanka's kings. The dialogue naturally leads to reflections on the fact that Renaissance art was made possible because some European societies lifted previous repressions, allowing the artists free expression of their feelings. They then painted human and nonhuman nature in their full unashamed beauty, while in the local paintings the human form is neither fully hidden under heavy clothes, as in European Medieval art, nor fully naked, as in the works of Michelangelo. These reflections present, in turn, an opportunity to discuss the need to reconnect body, mind, and spirit.

When working with people like these villagers of Sri Lanka, outside the formal education system, instructors act in the manner of folk storytellers. They use words that are as simple as possible to link the few statements on the card through a narration that flows through places, characters, facts, and a few figures when necessary. They frequently stop their narrative to invite the learners to express their fantasies and perceptions through questions and comments.

On another occasion, I was discussing with Professor Sunt Techakumpuch of Chulalongkorn University in Bangkok, Thailand, his difficulty in engaging students in a cultural integration program. His objective was to bring elements from humanities to students of science and engineering and to create technical awareness among students of humanities and social sciences.

I thought that *Pampedie* could be useful in this context, too, and chose the same card 10 of volume 14 to develop an appropriate scenario. The teacher in the program for science and engineering students encourages the participants to compare the composition and texture of painting materials available to a present-day artist with those available to an artist of the fifteenth century. Students also compare the manufacturing processes used in both periods. Discussion smoothly shifts from this comparison to the social and economic aspects of the Renaissance, the paradigms prevailing in the natural sciences at that time, and the lives and works of artists like Leonardo da Vinci and Michelangelo.

The same card, when used to integrate technological issues into the learning of students of humanities and social sciences, launches a discussion on the lives of Renaissance artists and proceeds from there to the evolution of the techniques for producing pigments—an evolution that led to the modern chemical industry. The increased alienation from nature that has occurred in the evolution of modern industry is then brought to the discussion. Students are urged to consider the difference in pace between changes in behavioral assumptions and social rules, and changes in industrial technologies.

My short acquaintance with *Pampedie* showed me that educational tools of this kind help to develop learning processes that excite the imagination and trigger new connections between the three parts of consciousness.[21] In a playful way, learners are enabled to critically analyze enculturation programs and modify them as needed. This empowers people to break through the enclosure of their often limited and limiting local societies, glimpsing the whole of humankind and its evolution, and developing a special sensitivity to nature. The latter allows people who are already accustomed to observe nature and make use of it, to also know more about it. Furthermore, they learn to integrate observations, actions, and knowledge into a feeling of unity and oneness with nature.

In a circular introducing *Pampedie*, Harrie Smeets, under whose direction *Pampedie* was developed, wrote: "Anybody who looks seriously at the whole reality of our world, including its history in all its dimensions, shall undoubtedly discover the same thing: there are so many common ideas, convictions, beliefs, working in humanity that real unity—understood as solidarity—becomes increasingly possible."[22] By transforming people's minds into change agents, educational tools like *Pampedie* promote changes in the whole structure of society. They often do this with more efficiency and at less cost than formal schooling, and they do not forget what schools often overlook: that "culture is the development of people's ability to love."[23]

EDUCATION WITH PRODUCTION

This is an effective and well-tested tool for reducing the burden imposed on households and governments alike by the cost of education. Instead of underrating manual work, education with production leads students to appreciate the contribution of manual work to the development of inferential knowledge, the tuning in to noninferential knowledge, and the application of knowledge to increase production efficiency, self-reliance, understanding of the self, and enjoyment of life.

In education with production, learning occurs in two contexts. One is related to the students' daily life. To satisfy their biological, psychological, and sociocultural needs, students *apply* knowledge to build and maintain the school's physical assets, manage its administrative services, and provide themselves with food, shelter, services for body care, and facilities for recreation. While performing these tasks, they establish physical, emotional, and spiritual communications with their peers and the faculty. The other learning environment includes conventional classrooms, laboratories, training workshops, and experimental fields. In this second environment, they *acquire* knowledge and the ability to develop new knowledge. Often, education with production schemes include a third context: neighbor societies and markets, in which students participate, contributing to local economic flows and cultural activities.

Education with production affects individual development in several ways. Because students and teachers participate in a variety of assignments that involve both mind and body, the prevailing hierarchical distinction between intellectual tasks and manual work is blurred. Students and teachers are in direct contact with the inputs to production processes, and participate in the transformation of these inputs into goods and services. This direct involvement develops the student's sensitivity to the complex characteristics of the artificial materials, natural elements, and machines used to sustain economic flows. Students also develop the ability to understand and cope with the complex interactions between managers, workers, and customers that take place in any process of producing and marketing goods and services.

In schools that practice education with production, students usually rotate through different tasks. For instance, during one study period, a group of students may be assigned with the task of cleaning the bathrooms, while in the next the same group may catalog books, or process apples and market the cider. This avoids a situation like the one I saw in China in 1987. Chinese students were working in external factories or offices, and this was called education with production. But the students were not taking care of their rooms, and they were living in dormitories where I saw accumulated dirt, broken windows, and a lack of minimal comforts. These dormitories were maintained by hired laborers, who had no interest whatsoever in creating healthy and enjoyable surroundings for the young people. Work by students outside the school, and work by wage-earners inside the school, was still being felt by both groups as an alienating task, not an integrative one. It created a hierarchical and social division between those who study and work in enterprises and those who work in menial domestic tasks. The aesthetic component of life was denied in both cases. There was neither a holistic perception of reality nor a friendly intimacy with one's own nature.

In some societies, education with production may help in overcoming a general disaffection toward the world of business and industry. In a seminar I facilitated for a group of science and technology policy-makers of French-speaking African countries, there was a negative reaction when I stressed the advantages for students, their households, and their societies that may derive from education with production. One of the participants stood up and said: "By toiling to give us an education at the highest level, our parents wanted to make sure that we would never have to work manually, as they did. And here you are, saying that an exposure to manual productive work could make of us more integrated and happy beings. Isn't this one more strategy to keep us underdeveloped, reduced to labor fields and work in foreign-owned factories?"

In an attempt to reverse their negative reaction, I invited the African policy-makers to come with me and visit an experiment in education with production at Warren Wilson College in Swannanoa, North Carolina. My intention was to show them that instead of being an "imperialist" conspiracy to keep the students underdeveloped, this form of education was a tool created in the heartland of the "empire" to help them develop better—at least, more humanely.

Warren Wilson College, founded in 1894, is one of several educational institutions in the United States that practice education with production.[24] It is a fully accredited four-year liberal arts college. Its 1070-acre campus included, at the time of our visit, a 300-acre farm, about 650 acres of forest, and housing for 500 students and 150 staff members. The students earned room and board in exchange for working 15 hours a week. They were doing all the electrical work, plumbing, landscaping, cleaning, and maintenance of the college's buildings and grounds. The students had built a magnificent chapel for the diversity of beliefs among the student body, and a library that held 84,000 volumes. Students were also doing office work for the college administration; growing vegetables; tending cows, pigs, and fowl; and processing some of the produce. Most of the produce was consumed within the college. Previously, students had prepared and served meals, but at the time of our visit, these services had been contracted out, not without protest from students and teachers alike.

A dean of work was responsible for the coordination of all the work crews that were necessary for college operation. Work grades were issued along with academic grades. A student who could not maintain an average work record would not graduate. In addition, the college required that each student complete a service project for a third party, whether on campus, in the surrounding community, or at home during summer breaks. This requirement could also be fulfilled through participation in international cooperation programs sponsored by the college. These programs had already led faculty and students to participate in community development programs in Sri Lanka, Mexico, Costa Rica, and the Dominican Republic.

It was easy to perceive the distinctive nature of Warren Wilson students compared with students of a purely intellectual college. There were neither formality, nor hippy-ness, nor yuppy-ness. The key words to describe them are openness, gaiety, and self-assurance. One of the students said: "I'm starting to be able to grasp the idea that I'm connected to everything else; I am a part of the Energy that flows through all aspects of existence. This makes me feel close to people, closer to nature, and closer to God. This brings a sense of peace to my soul."[25] Another confessed: "Once I understood that I must be at peace with myself, and resolved that conflict within myself, I was also able to accept others and not have conflicts with them."[26] And a third reflected that "with a positive attitude built upon self-knowledge and self-worth, we will not only be able to love ourselves but others as well."[27]

After listening to these youngsters and seeing what they did and were doing through their work and studies, the African policy-makers mellowed their response to the idea of education with production—even more so when they learned that in their own continent there was a growing movement toward this type of education. It was initiated by Patrick van Rensburg, who created the Foundation for Education with Production in Gaborone, Botswana, with the objective of disseminating information on this type of education and promoting its adoption by developing countries.[28]

Further evidence of the advantages of education with production was brought to the French policy-makers by my research assistant at the World Bank, Chris Hennin. He described his own experience with this type of education in Tepoztlan, Mexico. Hennin engaged rural youngsters who were attending the local high school in a supplementary curriculum of education with production at their boarding institution, the Asistencia Social a la Juventud Campesina (ASJC).[29] By the third year of the program, 69 percent of the recurrent costs of providing board and room were recouped by the students' work. In addition to productive work, there were creative and playful activities. The first ASJC graduates attained a high level of confidence and were motivated to pursue studies in nursing, agriculture, veterinary sciences, dentistry, accounting, mechanics, education, and music. These were youth who came from Mexican villages where only some 10 percent of the people could then read and write Spanish.

EXPERIMENTS IN VILLAGE DEVELOPMENT

We saw earlier the transformational efforts in which some businesspeople are engaged, attempting to dispel their existential uneasiness.

Are people at lower social, cultural, and economic levels of society, in poor villages and shantytowns, ready to undertake similar transformational processes that would make them masters of their own economic and cultural development? The answer from my experience and studies is yes! They are ready for a change, but they need facilitators to make clear for them the benefits that may accrue from change, and to guide their initial steps toward it. In poor rural areas of Sri Lanka and Thailand, I witnessed progress toward a self-sustained development under the guidance of those facilitators.

THE SARVODAYA MOVEMENT

If I have frequently referred in this book to my Sri Lankan experience, quoting from conversations with Sarvodaya leaders and from their writings and speeches, it is because my visit to Sri Lanka in 1979 was a turning point in my own evolution. Since the mid-1950s, I had been studying, reflecting, and writing on human issues in social and economic development while struggling to include those human aspects in the design and implementation of business projects in which I was involved. My thought then was this: If politicians change their way of thinking and doing politics, businesspeople change their way of thinking and doing business, and professionals and technicians change their way of applying science and technology, the whole society will change and start doing justice to those neglected at the bottom of the socioeconomic icebergs. After my visit to Sri Lanka in 1979, and a visit later to Thailand, my perception changed: People at the bottom do not need to wait for those at the top to change and become concerned with their lot. With appropriate facilitators, people at the bottom can easily change the structure of their consciousness. Operating from a new structure, they assure justice and progress for themselves, by themselves.

The transformational efforts in Sri Lanka were aimed at organizing a large network of progressive villages by restructuring the elementary rationality of their populations. It was a rationality easily permeated by magical and mythical elements springing up from its old foundations. Between the fourth century B.C.E. and the fourth century C.E., Buddhist rationality made good use of the opportunities provided by the island's environment and could overcome some of its threats, like the mosquitoes that carry the deadly malaria para-site. The elite of those times created for itself sophisticated physical and cultural surroundings[30] but also allowed some of its wealth and culture to trickle down to the poorest segments of the population. Al-though the voices from the unconscious were still heard as whispers from the devil, they were neither denied nor condemned. There was, instead, an incipient search for harmony: People were autho-rized to enjoy pleasure while trying to develop strong links with the divine.

In a comparative study of Buddhist and Freudian psychology, Pad-masiri da Silva paraphrases a Buddhist saying as follows:

A certain one, given to sensual pleasures, seeks wealth, unlawfully and by violence, so seeking wealth, he gets no ease, no pleasure for himself, he shares it not with others, he does no meritorious deeds. This is compared with the person who is given to sensual pleasures, seeks wealth by lawful means, without violence. So seeking it, he gets ease, gets pleasure for himself, shares it with others and does merito-rious deeds. But he makes use of his wealth, without greed and long-ing, he is guiltless of offense, he is heedful of danger and alive to his own salvation. Here instead of condemning the life of sensual plea-sure, an effort is made to work out the difference between the life of pleasure lived on correct principles and the life of pleasure which is unlawful.[31]

Successive invasions by foreign powers, from the fourth century C.E. onward, pitilessly exploited people and land, forcefully intro-duced competing ethnic groups, and destroyed the native social tis-sue. At the time of independence (1948), the rationality of the poorest sector of Sri Lanka's population was in a state of slumber. Ten years later, a Sri Lankan schoolteacher, A. T. Ariyaratne, began to work with his students in empowering those poor to become mas-ters of their own physical, mental, emotional, and spiritual develop-ment. This initial work grew to become the Sarvodaya Movement.[32]

When I visited Sri Lanka, the Sarvodaya villages varied in size from very small ones, like Manapitiya with only seventy inhabitants, to those providing social grounds for larger populations, such as Walana with six thousand members. Most of the villagers who were joining the movement owned no land and were earning less than $50 of cash income per year. The Movement was growing around regional extension centers and village-based developers. The former provided industrial and agricultural training and technical assistance to the latter.

Sarvodaya villages were ranked according to three levels of development. At the starting level, villages lacked any significant infrastructure. Often, their inhabitants had lost hope and self-esteem. At this level, the main aim of the Movement was to make the village population aware of the causes of their poverty and the breakdown of their social cohesion. This awareness was being awakened through the Shramadana[33] camps, where the satisfaction of the most pressing needs of a village was achieved by labor from the same village, sometimes with the help from nearby more developed Sarvodaya communities. The works undertaken by Shramadana camps were quite varied. They included, among others, construction of access roads, renovation of water reservoirs, opening of canals, engineering of water supply systems, digging of latrine pits, construction of schools, and opening of new farmland.

A Shramadana camp would last from a weekend to several weeks. Every day the participants would provide six to eight hours of labor and attend another two to four hours of educational meetings. From only three camps with 97 participants in 1958, the movement evolved to the point where it was able to organize some 400 camps a year, involving more than 70,000 people. Shramadana camps were building infrastructure in many rural areas at almost no cost to the Sri Lankan state. They were also helping to reduce generation and gender gaps by promoting dialogue between old and young, and men and women.

At the next level of development, villagers were able to organize various age and occupation groups whose activities were coordinated by a village reawakening council.[34] These activities aimed at cleaning and beautifying the environment, improving health conditions, and providing villagers with better clothes, food, housing, education, and communication with the rest of the country. Yet, at this stage, most of the development work was still undertaken on a problem-by-problem basis.

At the third level, the people would design a village development plan. It usually included the construction or renovation of tube wells, water supply systems, rainwater storage tanks, irrigation canals, houses, gardens, roads, drainage systems, schools, health rooms, temples, cemeteries, playgrounds, and public baths. Development plans often also included the organization of community shops and collective farms. The crops were insured, local savings systems were promoted, and arrangements were made with banks for securing loans that would finance the development plans. These introduced biogas and solar energy to the villages, promoted the planting of trees for firewood, and organized the local manufacture of clothes, furniture, and building materials. They also included the prevention of mosquito-breeding, the revival of indigenous medical systems, and the improvement of health-care services. To break the isolation of the villages from the country and the world, development plans usually included the organization of community services for receiving and dispatching mail, receiving radio broadcasts and newspapers, showing films, and bringing performers. Traditional gatherings and religious celebrations, as well as modern sports and cultural activities, were activated. By December 1979, the Sarvodaya Movement was planning a system of village enterprises, storage facilities, and village retail stores. The aim was to facilitate the exchange of products among villages and to market surplus production in local and foreign markets.

The Sarvodaya Movement was inspired by Buddhist philosophy and emerged from within the Sinhalese, a traditionally Buddhist ethnic group. However, the movement included all religious and ethnic groups in Sri Lanka, such as the Hindu Tamils and Christians. During our visits, we always found Christian and Hindu symbols displayed alongside images of the Buddha in school and community rooms of Sarvodaya villages.

Because of the bloody power struggle between the Sinhalese and Tamil ethnic groups, it was risky at the time of my visit to venture outside Sarvodaya villages through the rural routes of Sri Lanka. My wife and I felt safe and comfortable only within these villages. We were amazed to see the easy conviviality within them between two groups that were killing each other a few miles further up or down the road.[35] This convinced me that different pathways to the dialogue with the universal spirit do not divide people. It is the programs inspired by the *amour propre* of political and religious leaders that create separation and hatred. People passively receive these programs and blindly respond to them because the programmers purposely keep the receivers ignorant of their power to analyze and decide for themselves.

In his acceptance speech for the King Baudouin International Development Prize, Ariyaratne defined what the movement understands by awakening. He said:

> Firstly, I must continuously awaken myself to the real nature of my own psychophysical entity called my personality. Who am I? What is the path leading to my supreme happiness? Is it through increased greed, hatred and ignorance within me that I can find happiness or is it through a process of gradual decrease in these threefold defilements?
>
> Secondly, how do I awaken to the realities of society with all its complexities? What should be the nature of the moral, cultural, social, political, and economic environment which will help me to awaken my personality to the fullest?
>
> Thirdly, how do I awaken myself to the realities of my natural environment consisting as it does of land, water, air, sunshine, and various living beings including the plant kingdom?
>
> If I succeed in getting my personality to awaken in this three-fold dimension, then I believe that I am on the path to happiness which will help my inner life to be in harmony with the outer world.[36]

This awakening was leading Tamils and Sinhalese in the Sarvodaya villages to understand their common ever-present origin, rejecting socially programmed divisions. It was as if they had discovered that electrons that one day spin in the body of a Tamil villager, recording visions of Rama and Vishnu, may the next day be part of the body of a Sinhalese and start recording memories of the Buddha. In the Sarvodaya villages Sinhalese and Tamils sought to make the most of the space they shared. Outside those villages, they were programmed to see one group competing against the other, a competition that could end only by separating spaces or by one group dominating the other.

THE POPULATION AND COMMUNITY DEVELOPMENT ASSOCIATION

The efforts toward village development that I witnessed in 1980 in Thailand were similar in methods and inspiration to the Sri Lankan efforts. The Population and Community Development Association of Thailand, like the Sarvodaya in Sri Lanka, thought that its main task was to empower villagers for mastering their physical, mental, emotional, and spiritual development. However, while the Sarvodaya entry point into a village's life was usually the satisfaction of a pressing cultural or infrastructural need, for the PCDA it was the distribution of information and means for a responsible parenthood. The leaders of PCDA were convinced that it is impossible for rural people to improve their living conditions without controlling their population growth.

Their task was eased by the fact that Thai society is less repressive of sex drives than the Sinhalese is. Although the supreme goal in Thai society, as in other predominantly Buddhist societies, is to reach a higher spiritual level of development, most of the people feel that this is a state of mind that only a few enlightened people can achieve. While the majority struggle to join these enlightened few, the tensions they face between natural urges and social requirements are eased by a bonhomie that regards sex as just one of life's many pleasures.

In my short visit, I could not perceive much *amour propre* in the relations among villagers of the PCDA cluster. Instead, it was evident that *amour propre* was inspiring the behavior of Thai urban populations. Among the latter, sex, power, prestige, and status were all heavily commercialized.

Sri Lanka suffered a double cleavage: On one hand, between the Sinhalese and the Tamil, and on the other hand, between the poor of both ethnic groups, who were vegetating, and the rich, who wielded power and enjoyed life. Thailand suffered only from the second, and PCDA oriented its action toward decreasing the gap. By making the enjoyment of life safer for the peasantry, PCDA improved their bonhomie and began to break their dependency on urban rulers, whether government officials, merchants, gangsters, or armed forces.[37]

The Thai attitude of relaxing tensions between nature and society, and the PCDA's goal of building a deeper mastery of the population's physical, mental, and spiritual health, both led to the development of sound rational structures of consciousness. The people were still far from the integrative structures that rely on a deeper understanding of inner life. They still felt that "one does not expose all personal problems and frustrations, and deeper levels of one's stirrings are to be kept to oneself." Hence, these deeper stirrings "remained unvoiced and most often not even raised to the level of one's own consciousness."[38]

It was clear that the Thai bonhomie was not yet a product of the conscious opening of broad communication channels with the unconscious, which allows the establishment of individually appropriate trade-offs between nature's needs and social demands. Rather, it was a socially imposed trade-off that resulted in a socially controlled bonhomie.

Even so, this bonhomie made it easier for young Thais to stay home in the rural areas than it was for the youth of the Sarvodaya villages, where there was a more strict social control on relationships between young people. Some young Sri Lankans confessed that they chose to migrate to Colombo, although they were better fed and lodged at their villages, because it was only in the big city, far from the control of their families and their small rural societies, that they could feel free.

In 1980, some 300 staff members of PCDA coordinated the work of about 16,000 volunteers whom they had trained as village developers. These were integrating in their development work the professional expertise of PCDA's staff, the specialized knowledge of governmental extension services, and the traditional empirical expertise of the villagers themselves. Village developers helped peasants improve traditional practices of animal husbandry and folk medicine. The village developers also promoted the construction of manure-based methane generators, and of either cement-lined shallow wells or bamboo-reinforced concrete tanks for storage of rainwater.

In its fight against malnutrition, the PCDA shunned handouts of food. Charity was perceived as increasing dependency, inhibiting self-reliance, and failing to reach the root of the problem. Instead, the institution took a multidisciplinary approach that included teaching parasite control and nutrition, and promoting agricultural activities that make good nutrition possible. For this purpose it established a network of Village Appropriate Technology and Economic Development Centers that served as demonstration and training units and as distribution centers for agricultural products within a cooperative marketing system.

In 1980, the prices obtained through these PCDA marketing efforts were 20 to 30 percent better than the prices farmers could get by themselves. This meant that even after deducting PCDA's costs of packaging, transportation, and handling, the farmer's disposable income was higher than before, sometimes allowing savings to be generated. These savings could be invested in a development fund whose aim was to provide pensions and an insurance plan for farmers, finance the building of warehouses and rice mills, and purchase seeds and fertilizers in bulk.

There were many interesting spin-offs from various activities supported by the PCDA. The construction of systems for collecting and storing rainwater, for example, led to the development of cottage industries to produce and maintain roof-gutter systems. PCDA made loans available to local skilled workers to establish these industries and to villagers to buy the roof-gutters. Similarly, loans and training were made available to village groups to establish small crop-milling and animal-feeding operations, and to farmers for animal-growing activities and intercropping systems. The latter had the purpose of increasing local production of wingbeans, leucaena, and other fast-growing, high-protein legumes.

Also interesting was PCDA's approach to training village technicians. When the staff of PCDA perceived the need for certain skills in a village, or a cluster of villages, they worked with the village developers to select young villagers and tailor an educational program for them that would include theory and practice. Theoretical aspects could be either taught by consultants and staff from PCDA and the Industrial Services Institute of Thailand, or acquired through attendance at regular courses at technical schools and technological institutes. Practice was provided by work at private workshops and those of the Industrial Services Institute. Depending on the type of skill, the program would run from a few weeks to several months.

Afterward, the trainees earned their living marketing their services among villagers.

SIGNS OF HOPE

The business, educational, and village development experiments described in this chapter are just a few examples of the many transformational efforts that are taking place among different groups, in different locations. To record all of them would require much more than a chapter. It would require years of research and several books. Even if some of the experiments suffer setbacks, they have already put forth signs that others could capture and amplify. These signs say that an integration of technical and financial rationality with concerns for humans and ecosystems is possible. They say also that it is possible to awaken the rationality of large masses and impregnate it with love and life energies. Masses who are able to distinguish reality from illusions and delusions might cease swinging back and forth between the old left and the old right, lured by bright displays of magic and myths that politicians on both sides put up for them.

Of the three constituencies—businesspeople, educators, and village developers—businesspeople are by far the most powerful. The late Willis Harman said that he joined with several businesspersons to found the World Business Academy as a result of two convictions that he developed during sixteen years of work in strategic planning and research on the future. One of his convictions was that "the modern world is undergoing a period of fundamental transformation, the extent and meaning of which we who are living through it are only beginning to grasp." The other conviction was that "the role of business in that transformation is absolutely crucial."[39]

Businesspeople know too well the world of power and wealth, and some among them are suffering existential pains from their inability to resist the highly destructive gravitational field that power and wealth create. The pain of the few who acknowledge their suffering, and stubbornly attempt to transform themselves, could motivate many more to awaken to a world of integration and harmony, pushing themselves out of the black hole in which they have allowed themselves to be trapped.

As the number of businesspeople undergoing transformation reaches a critical mass, they might help steer the whole spaceship Earth away from a catastrophe. Yet, they cannot accomplish this by themselves. They need the energy provided by equally transformed masses. For this reason, businesspeople who are transforming themselves should promote and support educational reforms that will also advance the structure of consciousness of the existing population, and of generations to come. These businesspeople must come to realize that reforming education to lead the masses to a new integrative, harmonizing vision is the most cost-effective means of avoiding a tragic collapse of our spiritless rational constructions.

12

HISTORICAL EXAMPLES

T he Sri Lankan and Thai experiences described in the previous chapter show that it is possible to promote deep changes in the structure of consciousness of large segments of population with modest means. These experiences also show that when people's consciousness is restructured, their local economies and societies are also transformed.

Could similar efforts be designed on a national scale? Would they then be as cost-effective as they are at the village level? Could national educational systems provide an organizational base for these efforts? Attempting to find answers to these questions, I studied two national experiments of consciousness transformation: one that took place in Argentina at the end of the nineteenth century, and a more recent experiment in Costa Rica during the 1950s.

ARGENTINA: THE RISE AND FALL OF A NATION

From early in the sixteenth century until the beginning of the nineteenth century, Argentina was under Spanish rule. Spain was marginalized from the industrial and scientific revolution initiated by advanced rational structures of consciousness in other parts of Europe. The masses in Spain and its colonies were kept under predominantly magical and mythical structures of consciousness. With a few exceptions, even the rationality of the governing elites was deeply permeated by magic and myths.

250

However, by the end of the eighteenth century, the sons of local South American elites, educated in the few South American universities or abroad, were opening their minds to the intellectual products of those more advanced rational structures. These studious youth smuggled in the books of French philosophers and North American statesmen, and received esoteric teachings at Masonic lodges.

The invasion of Spain by Napoleon provided these South American elites with an opportunity to sever colonial ties. In Argentina, this happened in 1810. Soon thereafter, the country's independent life was threatened on two fronts. Internally, local caudillos unleashed anarchic forces that exploited the magical and mythical structures of the rural population. Externally, the Spanish monarchy regained strength after the defeat of Napoleon and was intent on reconquering its former colonies. The situation was so disheartening that for a moment, some members of the elite thought that they had only two options left to reestablish internal order and avoid a catastrophe on the battlefields. One option was to recall the Spanish king or to call on another available monarch. The other was to join a foreign nation as an autonomous state.[1] These were typical attitudes of rational structures of consciousness that, under a state of fear, rationalized solutions that they would otherwise have rejected as contrary to their republican convictions. The layers of magic and myth that underlie our rational structures often play tricks on even the most brilliant minds, making them believe that the pomp of symbols, or the power of external resources, can solve problems created by a deep-seated mind-set.

THE WAR OF INDEPENDENCE AND ITS HISTORICAL EXAMPLES OF AMOUR PROPRE VS. AMOUR DE SOI

Argentina was delivered from the external threat thanks to the combined actions of two military men, Argentinean José de San Martín and Venezuelan Simón Bolívar, who, while serving as young officers in the Spanish army, had opened their mind to new currents of thought by participating in Masonic lodges. When San Martín returned to Argentina in 1812, he founded, together with two other army comrades, a local lodge following the format of the Masonic lodges he had frequented in Spain. The purpose was to recruit local people who would share their ideals of obtaining total independence from Spain, bringing all of South America into a large political and economic union.[2] In 1822, after the memorable exploit of crossing the Andean mountains, chasing the Spanish army from Chile, and freeing Peru, San Martín met with Bolivar in Guayaquil, Ecuador. The latter was marching south with his troops after thwarting the Spanish threat to the northern part of South America.

San Martín decided to let Bolivar lead the final battles against the remnants of the Spanish army, returned to Argentina, and, resolved to stay out of the internal strife, exiled himself to France in 1824. He died there, at peace with himself, at the age of seventy-two. San Martín and Bolivar shared the dream of freeing South America from an inefficient and reactionary European absolutism. San Martín doggedly fought for the dream but refused to fight with Bolivar for the supreme command of the liberating forces that would give the final touch to its materialization. Guided by *amour de soi*, San Martín also refused to become involved in the civil strife that was afflicting Argentina. Thus, he revealed a profound respect for his own being and the well-being of his fellow citizens.

Bolivar, instead, full of *amour propre*, became involved in internal struggles, and, in a desperate attempt to save the political unity of the Republic of Colombia—then comprising what today are Venezuela, Colombia, and Ecuador—he assumed dictatorial powers. Soon after resigning these powers, in 1830, Bolivar died at the age of forty-seven. He was a disillusioned man, who felt the hatred of many among those whom he had given the possibility of building a new society.

From Anarchy to Organization

While independence from Spain was being secured in battlefields outside Argentina, the internal conflict was becoming increasingly anarchic, daunting repeated efforts to develop the newly established nation. Some forty years after San Martín's exile, a group of open-minded, courageous Argentine intellectuals finally faced the internal threat and undertook the task of organizing a free and modern country. They understood that this task had to start with a large-scale effort to expand the consciousness of the Argentine population, building sound rational structures on myths and magic. Juan Bautista Alberdi, one of the young thinkers in this group, stated their concerns thus: "It is the reflective and profound consciousness of its people that civilizes a nation. Before, it is only a conglomeration that moves instinctively and spontaneously, without knowing itself, and hence, incapable of determining the why, where, and how of its movements."[3]

We have seen repeatedly in this book how rational structures of consciousness often catalogue thoughts and behaviors into sharply opposing patterns, promoting one pattern and considering the other as harmful. The advanced rational structure of the leaders who built the Argentine nation was no exception. It led them to commit some excesses. In their despair to quickly build rational structures among the population, they rejected and repressed autochthonous cultural elements that might have contributed to a more integrative view of reality. It is now easy for us to criticize them, but we should realize that except for a few philosophers and mystics, the concepts of integration and harmony had to wait some hundred and fifty more years to begin emerging among humankind. And they have yet to reach global acceptance to start influencing the economic and social behavior of the society of nations.

Some of Alberdi's writings are good examples of the misconceptions to which a divisive rationality may lead. He wrote:

> Mathematics is the best tool to educate our Spanish heads in the practice of method, logic, and order. They discipline our exalted faculties, instill perseverance, and check our impetuous imagination. Commercial education, the teaching of arts and crafts, of practical methods to plow the land and improve the breeding of useful animals, the development of fondness and liking for mechanical matters, should all be among the highest objectives of popular education in these societies that, instead of struggling to dominate a savage nature and populate the desert with cities, are avidly killing people who dissent. The mission of the universities in South America should be to disseminate science rather than literature. Science appeases, literature exalts. Science

is light, reason, cold judgment, and reflective behavior. Literature is illusion, mystery, fiction, passion, eloquence, harmony, drunkenness of the soul.[4]

Another outstanding member of the intellectual group that organized the nation was an educator of humble origin, powerful intellect, and passionate curiosity. His name was Domingo Faustino Sarmiento. In 1847, after traveling through Europe to learn about the successes and failures of educational systems, he visited the United States and frequented the Bostonian group of intellectuals formed around Horace Mann, Henry Wadsworth Longfellow, and Ralph Waldo Emerson. The friendships he established then were further cultivated during his second sojourn as Argentine Ambassador to the United States from 1864 through 1868. When Sarmiento assumed the presidency of Argentina (1868–1874), Mary Mann, the widow of Horace Mann, was instrumental in sending a group of sixty-five American schoolteachers to Argentina to organize the first normal schools for educating Argentine teachers. On this cornerstone, Sarmiento and Nicolás Avellaneda, who was Sarmiento's minister of public education and his successor in the presidency, started building the country's educational system. The task was fully achieved by 1880, under the presidency of Julio A. Roca, when, by law, primary schooling became gratuitous, compulsory, and secular.

After Sarmiento's administration, the number of well-furnished schools constantly increased, and teachers received high social status and adequate monetary rewards. By restructuring the consciousness of indigenous populations and poor immigrants—who were arriving in increased numbers and with minds that were also deeply imbedded in magic and myth—the Argentine school system created the mental conditions that socioeconomic advancement required. The transformation of the institutes for higher education was slower, but when enraged students promoted the reform of the universities in 1918, they introduced advances that we have yet to see permanently established in Argentina, and which are rare even in highly industrialized countries. Among these advances we can mention parallel chairs,[5] the periodicity of the chairs,[6] and the participation of students and alumni in the university's governance.

Educational Reform Spearheads Economic Development

By the end of the nineteenth century, with a literacy rate of over 90 percent, many of the initial development objectives had been achieved. Included were the settling of immigrants, the development of railways, the regulation of property rights, the introduction of industries in the previously purely agrarian landscape, and the transformation of this landscape from open fields, where cattle grazed freely on wild pastures, to fenced, cultivated plots.

The old mercantile system, based on exporting the raw products of an uncultured land and importing everything else, began to make room for capitalist activities. Local industries began transforming indigenous raw materials. Local business undertook the maintenance of imported capital goods. Rural activities diversified to include the production of grains in the estancias (large ranches) and in smaller fields around immigrant colonies. Increased market opportunities led to the formation of a large middle class that began to share wealth with traditional landowners. Peasants and villagers shifted from being suppliers of food and cannon fodder for the caudillos' armies to becoming low-paid laborers on estancias and plantations, where their condition often was closer to that of serfs than modern wage-earners. Some moved to large cities, especially Buenos Aires, and joined immigrants in creating a working class that organized itself under a preponderantly democratic socialist leadership.

The progressive impulse of the early consciousness-restructuring efforts lasted seven decades, roughly from 1860 through 1930. In his study of Argentine history, David Rock comments:

> By the outbreak of World War I, per capita income equaled that in Germany and the Low Countries, and was higher than in Spain, Italy, Sweden, and Switzerland. Having grown at an average annual rate of 6.5 percent since 1869, Buenos Aires had become the second city of the Atlantic seaboard, after New York, and by far the largest city in Latin America. . . . By 1911, Argentina's foreign trade was larger than Canada's and a quarter of that of the United States. Argentina was the world's largest producer of corn and linseed, second in wool, and third in live cattle and horses. Though it ranked only sixth as a wheat producer, it was the third, and in some years the second, largest exporter.

255

Despite the competition for land from cattle and forage crops, the expansion of wheat farming after 1900 outpaced Canada's. . . . By and large, working-class conditions in Buenos Aires were much the same as in Western European cities. . . . By comparison with American [that is, U.S.] cities in this period, Buenos Aires was relatively free of ethnic ghettoes, and its highly mobile labor force made it also a city with little permanent unemployment.[7]

SHORTCOMINGS OF THE REFORM

The brightness of these figures hides the shadows and contradictions of the Argentine society and economy of that time. As Rock points out:

By 1914 Argentina had . . . evolved into an extremely mixed and diverse society. Across the regions extreme modernity and immutable backwardness coexisted. Expectations remained high that the imbalances would steadily recede as the present wave of growth continued, for there was still much to accomplish.[8]

Despite its evident success in launching the country into an era of accelerated economic growth and social progress, the educational reform suffered from shortcomings similar to those observable in the educational system that sprang up during the Age of Reason in the most advanced industrialized countries. They built a rational consciousness, but enculturated it into *amour propre* rather than *amour de soi*.

Machismo, a typical attitude supported by *amour propre*, continued to be a national trait, among poor and rich alike. It propelled the rich to struggle for control of political power and the accumulation of wealth. The poor machos, not being able to control either power or wealth, struggled to control their immediate surroundings: their group of friends, their women, and their children. Schools seldom told either rich or poor about the simple and pleasurable aspects of life of which they were deprived by that struggle for control.

Among the urban poor, this deprivation was compounded by the struggle to survive under miserable conditions. The "porteño machos"[9] expressed their loneliness,[10] frustration, and deep sadness through their popular music, the tango. Their subconscious rational programs were forcing them to display their machismo, but their

256

hearts were hurting "for reasons that their reason could not always understand." For instance, one of the tangos declares: "In my life I had many, many lovers, but never a partner."[11] Another sounds like a dispirited piece of cultural criticism written in the vernacular: "Among impostors and ambitious robbers, it is the same to be a priest, a mattress-maker, a scoundrel, or a bum."[12]

Among the rural poor, survival was also harsh, but at least their physical environment was more open than the city's and provided more gratuitous satisfiers, such as natural beauty, some food, and materials for shelter. In rural areas, it was often a hard-working poverty, rarely a disintegrating misery. In the immensity of a still underpopulated and virgin Argentina, nature facilitated the dialogue with the spirit, while the cement jungle of Buenos Aires hindered it. Hope and tenderness could crop up more easily and openly in country music than in the tango. For instance, a worker from the sugar cane fields sings to his beloved:

> Let's go, my love, to the harvest. We need to gather all the sweetness of the Earth drawn into the fibers of the sugar cane. I want you to have a baby boy to mend my wages because, while I pluck its leaves, the sugar cane is eating up my arms.[13]

A lonely driver of a pack of cows imagines the river talking to him:

> You, who still can, return, said the river while crying. The hills you love so much, he told me, are still there, waiting for you. It is sad to be a river. I wish I could instead be a pond, and hear the whispering of the willows when they are kissed by the moon. How close is your fate to mine. We both sing and suffer through our long life-paths.[14]

Amour propre, which feeds on comparisons, led the dominant classes to imitate foreign, more developed cultures and to despise their fellow citizens, who could attain neither wealth nor sophisticated culture. Somehow, the dominant classes managed to guide the enculturating process of the poor into replacing their previous mythical dependence on caudillos and priests with a rational obedience to the landed high class and the urban middle class. Schools fell short of giving the poor a vision of the world that would lead them to apply the rational tools they were receiving to the development of sound local economies. They were given tools to work for others, not to do things by themselves.

THE BEGINNING OF THE DOWNFALL

After World War I, education in Argentina failed to adjust to the accelerated scientific, technological, and cultural changes that were taking place in the world. Only a few intellectuals perceived this gap and attempted to close it. Most others, in early twentieth-century Argentina, were blind to events evolving before their eyes and were deluded by aspects of reality that they saw colored in an unrealistic way. For instance, the majority did not perceive the risk of having a growing working class with unsatisfied needs, and a peasantry without horizons. Nor did they perceive the risk of calling on the army to quell the protests of the poor. On the contrary, they saw a strong army as the best safeguard against workers who had begun to assert their rights, and who were perceived as potential revolutionaries that could establish an Argentine Soviet. Honest efforts by democratic socialists and progressive democrats to move the country toward more equitable socioeconomic structures were sometimes naively seen, and other times manipulatively presented, as leftist conspiracies to destroy the established order.

The dominant classes allied themselves with the military in opposing further reforms, and with the first coup d'état, in 1930, efforts to further expand the population's consciousness came to a halt. Moreover, after 1930 some of the Argentine administrations tried to move the clock backward. Argentina then started an economic and social downfall. By 1987 she was considered again an infant democracy,[15] a highly indebted[16] survivor of dirty internal and external wars and of long periods of mismanaged public finances and reckless populism.

However, some of the progress already made could not be abated. Governments attempted to reintroduce religious education in the schools, but secularism prevailed in the end. The universities never returned to teachings "subservient of theology."[17] The Argentine masses never returned to the magical and mythical pastoral past.

Making good use of rational structures of consciousness, people managed to create free spaces for their lives when governments attempted dogmatically to regulate their private behavior. Men and women alike would simulate compliance with regressive rules while behaving in whatever way pleased them in the shielded environment of their households. This explains why in a predominantly Catholic country, which was ruled for long periods by military juntas that promoted a high birth rate, the population grew at only 1.6 percent per year from 1965 to 1980.[18]

Argentina also continued its industrial development, although on a less sound basis than before 1930. *Amour propre* created a mirage in the rational mind of Argentine industrialists and politicians. Instead of expanding, perfecting, and humanizing the established industrialization of raw materials from a rich land, they invested in high-tech industries that did not generate much employment and created a heavy dependence on imported basic and intermediary inputs. Some politicians, intellectuals, and army members went so far as to dream of autarky.

Wealthy landowners, also guided by *amour propre*, neglected to improve their rural investments and shifted their profits toward industries with rapid payback. By contrast, the owners of smaller rural holdings around immigrant colonies became absentee landlords, managing their rural concerns from professional or business offices in the big cities.

Instead of a capitalist economy based on assuming risks in free markets, Argentina developed a capitalism of political patronage that constantly expanded the state sector at the expense of the private sector. "Among the country's thirty largest companies in the mid-1960s, state firms had 49 percent of total sales, foreign companies 41 percent, and private domestic manufacturers only 10 percent. . . . by the early 1980s some 700 state firms accounted for 42 percent of the gross domestic product."[19] The inefficiency of markets operating under heavy control of the state could be clearly seen from the fact that "between 1946 and 1955 production only crawled upward, but money in circulation increased eightfold." As a result, in just one year, 1952, "the cost of living rose by almost 40 percent."[20]

THE FUTURE: A TASK FOR A CONSCIOUSNESS ENCULTURATED INTO AMOUR DE SOI

Argentina's educational system suffered one blow after another from politicians with regressive ideologies and military leaders who did not hesitate to use up lean government revenues for their own purposes. The system is disintegrating, both physically and intellectually. It neither educates for life nor develops skills for an increasingly competitive national and international marketplace, where success depends on internal abilities and not on protection from a friend in the state bureaucracy.

> Half of students sampled in Buenos Aires scored 50 percent or lower on a Spanish proficiency test; 82 percent did that badly on a mathematics test; more than 40 percent of 13- to 18-year-old students are not enrolled in school; less than 5 percent of the education budget goes to teaching materials and the country's student-teacher ratios are the worst in the region.[21]

Sarmiento, Avellaneda, and Roca started the organization of the nation and of its educational system simultaneously with modest resources, but they had a strong vision of the future of the country and trust in the potential of its people to chart that future. The educational system now requires a restructuring of its physical assets, but more compelling yet is the need to fire a new vision. Argentina is ripe for the next leap in consciousness. From the springboard of a divisive, greedy, and often drowsy rationality, *amour de soi* might launch Argentine consciousness into integration and harmony. Education might develop these qualities and prepare the Argentine mind to increased knowledge of the vernacular and the foreign, integrating them. To achieve this, all Argentines, not only the rich, will need to practice convivial and unrestrained intercourse with the outside world. The Argentines living in the large metropolis will need to do the same with the now abandoned realm of Argentina's vast expanses of undeveloped land. *Amour de soi* might lead Argentines to free themselves from two delusions: one, that Buenos Aires, where half of the country's population is concentrated, is the whole of Argentina; two, that Buenos Aires, Paris, and New York are the navel of the world.

As we saw in the previous chapter, some Argentine businesspersons are already questioning their values and beliefs. At the same time, a new youth elite seems to be distancing itself from both the old politics of vicious alliances between wealth and power, and the calls to join in bloody regressive revolutions, often heard in the 1960s and 1970s. These youth are joining businesspeople in criticizing the capitalism of political patronage, and they may soon be ready to bring to the political arena and the marketplace a more harmonious, integrative consciousness, of which they are learning in small groups outside academic circles. They are slowly realizing that *amour de soi*, love mastering, and respect for nature are instruments that can heal old wounds from rebellion and repression, bridge artificial gaps between city and countryside, make good use of dormant natural resources, and awaken the creative forces that are within all of Argentina's people, not only her urban intellectuals and the rich.

Will Argentine businesspeople provide the leadership required by the progressive forces to coalesce and produce a renaissance that retakes the ascendant line followed by the country from 1860 to 1930? Will this confluence of minds undertake the necessary educational reform, making it again the key to an evolution toward more advanced structures of consciousness? Argentina needs desperately a new breed of schoolteachers to help students become simultaneously fully human and fully alive beings and efficient operators in the marketplace. The day schoolteachers recapture the status they had during the first evolutionary efforts, we may see Argentina maturing the incipient democracy that she regained in 1983, and offering again to the world a place in America where people try to realize the universal dream of bread, liberty, peace, love, and harmonious rapport with the land.

Costa Rica: Peace and Progress Amidst Violence

Costa Rica was discovered by Columbus on his last trip to the New World. He gave it that name, the Rich Coast, probably because of the gold ornaments worn by the indigenous people. Spanish rulers did nothing to develop this rich province. They enslaved and abused the local population, which soon decreased so much that at independence, the great majority of the people were descendants of early Spanish settlers.

Although Costa Rica declared its independence from Spain in 1821, it was not organized as an independent republic until 1848. In the interlude, it was included first in the Mexican empire dreamt by Agustín Iturbide, and later in the United Provinces of Central America. During the century that elapsed between 1848 and 1948, Costa Rica managed to live in peace and resolve disputes with its neighbors through arbitration. However, the social problems that began to erupt after World War II led to internal armed clashes.

> In 1948, a civil war cost some 2000 lives—the bloodiest event in Costa Rican history. The winning side of this civil war was headed by José Figueres Ferrer and his Social Democratic Party. Without forewarning, in a speech on December 6, 1948, he announced that the army was no longer needed and would be disbanded! "It is time," he said, "for Costa Rica to return to her traditional position of having more teachers than soldiers."[22]

Figueres took personal command of the Army and supervised its termination. He said he was abolishing the military "to reaffirm the principle of civil government."[23] A constitution was drafted, guaranteeing free elections with universal suffrage. Article 12 of this constitution states: "The Army as a permanent institution is proscribed. For vigilance and the preservation of public order, there will be the necessary police forces."[24] In 1953, with women voting for the first time, José Figueres was elected president by a large majority, and his party won most of the seats in the legislature. Under Figueres and his successors, the educational system of Costa Rica promoted the building of a new, more advanced structure of consciousness among the population.

RESULTS OF THE REFORM

Thirty-six years after the reforms, in 1989, Costa Rica, with a GNP per capita of $1780, spent only 1.7 percent of total government expenditures on defense. This is among the lowest recorded by the World Bank for that year, second only to Mauritius, for which the figure was 1 percent. In that same year, Panama with a GNP per capita quite similar ($1760) spent 7.9 percent, and El Salvador, with a lower GNP per capita ($1070), spent 27.9 percent of its government budget on defense.[25]

The permanence of Costa Rican reforms is further validated by its illiteracy rate in 1985, which was only 6 percent. We do not find a similarly low rate in any other Central American country. For that same year, the adult illiteracy rate was 12 percent in Panama, 28 percent in El Salvador, 41 percent in Honduras, and 45 percent in Guatemala.[26]

WEAKNESSES OF THE REFORM

The educational reform gave Costa Ricans powerful rational instruments for material progress but fell short in providing a sensual population with appropriate information and means in the field of family planning. The fast population growth—a yearly 2.7 percent for the period 1965–1980[27]—overtaxed Costa Rica's natural and financial resources.

Neither was the rational structure strong enough to resist the charm of the then popular myth that portrayed industrialization as the most expedient way to improve the well-being of the people. Between 1965 and 1980, while agriculture grew at only 4.2 percent per year, industrial production grew at 8.7 percent and services at 6.0 percent. In *Bordering on Trouble*, a book on resources and politics in Latin America, Walter LaFeber comments: "Particularly under the Central American Common Market, Costa Rican industry gained capital and diversity, while becoming controlled by a few wealthy families. Although Costa Rican industry made great strides, it also reduced many artisans to poverty and did not provide substitutes for expensive imports."[28]

PRESENT AND FUTURE

As a result of all these policies and behaviors, Costa Rica now struggles with high indebtedness (3.8 billion dollars of total debt in 1995)[29] and inflation (18.4 percent per year for the period 1985–1995).[30] This has made the country regress from its previously achieved social goals. Fortunately, the continuity of Costa Rican democratic governments has not, up to the present, been threatened. This holds out

THE TRANSFORMATIONAL PROCESS

hope for efforts to further evolve the structure of consciousness of the population.

Working under a more advanced structure of consciousness, Costa Ricans might create a society of abundance and well-being by prudently exploiting, in an environmentally safe way, their forests, plains, and coastal areas and by controlling the growth of their population. Costa Rica can count on three assets for future development of this kind: her advanced social security system, the high cultural level of her youth, and an educational system that stands ready to carry on new reforms after receiving appropriate financial and human resources.

COSTA RICA'S SOCIAL SECURITY SYSTEM

Costa Rica's social security system has demonstrated its efficiency by supporting the large number of people who were left unemployed, and often landless, by inappropiate, unstable, externally induced changes in its productive structure. Soon after Figueres' social and educational reforms, there was an expansion of cattle grazing, and the production of bananas and coffee shifted to large mechanized plantations. The people displaced by these practices from their jobs and their lands often squatted on land claimed by the plantations and cattle-grazers, but there was no army to violently evict them, as in other countries that went through similar changes, and the social security system and socialized medicine allowed relocation of the squatters to government-owned land without too much pain and misery.

Some say that the system is too costly. Perhaps it can be made more cost-effective, but it has already spared Costa Rica from the tragedies that have devastated other Central America countries. These tragedies have consumed more financial resources than what could have been wasted by the inefficiencies of the Costa Rican social security system, not to mention the costs in life and property destroyed.

Costa Rica's Youth

The positive effects on youth of the educational reform can still be perceived. I was able to witness some of these effects during my repeated visits to Costa Rica in the 1980s. Three anecdotes illustrate this point. During one of my visits, at the art museum of San José, Costa Rica's capital, I saw a rather large group of teenagers looking attentively at the pictures and commenting on them among themselves. I asked if they were fulfilling a school assignment. The answer was "No, Sir, we come often just because we like art."

Another time, a modest poster on a downtown sidewalk caught my attention. It announced a poetry reading by young poets. I went, befriended the youngsters, and got some of the books with their poems. A few stanzas of a poem written by one of them portray well their thoughts and feelings:[31]

PLANET

If closing my eyes

I could be born

with a world woven

of entwined hands

and could seal those tight lips

without smiles where to recharge myself.

If I could break

all the rules

and fences of my catechism

and throw myself into the streets

—naked—

without people nesting

my body

in their eyes of steel.

And if I could feel

a world equal and shared

where people find themselves

without need to mirror themselves on others

—life—

I would stuff myself with stars

to celebrate

the glory of a planet

in love.

Carlos Rubio

The third episode happened in Jicaral, a small rural community, where I was promoting an integrated village development project based on the conversion of an existing agricultural school to a center of education with production.[32] My wife, a physician, was talking with a group of women about advancing nutrition through better use of staples, and about cost-efficient means of improving health by using local herbs. In the next project-related meeting, those Jicaral women asked that a piece of the school's productive land be assigned to their care. They would use it to cultivate local herbs, applying the empirical traditional knowledge that a few old women of the village still remembered.

When the women were asked what kind of help they would like to receive from international aid organizations like the one I was representing, they answered:

We need some seed money, but more important for us is moral support. What we heard until now is that relying on herbs for the maintenance of our health was part of our primitive past. It is encouraging for us to now hear that advanced countries are relying more and more on similar natural healing methods. We know what to do and how to do it, but to put ourselves into the task, we need the stimulus of frequent visits from outsiders[33] that can bring information to update our basic knowledge, help us to connect with the markets, and make us feel that our effort has a meaning, and will have a reward.

266

LESSONS FROM THE TWO COUNTRY-WIDE EFFORTS

The examples of Argentina and Costa Rica show that it is possible and cost-effective to organize national efforts to restructure the consciousness of the people, building a more advanced structure of consciousness on the bases provided by the old. It is a relatively fast, and always sensitive, change process. In Jeffersonian terms, these are efforts to tailor new coats of values, beliefs, and behaviors for populations that have outgrown the old. In these two examples, the main agent in transforming consciousness was the public school system. Nowadays, in carrying on similar efforts, we would need to consider also the role that can be played by mass media and computer networks.

The two examples also show that a transformation of consciousness produces long-term socioeconomic effects. Once enlightened leaders spark the transformation, it acquires a life of its own. However, regression is always possible, even long after the reforms have been successfully implemented. Yet, the structure of consciousness built by the transformational process can never be fully destroyed. Overtly or covertly, it remains active and ready to offer support for building an even more advanced structure upon it.

Conversely, the examples below will show that socioeconomic transformations fail when they do not include efforts to restructure the consciousness of the population. When people are left wearing the coats designed by the systems previously in place, they neither participate actively in the implementation of the reforms nor assure their stability. Frozen structures of consciousness defeat change. The two cases to be discussed are those of Brazil and its new constitution, and the Russian Revolution from October 1917 to the onset of perestroika and glasnost.

BRAZIL AND ITS NEW CONSTITUTION

Beginning in 1964 and continuing for more than twenty years, Brazil was under a military dictatorship that favored agricultural exports and industrialization at the expense of staple food production. During this period, the fragile ecology of Amazonian rainforests was opened to the predatory activities of wealthy Brazilians and

267

powerful foreign interests. As a result, says LaFerbe, "Brazil became a major international debtor, and, in addition, scores of Indian tribes were virtually destroyed, large cattle ranges and agribusinesses drove out peasant populations, and attempts by the Indians and peasants to seek legal help and protection led to violence and repression by Brazilian officials."[34]

Brazil reemerged as a democracy by formulating a new constitution. It took a year and a half (1987–1988) for a rather democratic convention to promulgate its 245 articles and 70 temporary dispositions. During this period, there was strong popular participation. People submitted many proposals for analysis by the constitutional convention. To be considered, these proposals each had to gather at least 30,000 signatures.

Despite this high degree of popular participation, the new constitution is not a guarantee that the lot of the poorest Brazilians will be improved. The ministry for agrarian reform was suppressed three months after the new constitution was adopted. Commercial ventures continue to encroach onto the lands of indigenous peoples and to destroy rain forests. Violence is rampant in the streets of the large cities. There is hunger and despair everywhere.

The attempt to produce progressive changes in the social and economic structure of the country were not paralleled by efforts to lead the Brazilian masses and the wealthy elite to a more integrative, harmonizing view of both the country's reality and the people's inner personal reality. No attempts were made to change the enculturation patterns from *amour propre* to *amour de soi*. Hence, it should be no surprise that the approach of businesses to the use of Brazilian land and its people still is predominantly harsh and greedy. Only a change in the way in which Brazilian businesspeople think and do business might avoid a catastrophe.

Simultaneously, Brazilian poor should made aware of their dormant development potential through large-scale consciousness-expanding and consciousness-intensifying efforts, similar to those of the Sarvodaya or the PCDA described in the previous chapter. Among the Brazilian population, the magical and mythical layers of consciousness remain more active than in other Latin American countries. The shift to a new, more integrative, harmonizing consciousness should never attempt to repress this activity. On the contrary, it should blend magic and myth into a more awakened rationality, and enculturate the latter into *amour de soi*.

To avoid interference from magic and myths either when analyzing reality or working with it does not mean that people should be barred from playing with magic and myths when satisfying psychological, relational, and recreational needs. As I have said earlier, when magic and myths are recognized as such, they may enrich, rather than handicap, social and economic activities.

Brazilians love drumming. A transformation of consciousness could mean for them just marching to a different drummer. Instead of a drummer that excites *amour propre* among the rich and makes the poor doze off, they may choose a drummer that stirs *amour de soi* at both ends of the Brazilian social spectrum.

FROM THE RUSSIAN REVOLUTION TO PERESTROIKA

The two great revolutions of modern time—the French and the Russian—were attempts to violently and abruptly redistribute wealth. They both ended by adding, rather than erasing, pain and oppression. In chapter 5 I quoted from William Godwin, who said that: "A revolution of opinion is the only means of attaining a better distribution of wealth."[35] But a revolution—or better still an evolution—of opinion is never achieved through indoctrination. It requires a transformation of consciousness through reform of the educational systems and the media. Neither the French nor the Russian revolutions produced such a transformation. In both cases, the ideologies of the revolutionary leaders were quite different from the ideologies of those whom they overthrew, but the structures of consciousness were the same. Indoctrination replaces one set of belief programs with another in the subconscious hard disks of people's minds, but maintains the old patterns of interaction between the unconscious, the subconscious and the conscious mind.[36] Hence, there are no changes either in the interactions between mind, body, and spirit nor in the relationships that people establish among them and with nature.

When the European situation permitted Lenin to test the application of Marxist theory on the scale of a large country like Russia, the consciousness of neither the peoples of the Russian Empire, nor of those in the outside world, was ready for the experiment. The Russian revolutionaries concentrated on restructuring the ownership of the means of production; they completely forgot that socioeconomic transformations also need to restructure the minds. The revolutionary Marxists put tremendous effort into bringing scientific knowledge to the masses but kept their consciousness structured in molds similar to those used by the czars. On the subconscious of those old structures, the Marxists overwrote the myth of heaven and hell with the magic of a worker's paradise. This paradise had to materialize just because school and party books said it would happen. However, for it to happen, workers should never discuss the authority of the state. People previously indoctrinated into submission, obedience, and sacrifice to the czar and feudal lords were indoctrinated into submission, obedience, and sacrifice to the new Marxist state and its bureaucrats.

Some of the early revolutionaries, outstanding among them Anton Makarenko, thought that the revolution had to put in place educational systems through which the people could be empowered for the task of expanding and intensifying their consciousness. In his "Pedagogic Poem," Makarenko said that the pedagogic aim should be to accustom children to solve daily life problems by themselves, harmonizing individual freedom and social requirements.[37] Too soon, revolutionary mythoclasts like Makarenko were replaced by curators of new icons. The latter feared to free the Russian people from the old mental chains to which they themselves were enchained, perhaps without realizing.

The peoples of the Russian Empire were never educated to develop *amour de soi*, and without this healthy love of oneself, the spirit of service required to implement Marxist economic patterns could never spread in Soviet society. Because the minds of leaders and people alike were cast in the prison of old programs, it was inevitable that the dream of social freedom and economic justice would be replaced by the reality of corruption and oppression.

Initially, intellectuals from outside the Soviet Union followed the Marxist experiment in the hope that it would build a new, more humane, just, and free society. These intellectuals appealed to Western political leaders to join in the task of reconciling differences and producing an evolutionary leap for the whole of humankind, without necessarily adopting the economic theories of the Soviets.

In November 1918, French writer and scholar Romain Rolland sent President Woodrow Wilson a letter whose main passages are worth quoting:

> Peoples are breaking their chains. The time you forecasted has arrived. . . . From one extreme to the other of Europe, peoples are raising their will of assuming the administration of their destinies and of coming together to regenerate Europe. They are trying to reach each other over and beyond borders. But the chasm created by mistrust and mistakes is still open. A bridge should be built over it. The old fatalistic grip of nationalistic wars, that still holds strong in these peoples and blindly throws them into mutual destruction, should be conjured. They can't do it by themselves. They are asking for help. The world is anxious to hear a voice that will speak over nations and classes. Be you [President Wilson] the arbiter. I wish the future could hail you with the name of Reconciler.[38]

The American president couldn't reconcile the differences among his European colleagues, who never engaged in efforts to expand their vision of the world. The politicians of his own country were no exception. Their thought forms were also encased in structures that rationalized the separation between people of different genders, skin colors, and cultural beliefs, while the wealthy Americans who supported those politicians were speeding up the process of accumulating wealth and skewing the distribution of income. This last process, which started in the late nineteenth century, would end by producing the Great Depression.

Moreover, *amour propre* and power control led the rationality of business and political leaders of the capitalist countries to perceive the shift in the locus of ownership of the means of production from private hands to the Soviet state as a threat to their financial and geographical empires. Haunted by this threat, Western powers organized all kinds of attempts to cut the Soviet experiment short, which further reinforced in the Soviet leaders the idea that their experiment could survive only by ensuring blind obedience from their people and by getting other nations to join in the experiment through force or ruse.

In due time, the seeds of another global war, sown at Versailles, germinated and propagated. They were generously watered by *amour propre* and fertilized by the compost produced by decaying societies where poverty, ignorance, prejudice, and corruption fermented violence. Albert Einstein, who after World War I had joined Romain Rolland in signing a declaration of the independence of the spirit, after World War II called for a new way of thinking and doing politics, economics, and science. Einstein thought that a profound change in the way we see reality and act on it was essential for humankind's survival. His was an appeal to individual and collective reason.

Neither did this second call work. Reason was too heavily programmed into considering only rational figures, never listening to emotional calls. Reason could not develop wisdom either among Marxists or among capitalists because it was cut off from wisdom's main sources: nature, the body, and the spirit. Both sides lacked mythoclastic visionary leaders who would shake up the populations and awaken their sleepy reason. Hence, we continued behaving irrationally in the name of reason.[39]

Wisdom could have led to cooperation between free-market and centrally planned economies, seeking cross-fertilization and win-win solutions. Mutual fears and prejudices led instead to a buildup of the old conflict between Marxism and capitalism. The conflict concentrated around the two superpowers that emerged from World War II. It ended by damaging both economies and societies.

The United States ignored the advice of Dwight D. Eisenhower, the World War II hero, who, as president of the country, warned in 1953:

> Every gun that is made, every warship launched, every rocket fired, signifies in a final sense a theft from those who hunger and are not fed—those who are cold and not clothed. This world in arms is not spending money alone—it is spending the sweat of its laborers, the genius of its scientists, the hopes of its children.[40]

The United States overinvested in a giant military apparatus, neglecting to maintain and further develop its productive and social infrastructure, exhausting its treasury, and creating the largest public debt in history. All this, plus the increased greediness of the financial establishment and a strong belief in economies of scale among economists, engineers, and businesspeople, reduced opportunities for the emergence of new, small-scale, urban and rural businesses, which had previously provided the healthy tissue on which the American economy developed.

In the political and cultural arenas, for the United States the cold war meant a prolonged period of McCarthyism and a revival of the magic and myths of fundamentalisms. Governments increasingly shied away from intervening in the markets to assure a more equitable distribution of wealth, as had already been suggested by the father of the capitalist system.[41] Instead, the U.S. government increasingly encroached on aspects of private life that in a free-market democracy should be left to the citizens to decide in an unhindered dialogue with the spirit.

The Soviet Union, with its economy in shambles, slowly evolved from frustration and despair with post-Stalinist bureaucrats to hopes kindled by perestroika and glasnost. Finally, the Union of the Soviets broke, leaving its populations' consciousness still strongly influenced by the magic and myths of the pre-Marxist past and impregnated with the dogmatic, sleepy rationality of the Marxist period. The peoples of the former Soviet Union cannot clearly distinguish the positive and negative aspects of their previous Marxist forms of organization. Nor do they see clearly the lights and shadows of capitalism as it is practiced in the advanced industrialized countries of Europe and North America. Hence, they may end by adopting the worst of both systems instead of integrating the best of them in a new form of organization. In the economy, the crumbling of the centrally planned organization has created a vacuum that is being filled by a wild capitalism, which is unconcerned with human and ecological issues. Socially, the people are returning to the old fatalistic grip of nationalistic wars and religious fanaticisms.

Neither the United States nor the countries of the former Soviet Union will progress if they revive old divisive programs. They, and all other countries of the world, may instead benefit from reviving and updating the ideas of the brilliant group of American intellectuals who, at the end of the nineteenth century, helped Argentina accomplish its transformation. One of them, Horace Mann, said that "the common school is the greatest discovery ever made by man." The common school could speed up progress toward the new integrative, harmonizing structure of consciousness among large masses of population, ushering humankind into a new evolutionary leap.

The long decades of the cold war ended by freezing both the hand of the markets and the hand of the state, almost everywhere. They have both been deeply frostbitten, are becoming inoperative, and risk gangrenous decomposition. Only a new integrative, harmonizing consciousness can bring new warmth and restore the functions of both hands, healing the wounds and reestablishing a healthy, nonspeculative economic circulation adjusted to the carrying and cleansing capacity of every piece of land and the whole Earth. Unfortunately, most politicians, businesspeople, and households have not yet warmed up to these possibilities. Only a few leaders are attempting to meet, at least partially, the challenge. One of them is Vaclav Havel, the Czech leader, who is issuing a new invitation to the peoples of the world.

For Havel, "the salvation of this human world lies nowhere else than in the human heart, in the human power to reflect, in human meekness[42] and in human responsibility." And he adds: "Without a global revolution in the sphere of human consciousness, nothing will change for the better in the sphere of our being as humans."[43] Although I fully agree with the intention of Havel's call, and would subscribe to it without hesitation, I would never use the word revolution. Humankind went through too many revolutions that instead of producing a sustainable and pervasive change in society ended up proceeding as if in a circuit, back to very near the starting point. If humankind is to follow Havel's call, there will have to be an evolutionary leap rather than a revolution.

Epilogue

Hundreds of thousands of years ago, we emerged from the hordes of hominids to build human societies based first on magic, and later on myths. Subsequently, we started developing our rationality. The latter was instrumental in efforts to discover the earth, uncover some mathematical relationships between forces at play in the cosmos, cover them with beautiful scientific metaphors, compose music and poetry, invent different forms of art, and record in books and other media our thoughts, fantasies, and experiences. This was neither a linear nor a painless evolution. In the process, we destroyed cultures and their peoples; we scared and scarred the Earth; we killed, maimed, tortured, and enslaved fellow humans. We are now feeling increasingly dissatisfied with the world that our deficient rational structures of consciousness have created.

Gebser, and others after him, detected signals that a new evolutionary stage is in the making. Humankind is moving—again neither linearly, nor simultaneously in all places—beyond pure rationality to an integrative, harmonizing consciousness. The new structures may avoid the monsters engendered when an apparently rational programming of the mind actually puts reason to sleep. In this book, I have summarily pictured the most prominent monstrosities brought about by a drowsy rationality. I have also traced some of the signals of the new consciousness to their different sources: businesspeople; political, religious, and military leaders; educators; philosophers; and just common people—men and women who are slowly realizing that society makes life unnecessarily complicated and painful by manipulating our spiritually given nature.

The triangle of consciousness that I have designed makes it easy to capture the fact that we are simultaneously mind (the conscious), society (the subconscious), and nature (the unconscious enfolded in the cosmic consciousness). The emergence of this consciousness from the animal kingdom is part of one more experiment of that great experimenter, the cosmic consciousness. It is an audacious experiment, because by allowing us to shape our consciousness, at least partially, the cosmic consciousness gave us the right to be its partner in guiding the evolution of the planet Earth. Our decisions can make us either advance toward new horizons, or plunge back into the darkness and violence of evolutionary periods we thought were gone forever. Monsters unleashed by reason in its dreams may even wipe us out as a species.

When building our prevailing rational structures of consciousness, we devised enculturation processes that alienated our minds from our bodies and nature, betraying our ever-present spiritual origin. Instead of becoming rational masters of our own physical, mental, emotional, and spiritual health, we enculturated ourselves into accepting that it is society that should master our bodies, our minds, our emotions, and our communications with the spirit.

Society has denied the beauty of the body and vilified its love-and-life-giving functions. It is as if society knew that to estrange itself from the spirit, it had to control the body, which seldom betrays the spirit because most of its functions are unconsciously guided by the latter. As a result, our behavior is predominantly and irrationally guided by *amour-propre*–motivated desires for power control and wealth accumulation, rather than by the instinctive, natural motivations toward satisfying our biological, psychological, and sociocultural needs that *amour de soi* inspires. We have mastered many forces of nature, but few of the forces of love. We challenge death, but do not enjoy life as fully as the spirit intended us to do.

Humankind seems to be moving slowly beyond this unfinished rationality to a rationality that integrates and harmonizes ideas, feelings, and sensations. For a long time, we, as whole and hallowed mind/body units, have been separated from our parents, Mother Gaia and Father Sun, and from the holy spirit, which animates it all.

It seems we are now starting to come together again. This convergence is taking place at a much more highly developed level of integration and harmony than the archaic unity between creator and creatures of our origin. We are slowly learning to integrate and harmonize the satisfaction of instinctive biological needs, which spring from that archaic origin, and the satisfaction of psychological and cultural needs, which require us to be healthy individuals of healthy societies.

As we advance to integration and harmony, we are discovering that there is more than causality, matter, and energy in science; that there is more than rituals and dogmas in religion; that there is more than transactions in the markets; that there is more than management in enterprises; that there is more than relationship and economy in households; that there is more than transferring knowledge and social codes in education; that there is more than reacting to facts and figures in the making and application of laws; that there is more than training to kill in defense preparation; that there is more than drugs and procedures in healing. In all these domains there are also spiritual forces that animate life and reveal themselves as love. We are discovering that those forces are often chaotic, and that perhaps the purpose of the human experiment on Earth is to bring order out of the chaos by harmonizing social and natural needs. Furthermore, we are discovering that it is through love that we may accomplish the task—never through repression, neglect, or denial.

Once more advanced on our path to integration and harmony, we may design a Great Law of Peace, not just for a confederation of a few nations but for the whole Earth. We may even design not just a Great Law of Peace but a Great Law of Peace, Love, and Playfulness. Peace, Love, and Playfulness within each of us. Peace, Love, and Playfulness among humans. Peace, Love, and Playfulness with the Earth.

NOTES

Introduction

1. Quoted in Georg Feuerstein, *Structures of Consciousness: The Genius of Jean Gebser* (Lower Lake, California: Integral Publishing, 1987), p. 166.

Chapter 1

1. Robin Poynor, "Power concealed, power revealed," in *The Arts of Africa* (Daytona Beach, Florida: Museum of Arts and Sciences, 1986), p. 7.
2. Ibid.
3. J. E. Lovelock, *GAIA: A New Look at Life on Earth* (New York: Oxford University Press, 1979), p. 1.
4. I heard the words quoted here while sharing with Leloup a roundtable discussion at the III Brazilian and I Interamerican Holistic Congress, held in Canela (Rio Grande do Sul, Brazil) on September 15–19, 1992. Jean Yves Leloup was then the Director of the Institute pour la Rencontre et L'Etude des Civilizations (10 Faubourg du Rhin, Village Neuf 68128, France).
5. A Möbius strip is a long rectangular strip of paper bent in such a way that we can follow its contour from the inside to the outside and back without discontinuity. It suggests the idea of infinity within limits.
6. Because this is a book on the role of human consciousness in present life and future immediate changes, I prefer not to suggest precise dates in the evolution of the structures. I only want to give readers a sense of the span of time involved. I beg those who still believe the myth of a creation at a given date to recognize the myth as such, and, without abandoning the pleasure that it may bring to their lives, recognize that science, guided by the same spiritual forces as the myth, has advanced to the point of being able to date anthropological remains. I also ask them to understand that I may give to those creative forces a different name than the one they give to the Creator in their myth. Readers who would instead like to know more about the time frame of our ascent from the apes will find interesting discussions in the following works:

278

Richard Leakey, *The Making of Mankind* (London: Abacus, 1982).

Richard Leakey and Roger Lewin, *Origins Reconsidered* (New York: Anchor Books/Doubleday, 1992).

Ken Wilber, *Up From Eden* (Garden City, N.Y.: Anchor Press/Doubleday, 1981).

Georg Feuerstein, *Structures of Consciousness,* op. cit.

7. Readers can find more on Jean Gebser's studies of the structure of consciousness and its evolution in two books. One is his masterwork, *The Ever-Present Origin,* trans. Noel Barstad and Algis Mickunas (Athens, Ohio: Ohio University Press, 1985). The other is a synthesis of Gebser's ideas skillfully written by Georg Feuerstein, who overcame many of the difficulties of a heavy scholarly text: Georg Feuerstein, op. cit.

8. Poynor, op. cit., pp. 7–8.

9. Galbraith quotes Herodotus, for whom the invention of coined money is associated with the practice of prostitution in Asia Minor. Galbraith points out, however, that "there were much earlier experiences with coinage in the Indus Valley and China of which Herodotus was unaware." See John Kenneth Galbraith, *The Age of Uncertainty* (Boston: Houghton Mifflin Co., 1977), p. 163.

10. Although the newborn always starts developing from an archaic structure of consciousness, his or her gestation in the womb may not always be fully paradisiacal. We should remember that in the archaic stage we do not own our bodies, but we do feel. It has been shown that the fetus senses external energies and reacts differently when receiving positive peaceful loving and joyful vibrations than when such energies and vibrations are negative and violent. Toxic chemical materials that the mother's metabolism may produce, or that she may introduce through legal and illegal drugs and medical procedures like vaccinations, have an even stronger influence on the well-being of the fetus and the development of his or her biological terrain.

Chapter 2

1. Jean Jacques Rousseau, *Emile, or On Education,* introduction, translation and notes by Allan Bloom (New York: Basic Books, 1979), p. 484.

2. Ibid.

3. Matthew 22:40 in the New Testament, the Jerusalem Bible (Garden City, N.Y.: Doubleday & Co., 1966), p. 51. In the biblical context, *neighbor* sometimes means a companion, friend, associate, someone with whom a person has a specific relationship; at other times it is used in a much broader sense to mean a fellow being. The latter seems to be the meaning in Christ's command. See note 3c in the book of Proverbs of the Old Testament, op. cit., p. 937.

4. Luke 6:31 in the New Testament, op. cit., p. 102.

5. J. J. Rousseau, *Emile,* op. cit., p. 92.

6. Ibid., pp. 91–92.

7. The chronology of the different schools of thought mentioned in these paragraphs is as follows: Moses' leadership of the Jews in their exodus from Egypt could have happened about the thirteenth century B.C.E.; Confucius lived between 551 and 478 B.C.E.; it is known that verses from the Tao-te ching were transmitted orally during the sixth century B.C.E. and recorded in writing two centuries later; Heraclitus was born about 540 B.C.E. and died in 470 B.C.E.; Democritus's life spanned from 460 to 370 B.C.E., while Aristotle's went from 384 to 322 B.C.E. Islamic cultures began much later, after the seventh century C.E.

8. As quoted in Roger Garaudy, *Comment l'homme devint humain* (Paris: éditions j. a., 1979), p. 105. Translation by the author.

9. Teilhard de Chardin inspired me to use the expression *love-mastering* for identifying the trend in the history of civilization that aims at removing violence from nature and humankind. It is a trend that perceives love as the main shaping force in the relations among humans and between humans and nature. He said: "To dominate and canalize the powers of the air and the sea is all very well. But what is this triumph, compared with the world-wide mastery of human thought and love?" See Teilhard de Chardin, *Building the Earth* (Wilkes-Barre, Pa.: Dimension Books, 1965), p. 72.

10. The New Testament, op. cit., note 10 g, p. 169.

11. On the use of metaphors and parables by science, see Sir James Jeans, *Physics and Philosophy* (New York: Dover Publications, 1981).

12. See Bob Toben and Fred Alan Wolf, *Space, Time and Beyond* (New York: E. P. Dutton, Inc., 1982), pp. 50, 144.

13. I use the word *erotic* as a noun and as an adjective not in its connotation of being marked by, arousing, and satisfying sexual desire, but rather as derived from the myth of Eros, the Greek god of all forms of love, including agape, which denotes the love of God for humankind and by extension the unselfish love of one person for another without sexual implications. Erotic includes the amorous and the romantic as well as the carnal. For me, the erotic—the libido of the psychological language—includes all forms of human energy that, through a complex set of forces characterized by an intense somatic persistence and reserve of power, strive continuously to preserve and improve life.

14. John Maynard Keynes, "Newton, the Man," in *Essays in Biography* (New York: W. W. Norton & Co., 1963), p. 311.

15. Ibid., p. 313.

16. Albert Einstein, "The World As I See It," in *Einstein: A Centenary Volume,* ed. A. P. French (London: Heinemann Educational Books for the International Commission on Physics Education, 1979), p. 304.

17. G. J. Whitrow, "Einstein: The Man And His Achievements," in *Einstein: A Centenary Volume,* op. cit., p. 168.

18. Letter to Max Born of September 7, 1944, in *Einstein: A Centenary Volume,* op. cit., p. 275.

19. *The Book Of Angelus Silesius,* trans. and notes by Frederick Franck (Santa Fe, New Mexico: Bear & Co., 1985), p. 54. Angelus Silesius is the name adopted by Johannes Scheffler, a Silesian Lutheran physician, when he converted to Catholicism in 1653. As Franck notes, half a century after Johannes's death, the poetic work of the mystic was also reclaimed by Protestantism and became integrated in the shared heritage of Protestant and Catholic Europe.

20. As quoted in Matthew Fox, *The Coming of the Cosmic Christ,* (San Francisco: Harper & Row, 1988), p. 50.

21. Arthur I. Waskow, *Godwrestling* (New York: Schocken Books, 1978), pp. 50–51.

Chapter 3

1. C. A. Mallmann, "On the Satisfaction of Human Aspirations as the Development Objective," paper presented at the Symposium on Science, Technology and Human Values, cosponsored by the American Association for the Advancement of Science and the National Science and Technology Council of Mexico, Mexico City, July 2–3, 1973.

2. See Mario Kamenetzky, *Economia del Conocimiento y Empresa* (Buenos Aires: Paidos, 1976); Mario Kamenetzky, "The Economics of the Satisfaction of Needs," *Human Systems Management* (New York: North-Holland Publishing Co., 2, 1981), pp. 101–111; and Paul Ekins and Manfred Max Neef, eds., *Real-Life Economics* (London: Routledge, 1992), pp. 181–196.

3. Michel Tournier, *Vendredi, ou les limbes du Pacifique* (Paris: Gallimard, 1967).

4. Teilhard de Chardin, op. cit., p. 97.

5. A. R. Holmberg, *Nomads of the Long Bow: The Siriono of Eastern Bolivia* (New York: American Museum of Science Books, 1969).

6. There is a large amount of research on this issue. See among others the following books: Ashley Montagu, ed., *Culture and Human Development: Insights into Growing Human* (Englewood Cliffs, New Jersey: Prentice Hall Inc., 1974); Ashley Montagu, *Touching: The Human Significance of the Skin* (New York: Harper & Row, 1978); Paul Olsen, *The Future of Being Human* (New York: M. Evans and Company, Inc., 1975); and the seminal article by James W. Prescott, "Body Pleasure and the Origins of Violence," *The Bulletin of the Atomic Scientists,* Vol. XXXI, No. 9, (November 1975), pp. 10–20.

7. See on this subject the excellent analysis by Alfie Kohn, *No Contest: The*

Case Against Competition (Boston: Houghton Mifflin Co., 1986). He quotes Eisenhower who said that "the true mission of American sports is to prepare young people for war." (p. 145).

8. *The Chinese Barefoot Doctor's Manual*—the vogue in China just a few decades ago—stated that "if young people talk about love, marriage, and having children at too early an age, their energies will be dissipated, affecting their work and their study." As not only the recreational and relational aspects of sex were considered dangerous, but even reproduction was unwanted, the recommended behavioral pattern for young Chinese was to avoid all kinds of sexual activity until the age of 25! See *A Barefoot Doctor's Manual: The American translation of the official Chinese paramedical manual* (Philadelphia: Running Press, 1977), p. 173.

9. A quote from Mme de Rémusat's Memoirs (1880) in Will and Ariel Durant, *The Age of Napoleon* in *The Story of Civilization* (New York: MJF Books, 1975), XI, p. 203. Claire de Vergennes, Comtesse de Rémusat (1780–1821) and her husband were for a long time favorites of Napoleon. Claire became the lady-in-waiting to Josephine de Beauharnaise, Napoleon's first wife.

10. As quoted from Godwin's *Enquiry Concerning Political Justice* (1842) in Will and Ariel Durant, op.cit., XI, p. 361.

11. Ibid. p. 399.

Chapter 4

1. The command about our relation with the divinity uses the word *God* because in most Western societies the creative spirit is seen as a a unique supreme being. However, the command would read the same for cultures that believe in a society of gods. For atheists it reads instead: Science is what makes us powerful. She is our ally and will lead us to get power and wealth. If we become rich and powerful, it is because we know how to use her. If not, we are simpletons whose fate is to always be below the intelligent.

2. Adam Smith, *The Wealth of Nations,* 1776 (Chicago: The University of Chicago Press, 1976), II, p. 318.

3. J. J. Rousseau, *Emile,* op. cit., p. 46.

4. Roger Chartier, ed., Arthur Goldhammer, trans., "Passions of the Renaissance" in Philippe Ariès and George Duby, gen. eds., *A History of Private Life* (Cambridge, Mass.: Harvard University Press, 1989), III, p. 184.

5. Sources of the quotations included in this table are as follows:
    1 Samuel, the Old Testament, in the Jerusalem Bible (Garden City, N.Y., Doubleday & Co., 1966), pp. 361–362.
    Ecclesiasticus, ibid, p. 1076.
    The Koran, trans. N. J. Dagwood (London: Penguin Books, 1990), p. 236.

All others are from George Seldes, *The Great Quotations* (Secaucus, New Jersey: Castle Books, 1977). This book is arranged alphabetically by author and indexed by subject.

6. 1 John 2:15, in the New Testament, the Jerusalem Bible, op. cit., p. 413.

7. 1 John 4:7, in the New Testament, the Jerusalem Bible, op. cit., p. 416.

8. As quoted in Roger Garaudy, op. cit., p. 244. Translation from French by the author.

9. See St. Francis of Assisi, "The Canticle of Brother Sun," in David Herlihy, ed., *Medieval Culture and Society* (New York: Harper & Row, 1968), p. 304.

10. B. Z. Goldberg, *The Sacred Fire* (Secaucus, New Jersey: The Citadel Press, 1974), p. 257. See also the story of perfect happiness as taken from St. Francis's "Little Flowers" in Herlihy, op. cit., pp. 302–304.

11. The sources of the quotations for this table are as follows:

   Confucius, as quoted in Tama Starr, *The "Natural Inferiority" of Women* (New York: Poseidon Press, 1991), p. 123.

   Aristotle, *The Politics,* trans. T. A. Sinclair (London: Penguin Books, 1992), p. 92.

   Ecclesiasticus, in the Old Testament, the Jerusalem Bible, op. cit., p. 1070.

   The Koran, op. cit., p. 33.

   Macchiavelli, *The Prince,* trans. George Bull (London: Penguin Books, 1981), p. 133.

   All others are from George Seldes, op. cit.

12. World Bank,*World Development Report* 1993: *Investing In Health* (New York: Oxford University Press, 1993), p. 50.

13. It is interesting to elaborate on the etymology of two words that are used in Spanish cultures to denote these displays of gaiety and affection, which indeed always connote sexual seduction, or at least its possibility. One word is *piropo.* It comes from the Greek word *pyrôpos,* which describes a variety of garnet of an intense red color. Its use in Spanish for flattering gallantries suggests that the receivers of these gallantries often blush at hearing them. I suggest that while in the past *piropo* meant only men saying things and women blushing, it should now include actions by women that make men blush. The other word, which is used more in Spain than in Latin America, is *requiebro,* which means words that will break a man's or a woman's resistance to be seduced.

14. Erwin J. Haeberle, *The Sex Atlas* (New York: Seabury Press, 1978), p. 159.

15. However, many fathers, in a typical hypocritical double standard, often favor, or even push, their sons to have sexual experiences with prostitutes as soon as they reach puberty.

16. J. J. Rousseau, *Emile,* op. cit., p. 216.

17. On consensual crimes and their cost to society see the well-documented and amusing work by Peter McWilliams, *Ain't Nobody's Business If You*

Do: The Absurdity of Consensual Crimes in a Free Society (Los Angeles: Prelude Press, 1993). McWilliams calculates that in 1993 the United States economy spent $50 billion in punishing people for "crimes" that do not physically harm the person or property of another, and lost an additional $150 billion in tax revenue by resisting to bring "the underground economy of consensual activities [an economy made up of those harmless activities that are not being accepted by the law, being hence considered criminal] aboveground." op. cit., p. 183. Explanation in brackets is mine.

Chapter 5

1. Adam Smith, *The Theory of Moral Sentiments,* D. D. Raphael and A. L. Macfie, eds. (Indianapolis, Ind.: Liberty Press, 1982), p. 185.
2. I am making free use of a sentence commonly attributed to Lenin.
3. Adam Smith, *The Theory of Moral Sentiments,* op. cit., p. 141.
4. Ibid, p. 166.
5. Ibid, p. 166.
6. Ibid, p. 274.
7. We must forgive the old cultural philosopher for referring to *man* rather than *humankind,* and for uniting the creative spirit only with its rational creatures. We should remember that this was written in the second half of the eighteenth century. Two centuries later, the United States of America, the largest and most powerful capitalist country, has yet to approve equal rights for its female population.
8. John Kenneth Galbraith, op. cit., pp. 26–29.
9. Adam Smith, *The Wealth of Nations,* op. cit., II, p. 302.
10. Ibid.
11. Ibid., I, pp. 74–75.
12. Karl Marx and Friedrich Engels, "The German Ideology," as quoted in Lewis S. Feuer, ed., *Marx and Engels: Basic Writings on Politics and Philosophy* (New York: Anchor Books, 1959), p. 254.
13. In 1935 the government of the Soviet Union realized that the system was making workers indifferent to the quality and quantity of product output, so it developed a method to reward those who surpassed production quotas. The method was named after Aleksei Grigorevich Stakhanov, a coal miner whose productivity was the focus of a propaganda campaign.
14. As quoted in Will and Ariel Durant, op. cit., XI, p. 399.
15. Ibid., p. 7.
16. There were many more than the few intellectuals whom I name here. These few are those whose written work is familiar to me.
17. As quoted by George Seldes, op. cit., p. 448.
18. Ibid, p. 399.

19. I am referring here to weapons and services provided to military or paramilitary armies, not to guns sold to individuals in the marketplace. An evolution to an integrative, harmonizing consciousness may start by banishing the latter, and hopefully end with both the open trade between private citizens and retailers and the wholesale trade among governments, military-industrial complexes, and paramilitary groups.

20. As quoted in John Kenneth Galbraith, op. cit., p. 227.

21. Ibid.

22. The Bureau of the Public Debt, *Historical Public Debt Oustanding* (Internet: http://www.publicdebt.treas.gov/opd/opdhisto.htm, May 2, 1977).

23. See the section entitled "Smith's Plea for the Poor" in this chapter.

24. Robert L. Heilbroner and James K. Galbraith, *The Economic Problem,* rev. 8th ed. (Englewood Cliffs, New Jersey: Prentice-Hall, 1975), p. 95.

25. The Bureau of Public Debt, op. cit.

26. University of Virginia, Social Sciences Data Center, *National Income and Products Account* (Internet: http://www.lib.virginia.edu/ssdcbin/nipabin/nipa.cgi, May 2, 1997).

27. The Bureau of Public Debt, op. cit.

28. Economic Policy Institute, *Family Income Data Series* (Internet: http://epinet.org/fids02.html, May 2, 1997).

29. The Feminist Majority Foundation and New Media Publishing, *Individuals Are Paying a Larger Percentage of Federal Revenues—Corporations Are Paying Less* (Internet: http://www.feminist.org/other/budget/who pays.html, May 1, 1997).

30. The destructive effects were felt mainly in the United States, where homeopathy was flourishing by the beginning of this century, having established well-known hospitals and organized prestigious laboratories that supplied homeopathic medicines within and outside the country. Medical fundamentalism was less damaging to the European homeopathic and herbal establishments, which regained strength after World War II and are still growing.

31. Arms Control and Disarmament Agency, *Military Burden and Other Relative Indicators* (Internet: http://www.acda.gov/wmeat95/95milex.htm, May 2, 1997).

32. Heilbroner and Galbraith, op. cit., p. 101.

33. Arms Control and Disarmament Agency, op. cit.

34. Ibid.

35. Arms Control and Disarmament Agency, *Arms Export Trends* (Internet: http://www.acda.gov/wmeat95/95armexp.htm).

36. The World Bank, *World Development Report 1997: The State in a Changing World* (New York: Oxford University Press, 1997) pp. 214, 240. An international dollar is a unit of account that has the same purchasing power

over total GNP as does the U.S. dollar in a given year. It is calculated by converting GNP to U.S. dollars using purchasing power parities (PPP) instead of exchange rates as conversion factors. As the World Bank says in this report (p. 251), the international monetary unit takes into account the fact that "prices of goods and services not traded on international markets tend to vary substantially from one country to another, leading to large differences in the relative purchasing power of currencies and thus in welfare as measured by GNP per capita." The source of PPP data is the International Comparison Programme coordinated by the UN Statistical Division.

37. Adam Smith, *The Wealth of Nations,* op. cit., II, p. 455.
38. Ibid., pp. 462–463.
39. Lester Brown, "The Future of Growth," in Lester Brown et al., *State of the World* (New York: W. W. Norton, 1998), pp. 3–4.
40. "World Bank Offers New Yardstick to Measure Development," *World Bank News,* XVI, no. 13 (April 3, 1997), p. 3.
41. Thomas Robert Malthus, "Essay on the Principle of Population," 2nd ed., 1803, p. 571, as quoted in John Maynard Keynes, *Essays In Biography,* op. cit., p. 106.
42. *Population Reports,* Series L, no. 9 (Baltimore: The Johns Hopkins School of Hygiene and Public Health, June 1993), p. 1.
43. "The World Bank Responds To AIDS," *World Bank News,* XIII, no. 45 (December 1, 1994), p. 1.
44. Ibid.
45. Ibid., p. 2.
46. Ibid., p. 4.
47. Joel Kurtzman, *The Death of Money* (Boston: Little, Brown and Company, 1993), pp. 206–207.
48. The concept of economies of scale was a typical product of a rational consciousness that separated the mathematics of economics from the reality of daily life, rationalizing economic magic and mythology. Engineers and economists believed that if cheaper products were produced, more and more people would have access to them. To some extent, this did happen. However, as with the magic of painting a deer on the wall of a cave to facilitate its hunt, economies of scale often failed to reach the objective of expanding markets. They generated unemployment and chased smaller entrepreneurs out of the markets, thereby reducing the number of people with the capacity to buy the products that the large installations were producing. Often, giant installations crushed hopes of their designers. The purposes of lower costs and higher profits were often defeated by a combination of circumstances, among them the need to pay higher wages to more skilled personnel, the frequent shutdowns of equipment of increased complexity, the proneness to accidents,

the financial burden of larger investments, the requirement that the plants be located in costly urban environments to assure the high quality of ancillary services and technical labor they demanded.

49. All quotes are taken from Kurtzman, op. cit., pp. 209–214.
50. Ibid., p. 12.
51. Ibid., pp. 39–40.

Chapter 6

1. As reprinted in the *Daytona Beach News-Journal* (July 6, 1992), p. 1A. The next day, the same newspaper reported that 9000 police officers from all sixteen German states had turned the city center of Munich into an armed camp.
2. American Indians knew that drinking tea from the bark and leaves of the arbor vitae (*Thuja occidentalis*) prevented a winter disease marked by swollen and bleeding gums, red spots on the skin, and prostration. Now we call this disease scurvy and know it is due to a diet lacking vitamin C. *Thuja* is a good natural source of vitamin C.
3. See chapter 5, p. 80.
4. See "A Steel Mill Project" in Mario Kamenetzky, Robert Maybury, and Charles Weiss, Jr., *Choice and Management of Technology in Developing Countries* (Washington, D.C.: The World Bank, Projects Policy Department, 1986), II, p. 131.
5. I must recognize that by the time I was gathering those experiences, the World Bank, the United Nations Development Program, the United States Agency for International Development, and other bilateral aid agencies were making the first efforts to develop aid programs for providing financial assistance to small-scale entrepreneurs in developing countries. The knowledge and perseverance that some staff members of these institutions applied to this purpose should be praised. They often had to fight against the narrow vision of their own bosses, whose consciousness was heavily enculturated into listening only to the tunes of fundamentalist economics sung by academia.
6. Speech at a conference on development held at Columbia University, as quoted in John L. Maddux, *The Development Philosophy of Robert S. McNamara* (Washington, D.C.: The World Bank, 1981), p. 13.
7. Ibid., p. 15.
8. Ibid., p. 16.
9. Ibid., p. 17.
10. We will see more about this struggle among businesspeople in chapter 11.
11. Deborah Shapley, *Promise and Power: The Life and Times of Robert McNamara* (Boston: Little, Brown and Company, 1993), p. 539.
12. See chapter 11.
13. Maddux, op. cit., p. 30.

14. The five most affluent countries of the North and their respective GNP per capita in 1995, were Luxembourg ($41,210), Switzerland ($40,630), Japan ($39,640), Norway ($31,250), and Denmark ($29,890). The five poorest countries of the South and their respective GNP per capita in that same year were Mozambique ($80), Ethiopia ($100), Zaire ($120), Tanzania ($120), and Burundi ($160). Data taken from *World Bank News,* XVI, no. 13 (April 3, 1997), p. 3. *The World Bank News* can be read on the Internet at http://www.worldbank.org/html/extctr/extcs/news.html.

15. Ibid.

16. This information has been gathered from an article by the Associated Press correspondent Clare Nullis that comments on a report by the International Labor Organization. Clare Nullis, "Millions of Kids Labor Worldwide," in the *Daytona Beach News-Journal* (June 2, 1992), p. 14 A.

17. Julius Nyerere, in an interview with the editor of *Third World Quarterly,* as quoted in *World Development Forum,* a publication of the Hunger Project, 4, no. 8 (April 30, 1986).

18. See the case of Argentina in chapter 12.

19. Mohsin S. Khan and Nadeem Ul Haque, "Capital Flight from Developing Countries," *Finance and Development,* (March 1987), p. 2. The percentages given are those obtained when the cumulated capital flight is calculated as total private capital flows minus private capital flows calculated on basis of reported interest income.

20. Calculated from tables 1, 11, and 20 of World Bank, *World Development Report 1991: The Challenge of Development* (New York: Oxford University Press, 1991), pp. 204, 224, 242.

21. Claude Julien, "Le Prix Des Armes," *Le Monde Diplomatique,* no. 412 (July 1988), p. 5.

22. World Bank, *World Development Report 1985: International Capital and Economic Development* (New York: Oxford University Press, 1985), p. 66.

23. Hector Gary, "Nervous Money Keeps on Fleeing," *Fortune* (December 23, 1985), p. 103.

24. World Bank, *World Development Report 1988: Financial Systems and Development* (New York: Oxford University Press, 1988), pp. 106–107.

25. Ibid. (See also chapter 5, "Cutting Military Expenses.")

26. Ibid.

27. World Bank, *World Development Report 1991,* op. cit., pp. 140–143.

28. Ibid., p. 142.

Chapter 7

1. George Seldes, op. cit., p. 125.

2. Henry Ford provides a good example of a divisive and divided rationality. On one hand, Ford lucidly applied reason to product development and business organization. This lucid rationality is also reflected in some

of his social criticisms. On the other hand, he let mythical prejudices put reason to sleep when he became virulently anti-Semitic.

3. George Seldes, op. cit., p. 253.
4. From *Leonardo da Vinci's Notebooks,* arranged, rendered into English, and introduced by Edward MacCurdy, New York, 1938, two vols. as quoted in Will and Ariel Durant, op. cit., V, p. 216.
5. See chapter 3.
6. I am paraphrasing here a song of the popular Spanish songwriter and singer Joan Manuel Serrat: "De vez en cuando la vida" (Once in a while life) in the album "Cada loco con su tema" (Each crazy has a particular theme), edited and distributed by Ariola-Eurodisc, 1983.
7. Homosexual partnerships could also include children either by adoption or by engendering them with outside mates. In some cases they are children from previous heterosexual partnerships. I know of two households, one lesbian, the other gay, where two children, a girl and a boy, have been parented by artificially fertilizing one of the lesbian women with semen from one of the gay men. The two children are growing well and have found loving support and care from four parents and their respective grandparents.
8. Experiments in community building are described in the following books:
     Corinne Mc Laughlin and Gordon Davidson, *Builders of the Dawn: Community Lifestyles in a Changing World* (Walpole, N.H.: Stillpoint Publishing, 1985).
     Cris and Oliver Popenoe, *Seeds of Tomorrow: New Age Communities That Work* (San Francisco: Harper & Row, 1984).
9. Robert Salmon, *Tous Les Chemins Mènent à l'Homme* (Paris: InterEditions, 1994), pp. 150–156.
10. Ibid., p. 154. Translation from French by the author.
11. Ibid., p. 156. Free translation by the author.
12. See in chapter 8, a discussion about the meanings of these different kinds of time.
13. I am freely using the beautiful words by Agnes de Mille, the famous choreographer and dancer, as they are quoted in *The Sun* (August 1992), no. 200, p. 40. He says that we need to "reach beyond the faces across our tables, learn to investigate the wilderness in the seat next to us, and explore the constellations locked up in our skulls." I would add that bright constellations are locked up not only in our skulls but also beneath the whole of our skin.
14. I am freely using concepts expressed by John Stuart Mill in his essay *On Liberty* (London: Penguin Classics, 1985), p. 72.
15. François René, Vicomte de Chateaubriand (1768–1848), a French writer and statesman, is considered one of the masters of the Romantic

movement that prevailed in art, literature, music, and philosophy from the end of the eighteenth century to almost the end of the nineteenth century. We may trace its beginnigs to the return-to-nature philosophy of Jean Jacques Rousseau (1712–1778). Other exponents of romantic literature are Samuel Richardson (1689–1761) in England, Johann Wolfgang von Goethe (1749–1832) in Germany, Victor Marie, Viscount Hugo (1802–1885) in France, and Nathaniel Hawthorne (1804–1864) in the United States, to name just a few.

16. René de Chateaubriand, *Atala and René,* trans. Irving Putter, (Berkeley, California: University of California Press, 1980), p. 97.

17. Ibid., p. 109.

18. Jean Jacques Rousseau, *Eloisa,* trans. William Kenrick, 1803 (Oxford: Woodstock Books, 1989), I, letter IV, p. 57.

19. Ibid., letter XXIX, p. 153.

Chapter 8

1. With this title, Tibor Scitovsky has written a book inquiring into human satisfaction and consumer dissatisfaction. He says that "we get and pay for more comfort than it is necessary for the good life, and some of our comforts crowd out some of the enjoyments of life." Tibor Scitovsky, *The Joyless Economy* (New York: Oxford University Press, 1977), p. 284.

2. Erasmus, *In Praise of Folly,* 1515 (New York: Penguin Books, 1982), pp. 73–74.

3. The English language distinguishes labor, with its connotations of hard, fatiguing, dispiriting toil and drudgery, from work that connotes exertion of body and mind in performing or accomplishing something. Academic Spanish provides only one word, *trabajo,* for both situations. However, a vernacular Spanish from Buenos Aires, the *lunfardo,* has borrowed from English and coined a word for toil and drudgery: *laburo.*

4. Jean Gebser, op. cit., p. 537.

5. Some economists may argue that the moment we take something from nature by fishing, and even more so when we consume the catch, a cost is incurred. In theory I agree, but in a practice guided by a new consciousness, it still is a gratuitous activity, as long as the elements taken out of nature do not overpower nature's regenerative capacity. For instance, when rural people cut wood for their own cooking and heating without destroying the surrounding forests they are exercising a gratuitous activity—an activity that in certain places, like Finland, has been regulated so that people may not chop their own forests beyond that equilibrium point. However, when the population grows beyond the carrying capacity of the land, as in some regions of Africa, destruction of the forests is inevitable. A harmonizing consciousness would avoid reaching this point by promoting family planning.

290

6. Robert L. Heilbroner and James K. Galbraith, op. cit., p. 124.
7. Ibid, p. 125.
8. Peter Russell, *The White Hole in Time: Our Future Evolution and the Meaning of Now* (San Francisco: HarperSanFrancisco, 1992), p. 170.
9. See especially the following publications by Herman Daly:
   Beyond Growth: The Economics of Sustainable Development (Boston: Beacon Press, 1996).
   Steady-State Economics (Washington, D.C.: Island Press, 1991) with John Cobb, *For the Common Good* (Boston: Beacon Press, 1989).
   Economics, Ecology, Ethics (San Francisco: W. H. Freeman Co., 1980).
10. For all practical purposes in an economic analysis, the Earth may be considered a closed system, although the planet, which exchanged matter with other parts of the universe during its formation, not only receives energy from the sun, but radiates energy back to the universe. Moreover, life on Earth is not independent of the gravitational fields, planetary and galactic movements, and other cosmic forces.
11. From here on I will use the word *artifacts* in the sense in which Daly uses it—that is, to represent all the productive equipment, durable and nondurable consumer goods, and installations of the society's infrastructure that can be inventoried at a particular point in time in a given economy.
12. The Iroquois recommended that their people keep in mind seven generations when making social and economic decisions. In the case of fossil fuels, a horizon of seven generations is not enough. It took nature millions of years to build the stocks. Moreover, the geological conditions that originated them may never again be reproduced. Fossil fuels are irreversibly destroyed when they are used to produce energy. Minerals can instead be recycled to some extent. Some products that result from industrial processes in which fossil fuels are used as sources of matter can also be partially recycled.
13. About the flight of capital from developing countries, see chapter 6, p. 114. About the global financial flows, see chapter 5, pp. 97–101.
14. It is beyond the scope of this book to include a description of the environmental problems generated by economic activities that ignore the limits within which an economy can make use of nature's resources and services. There is already a vast literature on the subject. Of particular interest for the reader may be the yearly updates on *The State of the World* published by the Worldwatch Institute, Washington, D.C.
15. See chapter 5, p. xxx.
16. Data for Sri Lanka (1970) and United States (1980) from World Bank, *World Development Report 1985*, op. cit., pp. 228–229. Data for Sri Lanka (1986) and United States (1985) from World Bank, *World Development Report 1993*, op. cit., pp. 296–297.

17. See chapter 7, pp. 124–125.
18. See chapter 5, p. 80.
19. Khalil Gibran, *Obras Completas* (Barcelona: Ediciones Teorema, 1982), II, pp. 363–365. Translation from Spanish by the author.
20. Joel de Rosnay, "Modernes Activités, Emplois Nouveaux: ce que va changer la révolution informationnelle," *Le Monde Diplomatique* (August 1996), p. 19. Translation by the author.
21. Ted McIlvenna and Laird Sutton, *Meditations on the Gift of Sexuality* (San Francisco: Specific Press, 1977), p. 13.
22. Mircea Eliade, *Images and Symbols* (New York: Sheed & Ward, 1969), p. 14, as quoted in Matthew Fox, op. cit., p. 173.
23. Dorothee Soelle, *To Work and to Love: A Theology of Creation* (Philadelphia: Fortress Press, 1984), pp. 139, as quoted in Matthew Fox, op. cit., p. 173.
24. George Seldes, op. cit., p. 231.
25. Guy Breton, *Histoires d'Amour de l'Histoire de France* (Paris: Presses Pocket, 1965), I, p. 5. Free translation by the author.
26. Hazel Henderson, *Paradigms in Progress: Life Beyond Economics* (Indianapolis, Ind.: Knowledge Systems, 1991). In this book, Hazel Henderson extensively discusses the limitations of the old purely material indicators and the different proposals to improve them with newer indicators of the satisfaction of human needs and the enjoyment of life.
27. The figures, except for the sales of do-it-yourself home-repair kits, are taken from the summary of a presentation by B. Stokes to the Society for International Development Conference Panel on alternative ways of life in industrialized societies. The conference took place in Baltimore, Maryland, in 1982. The figures for the do-it-yourself home-repair kits are from the 1986 report of the Building Supply Home Centers.
28. See how this can be done in the books that follow, among others, which have been written to make it easier for parents to know the constitutional types of their children and to deal better with their illnesses:
   Paul Herscu, *The Homeopathic Treatment of Children: Pediatric Constitutional Types* (Berkeley, California: North Atlantic Books, 1991).
   Andrew Lockie, *The Family Guide to Homeopathy* (New York: Simon & Schuster, 1989).
29. Robert Salmon, op. cit., p. 241. Free translation by the author.
30. Free translation from French of the title of chapter 18 in Salmon, op. cit., p. 247. See more about these changes in the mind-set of entrepreneurs in chapter 11 of this book.
31. See Hazel Henderson, op. cit., pp. 22–44.

NOTES

Chapter 9

1. The list has been taken from Paula Underwood, *The Great Tree of Peace: Iroquois Contributions to the U.S. Constitution, 1987*. It is part of the Living Legacy Program of the National Commission on the Bicentennial of the United States Constitution. Available from The Learning Way Center, P.O. Box 216, San Haselmo, CA, 94979. Tel.: 1-800-995-3320. Readers can find more about the Iroquois society and its influence on the United States Constitution in the following books, among others:

   Jack Weatherford, *Indian Givers* (New York: Crown Publishers, 1988).

   Congressional Resolution 76, *Iroquois Contributions to the U.S. Constitution, 1987*.

   Lewis Henry Morgan, *League of the Iroquois* (New York: Carol Publishing Group, 1993).

   Frederick Engels, *The Origin of the Family, Private Property, and the State 1884* (New York: Pathfinder Press, 1979).

2. On the exile of the spirit from the rational mind, see chapter 1, pp. 25–27.

3. I quote here freely from delightful conversations I had with Paula Underwood, an American educator of Oneida descent. She undertook the task of organizing in written form the tradition that Iroquois scions receive orally from their parents. The result is a book: *The Walking People: A Native American Oral History* (San Anselmo, California: A Tribe of Two Press, 1993). Paula, whose native name is Turtle Woman Singing, taught me more about the Iroquois, and in a more pleasant way, than a large collection of scholarly books could do.

4. Leon Felipe, *Antologia Rota* (Buenos Aires: Losada, 1984), p. 170.

5. I will suggest only two organizations; many more may come to the reader's mind. Those whose information might be trusted are Amnesty International and the International Association of Students in Economics and Management (AIESEC). They may not be ideal, in the sense that they may not be working fully yet under the new consciousness, but they represent forces of transformation. Amnesty keeps a watchful eye on human rights violations and has saved many lives from the clutches of vicious tyrants. According to information posted in the World Wide Web (http://www.amnesty.org), Amnesty has around one million members in 162 countries as of 1993. AIESEC is a student-managed association that operates in more than 750 academic institutions in some 85 countries. Through multicultural meetings, leadership workshops, and exchange programs, it attempts to develop students who are globally minded and responsible members of society and who think about, and act on, issues beyond the technical and financial rationality of business and economics. This institution could also help in organizing the youth

293

council proposed in the section of this chapter devoted to democratizing and rejuvenating the United Nations.

6. See previous note.
7. I am again using words by Agnes de Mille quoted in note 13 of chapter 7. I am also making a distinction between leaders and managers—a distinction that appears also in other sections of this book. In this, I follow Perry Pascarella and Mark Frohman, who say that leaders light fires while managers fight fires. I feel that we should further qualify as leaders only those who light fires that illuminate new avenues of thought and behavior, never fueling fires that end by burning people and land. These are just managers—and bad managers, for that matter. The words by Pascarella and Frohman are from Robert Salmon, op. cit., p. 261.
8. This statement is traditionally attributed to Albert Einstein.
9. See note 7 above.
10. See Alan F. Kay and Hazel Henderson, United Nations Security Insurance Agency, Participant Paper 2A, UNDP Stockholm Roundtable on "Change: Social Conflict or Harmony?", July 22–24, 1994.
11. Daniel M. Smith, "The United Nations Security Insurance Agency (UNSIA) Proposal: A Preliminary Assessment" in *The United Nations: Policy and Financing Alternatives,* eds. Harlan Cleveland, Hazel Henderson, and Inge Kaul (Washington, D.C.: The Global Commission to Fund the United Nations, 1996), pp. 209–213.
12. For more details on the UNSIA proposal, see Hazel Henderson, *Building a Win-Win World: Life Beyond Global Economic Warfare* (San Francisco: Berret-Koehler Publishers, 1996), pp. 322–324.
13. *The United Nations: Policy and Financing Alternatives,* op. cit.
14. See note 5 above.
15. See "The Requiem of Unfulfilled Dreams" in chapter 6.
16. The World Bank, *World Development Report 1992: Development and the Environment* (New York: Oxford University Press, 1992), p. 4.
17. See chapter 5, Figure 10, and chapter 8, Figure 13.
18. Hazel Henderson, *Paradigms in Progress: Life Beyond Economics* (Indianapolis, Ind.: Knowledge Systems, 1991).
19. Robert Salmon, op. cit., p. 148.
20. Ibid., p. 149.
21. Data from the World Bank, *World Development Report 1993,* op. cit., pp. 240–241 and 288–289.
22. Following on my iceberg metaphor, I should perhaps call them deep-water organizations.

Chapter 10
1. Merril D. Peterson, ed., *The Portable Thomas Jefferson* (New York: Viking Penguin Inc., 1987), pp. 399–400.

2. World Bank, *World Development Report 1991,* op. cit., p. 43.

3. Ibid., pp. 55–56.

4. Ibid., p. 52.

5. George Seldes, op. cit., p. 656.

6. Ibid., p. 412.

7. Ibid., p. 611.

8. Ibid., p. 320.

9. *From the Fires of Revolution to the Great War,* ed. Michelle Perrot, trans. Arthur Goldhammer, in Philippe Ariès and George Duby, gen. eds., *A History of Private Life* (Cambridge, Massachusetts: Harvard University Press, 1990), IV, pp. 196–219.

10. For the distinction between leaders and managers, see chapter 9, pp. 176 and 177, and endnote 7.

11. See Arthur Waskow's reflection on the meaning of sacred texts in chapter 2, pp. 41–42.

12. Adam Smith, *The Wealth of Nations,* op. cit., II, p. 309.

13. Ibid., pp. 292–293.

14. Ibid., p. 319.

15. Ibid., p. 306.

16. See chapter 9, p. 173.

17. George Seldes, op. cit., p. 92.

18. Guy Breton, op. cit., p. 5.

19. Quoted in J. K. Galbraith, op. cit., p. 204.

20. The World Bank estimates that 85 million to 114 million women in the world have experienced genital mutilation. Clitoridectomy, the removal of the clitoris, accounts for 80 to 85 percent of the cases worldwide. Infibulation, which involves in addition the removal of tissue from the labia and the stitching together of the vulva, leaving a small opening for the passage of urine and menstrual blood, accounts for the remaining cases. The consequences of both procedures can include hemorrhage, tetanus, infection, urine retention, and shock. Infibulation carries the added risk of long-term complications because of the repeated cutting and stitching at marriage and with each childbirth. See World Bank, *World Development Report 1993,* op. cit., p. 50.

21. See chapter 4.

22. Ariès and Duby, op. cit., IV, p. 211.

23. In 1918, a student movement to reform college education in Argentina promoted the participation of students in the governing bodies of the universities and the right to establish parallel, "free" chairs when tenured professors did not update the information related to their subjects or when they presented them in a biased way. The idea was that personalities external to the college could bring refreshing or broader views and better information, and that students should have the right to

choose between the tenured and the free-chair teachers. Some of the proposals were implemented for short periods during democratic governments. Indeed, they were rejected by the different military dictatorships that Argentina suffered between 1930 and 1983.

24. See chapter 7, pp. 125–126.
25. About the Sarvodaya movement, see chapter 11.
26. George Seldes, op. cit., p. 205.
27. J. Krishnamurti, *Education and the Significance of Life* (San Francisco: Harper and Row, 1981), p. 11.
28. Ibid., p. 17.
29. I am using again the beautiful words by Agnes de Mille, already quoted in chapter 7, note 13.
30. Frederick Franck, *A Little Compendium on That Which Matters* (Arlington, Virginia: Great Ocean Publishers, 1989), p. 7.
31. Once more I refer the reader to Arthur Waskow's reflections. See note 11 above.
32. Pancakes made of grated potatoes that Jews cook traditionally for Hanukkah.
33. See, for instance, Idries Shah's *Tales of the Dervishes: Teaching Stories of the Sufi Masters over the Past Thousand Years* (London: The Octagon Press, 1982).
34. *The Mahabharata,* directed by Peter Brooks (1989), 3 videocassettes (328 minutes).
35. See Piyasena Dissanayake, *Political Thoughts of the Buddha* (Colombo, Sri Lanka: Ratnakara Press, 1977), and Padmasiri de Silva, *Buddhist and Freudian Psychology* (Colombo, Sri Lanka: Lake House Printers & Publishers, 1978).
36. Paula Underwood, *Who Speaks for Wolf: A Native American Learning Story* (San Anselmo, California: A Tribe of Two Press, 1991).
37. Miguel Chase-Sardi, *Pequeño Decameron Nivacle* (Asunción, Paraguay: Ediciones Napa, 1981).
38. Martin Scorsese's film, based on a screenplay by Paul Schrader which in turn is loosely based on the novel of the same title by the Greek author Nikos Kazantzakis.
39. See chapter 12.
40. Sigmund Freud, *Civilization and Its Discontents,* trans. and ed. James Strachey (New York: W. W. Norton & Co., 1961), p. 44.
41. See the sense in which I use the words *erotic* and *libido* in endnote 13 of chapter 2.
42. Havelock Ellis in *The Dance of Life,* as quoted in George Seldes, op. cit., p. 231.
43. Pierre Teilhard de Chardin, op. cit., p. 88.

44. Ibid., pp. 44, 49, and 75.
45. Freud, op. cit., p. 81, note 1.
46. Erwin J. Haeberle, *The Sex Atlas* (New York: The Seabury Press, 1978), pp. 159–160.
47. Teilhard de Chardin, op. cit., p. 72.

Chapter 11

1. See the example of a decision made by Winston Churchill in 1925 as Chancellor of the Exchequer in chapter 10, p. XXX.
2. John Maynard Keynes, "My Early Beliefs," in *Two Memoirs* (London: Rupert-Hart Davis, 1949), p. 83.
3. The link of business with constant activity is also reflected in the Spanish language: *negocio* comes from Latin and means the denial of idleness, the opposite of leisure.
4. A full report on this meeting can be seen in Mario and Sofia Kamenetzky, "Are Businesses Changing Their Ethics and Values?" *Bulletin of Science, Technology and Society* 10, no. 3 (1990), pp. 137–145. The Argentine entrepreneurs organized themselves as an association of businesspeople for the expansion of consciousness (Gente de Empresa Para la Expansion de la Conciencia, GEPEC).
5. Willis Harman, who died on January 30, 1997, pioneered studies on the challenges that human consciousness presents to science and society. He was President of the Institute of Noetic Sciences, a research foundation, educational institution, and membership organization based in Sausalito, California, whose purpose is to investigate on the workings of the mind and the structure of our consciousness (noetic means mind, intelligence, ways of knowing). In 1987, Willis Harman inspired a small group of businesspeople to create the World Business Academy. The objective was to promote a shift in the way businesspeople think and do business, providing a meeting ground where business leaders and scholars can discuss the crucial role of business in shaping the future of our societies and economies. The message to the meeting in Mendoza, Argentina, was sent through the author, who read it at the inaugural session.
6. Robert Salmon, op cit., p. 2.
7. Ibid, p. vii.
8. James Liebig, *Merchants of Vision* (San Francisco: Berrett-Koehler, 1994).
9. Affiliations and positions are those the persons interviewed held at the time of the interviews.
10. In addition to James Liebig's work, readers may find examples in the following books and periodicals, among others:
    Michael Ray and Alan Rinzler, eds., *The New Paradigm in Business* (Los

Angeles: Jeremy P. Tarcher, 1993). The book contains contributions from businesspeople as well as scholars in business administration.

Michael Phillips and Salli Rasberry, *Honest Business* (New York: Random House, 1981). The book is based on the authors' experience in organizing a network of some 450 small businesses in the San Francisco Bay area, where entrepreneurs tried to fulfill three main objectives: be honest; be gentle to themselves, those who work with them, and the surrounding community; and have fun with what they were doing.

Perspectives, a quarterly journal from the World Business Academy, published by Berrett-Koehler, San Francisco.

Business Ethics, a bimonthly magazine published by Business Ethics, Chaska, Minnesota.

At Work: Stories of Tomorrow's Workplace, a bimonthly publication by Berrett-Koehler, San Francisco.

11. Frank Rose, "A New Age For Business?" *Fortune,* October 8, 1990.

12. In 1984, Willis Harman and Howard Rheingold argued the necessity of liberating the unconscious from socially imposed constraints in order to produce breakthrough insights. More recently, Harman dealt with causality-related anomalies in our thought processes. He and Jane Clark asked whether the fundamental assumptions embedded in the current scientific paradigm place blinders—or at least boundaries—on what contemporary science is free to discover. See the following books:

Willis Harman and Howard Rheingold, *Higher Creativity* (Los Angeles: Tarcher, 1984).

Willis Harman, *A Re-examination of the Metaphysical Foundations of Modern Science* (Sausalito, California: Institute of Noetic Sciences, 1991).

Willis Harman and Jane Clark, *New Metaphysical Foundations of Modern Science* (Sausalito, California: Institute of Noetic Sciences, 1994).

13. As quoted in Perspectives, 3, no. 1 (January 1989), p. 5.

14. See chapter 8, p. 142.

15. Willis Harman, *Global Mind Change* (New York: Warner Books, 1988).

16. A paraphrase of Teilhard de Chardin, op. cit., p. 70.

17. Ibid.

18. See chapter 10, p. 219.

19. *Pampedie* was developed under the direction of Harrie Smeets. When I became acquainted with this educational tool in 1982, it had been tested only in the Netherlands and the Philippines. I was then working at the World Bank, saw its potential for expanding the consciousness of poor, illiterate villagers, and established contact with Harrie Smeets, who was then living in Stevensbeek, The Netherlands. When I undertook the

writing of this book and tried to reach Mr. Smeets again, he had evidently moved elsewhere, and I could not find any recent reference to *Pampedie*. Mr. Smeets' efforts may not have found a sustainable market for their development, but the idea deserves further testing. Now, through the Internet and the Web, it might be easier to make the idea known to wider audiences, and find educators and village developers ready to experiment with it.

20. See the section in this chapter on experiments in village development.

21. See chapter 1, pp. 10–11.

22. From a copy of a circular, dated February 22, 1985, sent to the author by Harrie Smeets.

23. Words from the French sociologist de Jouvenel, quoted in Harrie Smeets' circular of February 22, 1985. I dared to change *man,* which is the word that de Jouvenel uses, into *people.*

24. Berea College in Berea, Kentucky, is another four-year educational institution where all students work to keep operational costs at a minimum. I have read about this college but never have had a chance to visit it.

25. Catharine Finks in *Life Is My Teacher: The Birth of a New Student* (Swannanoa, North Carolina: Warren Wilson College, 1987), p. 1-1. Between September 11 and September 24, 1987, the author and his wife arranged for the late Luis Frejtman, an Argentine lawyer and youth leader, to hold a series of eleven talks and dialogues with teachers and students at Warren Wilson College. The students collected Frejtman's talks and the thoughts they expressed during the dialogues in the above-mentioned mimeographed book.

26. Ibid., Bobby Coker, p. 3-1.

27. Ibid., Janie Bowen, p. 5-9.

28. The World Bank supported a project of education with production, called Youth Brigades, in Botswana. Nat Colleta, its architect, in collaboration with Paul Bundick, described the project in Mario Kamenetzky, Robert Maybury, and Charles Weiss, Jr., eds., *Choice and Management of Technology,* op. cit., II, pp. 115–130.

29. Social Assistance to Rural Youth.

30. I saw in some old monasteries an artifact similar to our modern bidets. It seems that the old elite were washing even the parts that, later on, the Europeans would consider as devilishly dirty, hence not deserving of any care. I was also amazed by the works of art that adorned the complex of gardens, fountains, and bathing pools in the palace that an early Buddhist king built on top of the Sigiraya Rock.

31. Padmasiri de Silva, op. cit., p. 99.

32. *Sarvodaya* is a word coined by Mahatma Gandhi from *sarva,* which means "all," and *udaya,* which means "awakening."

33. *Shrama* means "labor," and *dana* is "sharing."
34. Villagers would usually organize themselves in a preschool group of children between 3 and 6, a children's group of those between 7 and 16, a youth group, a mothers' group, a farmers' group, and a group of elders.
35. During the 1980s and early 1990s the conflict worsened and affected Sarvodaya's work in some areas, but on May 11, 1998 Ariyaratne told me that the situation has changed. The Sarvodaya Movement is working again in Jaffna, a Tamil stronghold, and Ariyaratne is continuing his mission toward a peaceful resolution of the conflict, at both the grassroots and national levels. He says that Sarvodaya works now in 11,300 villages.
36. A. T. Ariyaratne, *Vishvodaya Through Vishvadana*, address delivered at the Royal Palace in Brussels on November 24, 1982. It is included in A. T. Ariyaratne, *Collected Works* (Sri Lanka: Vishva Lekha, 1985), III, pp. 71–78.
37. See a clever interpretation of the social structures of Thailand in Niels Mulder, *Everyday Life in Thailand* (Bangkok: Editions Duang Kamol, 1979).
38. Ibid., p. 102.
39. Willis Harman, *Why a World Business Academy?* (Burlingame, California: World Business Academy, 1990), p. 1.

Chapter 12

1. See Carlos A. Floria and César A. García Belsunce, *Historia de los Argentinos* (Buenos Aires: Larousse Argentina, 1992), I, pp. 380–385 and 403–407.
2. Ibid., pp. 335–336 and 439–449.
3. Jorge Mayer, *El Pensamiento Vivo de Alberdi* (Buenos Aires: Losada, 1984), p. 33. Free translation to English by the author of this book.
4. These are all free translations by the author of quotes from Alberdi's writings included in Jorge Mayer, op. cit., pp. 43, 61, 106.
5. See chapter 10, endnote 23.
6. There was no tenure for life. Every seven years, professors had to renew their right to occupy a chair through a contest.
7. David Rock, *Argentina 1516–1987: From Spanish Colonization to Alfonsín* (Berkeley, California: University of California Press, 1987), p. 172.
8. Ibid., p. 182.
9. The inhabitants of Buenos Aires are also known as *porteños*, which means "those who live at the port." *Machismo* is a Spanish expression for the attitude known as male chauvinism, and *macho* refers to a man with exaggerated physical and cultural attributes of manhood.
10. David Rock comments that prostitution in Buenos Aires reflected the marked lack of women immigrants, and adds: "Early in the twentieth

century Buenos Aires had ill-fame as the center of a white-slave traffic from Europe, with some three hundred registered brothels in the city in 1913. Many other expressions of misery and wretchedness prevailed. Among the large foreign employers, the meat-packing plants were notorious for low wages and oppressive working conditions. Some of the worst abuses against workers were perpetrated by the immigrant middle-class store owners, who paid paltry wages and made eighteen-hour shifts commonplace." See David Rock, op. cit., p. 176.

11. Words from the tango "El Patotero Sentimental" (The Sentimental Brawler) written by Manuel Romero (1891–1954). The words, freely translated by the author, have been taken from José Gobello and Jorge Bossio, *Tangos y Letristas* (Buenos Aires: Plus Ultra, 1979), p. 168. The words in Spanish are "En mi vida tuve muchas, muchas minas, pero nunca una mujer." The word *mina*, which is a slang expression, could mean a lover or a prostitute; it is a woman whom one dates or with whom lives, who is part of one's possessions, and whom one may even exploit.

12. This tango was written by Enrique Santos Discepolo (1901–1951). Some words in the Spanish version are from the *porteño* slang called *lunfardo*. Others are colloquial forms. As in the previous case, the words have been taken from José Gobello and Jorge Bossio, op. cit., p. 65, and freely translated by the author.

13. From "Vamos a la Zafra," a folk song with music by Eduardo Falú and words by Jaime Dávalos, in a free translation by the author.

14. From the folk song "Tu Que Puedes Vuelvete" by Atahualpa Yupanqui.

15. An expression used by David Rock, op. cit., p. 390.

16. According to the World Bank, the total long-term debt was $50.3 billion in 1987, representing 65.5 percent of the country's GNP. The service of this debt consumed 52 percent of the exports of goods and services that year. World Bank, *World Development Report 1989* (New York: Oxford University Press, 1989), table 23, p. 209.

17. I repeat here a quotation from Adam Smith, *The Wealth of Nations*, op. cit., II, pp. 292–293. See more about his views on school teachings subservient of theology in chapter 10, p. 200.

18. World Bank, *World Development Report 1992*, op. cit., p. 269. An anecdote is to the point. For a while, my wife practiced gynecology at one of the hospitals of a labor union. Women would come and say: "Let our husbands talk politics and decide we should have larger families; you help us to control pregnancies—at home our men agree with us."

19. David Rock, op. cit., p. 326.

20. Ibid., p. 265.

21. *World Bank News* XIII, no. 35 (September 22, 1994), p. 1.

22. Benjamin B. Ferencz and Ken Keyes, Jr., *Planethood* (Coos Bay, Oregon: Love Line Books, 1991), pp. xi–xii.
23. Ibid.
24. Ibid.
25. World Bank, *World Development Report 1991,* op. cit. The figures for the GNP per capita are all in 1989 dollars; they are on Table 1, pp. 204–205. The data for defense expenditures as a percentage of central government expenditures are on Table 11, pp. 224–225. For Costa Rica and Panama, they are related to the central government's consolidated accounts; for El Salvador to the government's budget. In the latter case, the figures may be understated because they may exclude units, like the military, that often have discretionary, nonpublicized budgets. There are no figures for other Central American countries.
26. Ibid., Table 1, pp. 204–205. There is no data on Nicaragua.
27. Ibid., Table 26, p. 255.
28. Walter LaFeber, "Alliances in Retrospect," in *Bordering on Trouble,* Andrew Maguire and Janet Welsh Brown, eds. (Bethesda, Maryland: Adler & Adler, 1986), p. 370.
29. World Bank, *World Development Report 1997,* op. cit., Table 17, p. 247.
30. Ibid., Table 2, p. 217. The average annual rate of inflation is measured by the growth rate of the gross domestic product (GDP) deflator, which is the ratio between the GDP at current values over the GDP at constant values, both in national currency.
31. Carlos Rubio, *La Vida Entre los Labios* (San Jose, Costa Rica: Editorial Costa Rica, 1985), p. 19. English version by the author.
32. A full description of the project can be seen in Hernan Alvarado, Fred Herrera, and Mario Kamenetzky, "Development of a Rural Community" in Mario Kamenetzky, Robert Maybury, and Charles Weiss, Jr., eds., *Choice and Management of Technology,* op. cit., II, pp. 1–21.
33. By outsiders they meant not only people like myself and my wife from outside Costa Rica, but also people from Costa Rican academic institutions who were participating in the project, and who joined me in that visit.
34. Walter LaFerbe, op. cit., p. 364.
35. See chapter 5, p. 82, and endnote 14.
36. See chapter 1.
37. Maurice Crouzet, *La Epoca Contemporanea: En Busca de Una Nueva Civilización,* vol. VII in *Historia General de las Civilizaciones* (Barcelona: Ediciones Destino, 1961), p. 294. Translation from Spanish by the author.
38. Romain Rolland, "Open Letter to President Wilson," translation by the author from the Spanish version included in Roman Rolland, *El Espíritu Libre* (Buenos Aires: Librería Hachette, 1956), p. 273.

39. Ashley Montagu is quoted as saying: "Human beings are the only creatures who are able to behave irrationally in the name of reason." See *Daytona Beach News Journal,* February 7, 1994, p. 2A.
40. As quoted in Benjamin B. Ferencz and Ken Keyes, Jr., op. cit., p. xii.
41. See chapter 5, pp. 87–88.
42. I assume that Havel is using this word in its rather obsolete connotation of gentleness and kindness, and not in its now more accepted meaning of submission, compliance, tameness, and spiritlessness.
43. *The Washington Post,* Text of Havel's Speech to Congress, Thursday, February 22, 1990, p. A28.

BIBLIOGRAPHY

A Barefoot Doctor's Manual: the American translation of the official Chinese paramedical manual. Philadelphia: Running Press, 1977.

Ariès, Philippe, and George Duby, eds. *A History Of Private Life,* 5v. Cambridge, Mass: Harvard University Press, 1989.

Aristotle. *The Politics,* tr. T. A. Sinclair. London: Penguin Books, 1992.

Ariyaratne, A. T. *Collected Works,* 3v. Sri Lanka: Vishva Lekha, 1985.

Arms Control and Disarmament Agency. *Military Burden and Other Relative Indicators.* Internet: http://www.acda.gov/wmeat95/95 milex.htm. May 2, 1997.

The Book of Angelus Silesius. Trans. and notes by Frederick Franck. Santa Fe, New Mexico: Bear & Co., 1985.

Breton, Guy. *Histoires d'Amour de l'Histoire de France,* 8 v. Paris: Presses Pocket, 1965.

Brown, Lester, et al. *State of The World: A Worldwatch Institute Report on Progress Towards a Sustainable Society.* New York: W. W. Norton & Co., 1992.

Bureau of the Public Debt. *Historical Public Debt Outstanding.* Internet: http://www.publicdebt.treas.gov/opd/opdhisto.htm. May 2, 1997.

Chase-Sardi, Miguel. *Pequeño Decameron Nivacle.* Asunción, Paraguay: Ediciones Napa, 1981.

Chateaubriand, René de. *Atala & René,* 1801, Irving Putter, trans. Berkeley, California: University of California Press, 1980.

Cleveland, Harlan, Hazel Henderson and Inge Kaul, ed. *The United Nations: Policy and Financing Alternatives.* Washington, D.C.: The Global Commission to Fund the United Nations, 1996.

Congressional Resolution 76. *Iroquois Contributions to the U.S. Constitution,* 1987.

Crouzet, Maurice. *Historia General de las Civilizaciones,* 7 v. Barcelona: Ediciones Destino, 1961.

Daly, Herman, and John Cobb. *For the Common Good.* Boston: Beacon Press, 1989.

Daly, Herman. Beyond Growth: *The Economics of Sustainable Development.* Boston: Beacon Press, 1996.

———. *Economics, Ecology, Ethics.* San Francisco: W. H. Freeman Co., 1980.

———. *Steady-State Economics.* Washington D.C.: Island Press, 1991.

Daytona Beach News-Journal. February 7, 1994.

———. July 6, 1992.

Dissanayake, Piyasena. *Political Thoughts of the Buddha.* Colombo, Sri Lanka: Ratnakara Press, 1977.

Durant, Will and Ariel. *The Story of Civilization,* 11v. New York: MJF Books, 1975.

Economic Policy Institute. *Family Income Data Series.* Internet: http://epinet.org/fids02.html. May 2, 1997.

Einstein: A Centenary Volume, ed. A. P. French. London: Heinemann Educational Books for the International Commission on Physics Education, 1979.

Ekins, Paul, and Manfred Max Neef, eds. *Real-Life Economics.* London: Routledge, 1992.

Eliade, Mircea. *Images and Symbols.* New York: Sheed & Ward, 1969.

Engels, Frederick. *The Origin of the Family, Private Property, and the State,* 1884. New York: Pathfinder Press, 1979.

Erasmus. *In Praise of Folly,* 1515. New York: Penguin Books, 1982.

Felipe, Leon. *Antologia Rota.* Buenos Aires: Losada, 1984.

The Feminist Majority Foundation. New Media Publishing. *Individuals Are Paying a Larger Percentage of Federal Revenues—Corporations Are Paying Less.* Internet: http://www. feminist.org/other/budget/whopays.html. May 1, 1997.

Ferencz, Benjamin B., and Ken Keyes, Jr. *Planethood.* Coos Bay, Or.: Love Line Books, 1991.

Feuer, Lewis S. ed. Marx & Engels: *Basic Writings on Politics and Philosophy.* New York: Anchor Books, 1959.

Feuerstein, Georg. *Structures of Consciousness: The Genius of Jean Gebser.* Lower Lake, Calif.: Integral Publishing, 1987.

Floria, Carlos A., and César A. García. *Belsunce, Historia de los Argentinos.* Buenos Aires: Larousse Argentina, 1992.

Fox, Matthew. *The Coming of the Cosmic Christ.* San Francisco: Harper & Row, 1988.

Franck, Frederick. *A Little Compendium on That Which Matters.* Arlington, Va.: Great Ocean Publishers, 1989.

Freud, Sigmund. *Civilization and Its Discontents,* 1930. trans. and ed. James Strachey. New York: W. W. Norton & Co., 1961.

Galbraith, John Kenneth. *The Age of Uncertainty.* Boston: Houghton Mifflin Co., 1977.

Garaudy, Roger *Comment l'homme devint humain.* Paris: éditions j. a., 1979.

Gary, Hector. "Nervous Money Keeps on Fleeing." *Fortune,* December 23, 1985.

Gebser, Jean, *The Ever-Present Origin.* Trans. Noel Barstad and Algis Mickunas. Athens, Ohio: Ohio University Press, 1985.

Gibran, Khalil. *Obras Completas,* 3v. Barcelona: Ediciones Teorema, 1982.

Gobello, José, and Jorge Bossio. *Tangos y Letristas.* Buenos Aires: Plus Ultra, 1979.

Goldberg, B. Z. *The Sacred Fire.* Secaucus, N.J.: The Citadel Press, 1974

Haeberle, Erwin J. *The Sex Atlas.* New York: Seabury Press, 1978.

Harman, Willis, and Howard Rheingold. *Higher Creativity.* Los Angeles: Tarcher, 1984.

Harman, Willis, and Jane Clark. *New Metaphysical Foundations of Modern Science.* Sausalito, Calif.: Institute of Noetic Sciences, 1994.

Harman, Willis. *A Re-examination of the Metaphysical Foundations of Modern Science.* Sausalito, Calif.: Institute of Noetic Sciences, 1991.

———. *Global Mind Change.* New York: Warner Books, 1988.

———. *Why a World Business Academy?* Burlingame, Calif.: World Business Academy, 1990.

Heilbroner, Robert L., and James K. Galbraith. *The Economic Problem,* rev. 8th ed. Englewood Cliffs, N.J.: Prentice-Hall, 1975.

Henderson, Hazel. *Building a Win-Win World: Life Beyond Global Eco-*

nomic Warfare. San Francisco: Berret-Koehler Publishers, 1996.

———. *Paradigms in Progress: Life Beyond Economics.* Indianapolis, Ind.: Knowledge Systems, 1991.

Herlihy, David, ed. *Medieval Culture and Society.* New York: Harper & Row, 1968.

Herscu, Paul. *The Homeopathic Treatment of Children: Pediatric Constitutional Types.* Berkeley, Calif.: North Atlantic Books, 1991.

Holmberg, A. R. *Nomads of the Long Bow: The Siriono of Eastern Bolivia.* New York: American Museum of Science Books, 1969.

Hunger Project, The. *World Development Forum,* 4, no. 8, April 30, 1986.

Jeans, Sir James. *Physics and Philosophy.* New York: Dover Publications, 1981.

Jerusalem Bible, The. Garden City, New York: Doubleday & Co., 1966.

Johns Hopkins School of Hygiene and Public Health. Population Reports, Series L, no. 9, June 1993.

Julien, Claude. "Le Prix des Armes." *Le Monde Diplomatique,* no. 412, July 1988.

Kamenetzky, Mario. *Economía del Conocimiento y Empresa.* Buenos Aires: Paidos, 1976.

———. "The Economics of the Satisfaction of Needs." *Human Sys-tems Management,* 2. New York: North-Holland Publishing Co., 1981.

Kamenetzky, Mario, Robert Maybury, and Charles Weiss, Jr. *Choice and Management of Technology in Developing Countries,* 2v. Washington D.C.: The World Bank, Projects Policy Department, 1986.

Kay, Alan F., and Hazel Henderson. *United Nations Security Insurance Agency,* Participant Paper 2A. UNDP Stockholm Roundtable on "Change: Social Conflict or Harmony?", July 22–24, 1994.

Keynes, John Maynard. *Essays in Biography.* New York: W. W. Norton & Co., 1963.

———. *Two Memoirs.* London: Rupert-Hart Davis, 1949.

Khan, Mohsin S., and Nadeem Ul Haque. "Capital Flight from Developing Countries." *Finance and Development,* March 1987.

Kohn, Alfie. *No Contest: The Case Against Competition.* Boston: Houghton Mifflin Co., 1986.

Koran, The. London: Penguin Books, 1990.

Krishnamurti, J. *Education and the Significance of Life*. San Francisco: Harper & Row, 1981.

Kurtzman, Joel. *The Death of Money*. Boston: Little, Brown and Company, 1993.

Leakey, Richard, and Roger Lewin. *Origins Reconsidered*. New York: Anchor Books/Doubleday, 1992.

Leakey, Richard. *The Making of Mankind*. London: Abacus, 1982.

Liebig, James. *Merchants of Vision*. San Francisco: Berrett-Koehler, 1994.

Lockie, Andrew. *The Family Guide to Homeopathy*. New York: Simon & Schuster, 1989.

Lovelock, J. E. *GAIA: A New Look at Life on Earth*. New York: Oxford University Press, 1979.

Macchiavelli. *The Prince*, trans. George Bull. London: Penguin Books, 1981.

Maddux, John L. *The Development Philosophy of Robert S. McNamara*. Washington D.C.: The World Bank, 1981.

Maguire, Andrew and Janet Welsh Brown, eds. *Bordering on Trouble*: Bethesda, Md.: Adler & Adler, 1986.

Mallmann, Carlos A. "On the Satisfaction of Human Aspirations as the Development Objective." *Symposium on Science, Technology and Human Values*. Mexico City, July 2-3 1973.

Mayer, Jorge. *El Pensamiento Vivo de Alberdi*. Buenos Aires: Losada, 1984.

McIlvenna, Ted, and Laird Sutton. *Meditations on the Gift of Sexuality*. San Francisco: Specific Press, 1977.

McLaughlin, Corinne, and Gordon Davidson. *Builders of the Dawn: Community Lifestyles in a Changing World*. Walpole, N.H.: Stillpoint Publishing, 1985.

McWilliams, Peter. *Ain't Nobody's Business If You Do: The Absurdity of Consensual Crimes in a Free Society*. Los Angeles: Prelude Press, 1993.

Mill, John Stuart. *On Liberty*, 1859. London: Penguin Classics, 1985.

Montagu, Ashley, ed. *Culture and Human Development: Insights into Growing Human*. Englewood Cliffs, N.J.: Prentice Hall Inc., 1974.

Montagu, Ashley. *Touching: The Human Significance of the Skin*. New York: Harper & Row, 1978.

Morgan, Lewis Henry. *League of the Iroquois.* New York: Carol Publishing Group, 1993.

Mulder, Niels. *Everyday Life in Thailand.* Bangkok: Editions Duang Kamol, 1979.

Nullis, Clare. "Millions of Kids Labor Worldwide." *The Daytona Beach News-Journal.* June 2, 1992.

Olsen, Paul. *The Future of Being Human.* New York: M. Evans and Company, Inc., 1975.

Peterson, Merril D., ed. *The Portable Thomas Jefferson.* New York: Viking Penguin Inc., 1987.

Phillips, Michael, and Salli Rasberry. *Honest Business.* New York: Random House, 1981.

Popenoe, Cris and Oliver. *Seeds of Tomorrow: New Age Communities That Work.* San Francisco: Harper & Row, 1984.

Poynor, Robin. "Power concealed; power revealed." *The Arts of Africa.* Daytona Beach, Fla.: Museum of Arts and Sciences, 1986.

Prescott, James W., "Body Pleasure and the Origins of Violence." *The Bulletin of the Atomic Scientists,* vol. XXXI, no. 9, November 1975: 10–20.

Ray, Michael, and Alan Rinzler, eds. *The New Paradigm in Business.* Los Angeles: Jeremy P. Tarcher, 1993.

Rock, David. *Argentina 1516–1987: From Spanish Colonization to Alfonsín.* Berkeley, Calif.: University of California Press, 1987.

Rolland, Roman. *El Espíritu Libre.* Buenos Aires: Librer'a Hachette, 1956.

Rose, Frank. "A New Age For Business?" *Fortune.* October 8, 1990.

Rosnay, Joel de. "Modernes Activités, Emplois Nouveaux: ce que va changer la révolution informationnelle." *Le Monde Diplomatique.* August 1996.

Rousseau, Jean Jacques. *Eloisa* (Julie or La Nouvelle Heloise, 1761). William Kenrick, trans., 1803. Oxford: Woodstock Books, 1989.

—————. *Emile, or On Education.* Introduction, translation and notes by Allan Bloom. New York: Basic Books, 1979.

Rubio, Carlos. *La Vida entre los Labios.* San Jose, Costa Rica: Editorial Costa Rica, 1985.

Russell, Peter. *The White Hole in Time: Our Future Evolution and the Meaning of Now.* San Francisco: HarperSanFrancisco, 1992.

Salmon, Robert. *Tous les Chemins Mènent à l'Homme*. Paris: InterEditions, 1994.

Scitovsky, Tibor. *The Joyless Economy*. New York: Oxford University Press, 1977.

Seldes, George. *The Great Quotations*. Secaucus, N.J.: Castle Books, 1977.

Shah, Idries. *Tales of the Dervishes: Teaching Stories of the Sufi Masters over the Past Thousand Years*. London: The Octagon Press, 1982.

Shapley, Deborah. *Promise and Power: The Life and Times of Robert McNamara*. Boston: Little, Brown and Company, 1993.

Silva, Padmasiri de. *Buddhist and Freudian Psychology*. Colombo, Sri Lanka: Lake House Printers & Publishers, 1978.

Smith, Adam. *The Theory of Moral Sentiments*. D. D. Raphael and A. L. Macfie, eds. Indianapolis, Ind.: Liberty Press, 1982.

———. *The Wealth of Nations*, 1776. Chicago: The University of Chicago Press, 1976.

Soelle, Dorothee. *To Work and To Love: A Theology of Creation*. Philadelphia: Fortress Press, 1984.

Starr, Tama. *The "Natural Inferiority" of Women*. New York: Poseidon Press, 1991

Sun, The. no. 200. August, 1992.

Teilhard de Chardin, Pierre. *Building the Earth*. Wilkes-Barre, Pa.: Dimension Books, 1965.

Toben, Bob, and Fred Alan Wolf. *Space, Time and Beyond*. New York: E. P. Dutton, Inc., 1982.

Tournier, Michel. *Vendredi, ou les limbes du Pacifique*. Paris: Gallimard, 1967.

Underwood, Paula, *The Great Tree of Peace: Iroquois Contributions to the U.S. Constitution*. San Anselmo, Calif.: LearningWay Center, 1987.

———. *The Walking People: A Native American Oral History*. San Anselmo, Calif.: A Tribe of Two Press, 1993.

———. *Who Speaks for Wolf: A Native American Learning Story*. San Anselmo, Calif.: A Tribe of Two Press, 1991.

University of Virginia, *Social Sciences Data Center. National Income and Products Account*. Internet: http://www.lib.virginia.edu/ssdcbin/nipabin/nipa.cgi. May 2, 1997.

310

Washington Post, The. February 22, 1990.

Waskow, Arthur I. *Godwrestling.* New York: Schocken Books, 1978.

Weatherford, Jack. *Indian Givers.* New York: Crown Publishers, 1988.

Wilber, Ken. *Up From Eden.* Garden City: Anchor Press/Doubleday, 1981.

World Bank, The. "The World Bank Responds to AIDS." *World Bank News,* XIII, no. 45. December 1, 1994.

———. "World Bank Offers New Yardstick to Measure Development." *World Bank News,* XVI, no. 13. April 3, 1997.

———. *World Bank News,* XIII, no. 35. September 22, 1994.

———. *World Development Report 1985 : International Capital and Economic Development.* New York: Oxford University Press, 1985.

———. *World Development Report 1988: Financial Systems and Development.* New York: Oxford University Press, 1988.

———. *World Development Report 1989.* New York: Oxford University Press, 1989.

———. *World Development Report 1991: The Challenge of Development.* New York: Oxford University Press, 1991.

———. *World Development Report 1992: Development and The Environment.* New York: Oxford University Press, 1992.

———. *World Development Report 1993: Investing in Health.* New York: Oxford University Press, 1993.

———. *World Development Report 1997: The State in a Changing World.* New York: Oxford University Press, 1997.

World Resources Institute, The. The United Nations Environment Programme, and The United Nations Development Programme. World Resources. New York: Oxford University Press, 1994.

INDEX

314